COGNITIVE METHODS

COGNITIVE METHODS

and Their Application to Clinical Research

Edited by
Amy Wenzel
David C. Rubin

AMERICAN PSYCHOLOGICAL ASSOCIATION • WASHINGTON, DC

Published by
American Psychological Association
750 First Street, NE
Washington, DC 20002
www.apa.org

To order
APA Order Department
P.O. Box 92984
Washington, DC 20090-2984
Tel: (800) 374-2721; Direct: (202) 336-5510
Fax: (202) 336-5502; TDD/TTY: (202) 336-6123
Online: www.apa.org/books/
E-mail: order@apa.org

In the U.K., Europe, Africa, and the Middle East, copies may be ordered from
American Psychological Association
3 Henrietta Street
Covent Garden, London
WC2E 8LU England

Typeset in Goudy by Stephen McDougal, Mechanicsville, MD

Printer: United Book Press, Inc., Baltimore, MD
Cover Designer: Naylor Design, Washington, DC
Technical/Production Editor: Rosemary Moulton

The opinions and statements published are the responsibility of the authors, and such opinions and statements do not necessarily represent the policies of the American Psychological Association.

Library of Congress Cataloging-in-Publication Data

Cognitive methods and their application to clinical research / edited by Amy Wenzel, David C. Rubin ; contributors, Amy Wenzel ... [et al.].
    p. cm.
    ISBN 1-59147-185-0 (alk. paper)
    1. Clinical psychology—Methodology. 2. Cognition. I. Wenzel, Amy. II. Rubin, David C.

    RC467.8.C64 2004
    616.8—dc22   2004013986

British Library Cataloguing-in-Publication Data
A CIP record is available from the British Library.

Printed in the United States of America
First Edition

CONTENTS

CONTRIBUTORS

Nader Amir, PhD, Department of Psychology, University of Georgia, Athens

Nelson Cowan, PhD, Department of Psychological Sciences, University of Missouri, Columbia

Lisa Geraci, PhD, Department of Psychology, Washington University, St. Louis, MO

Jonathan M. Golding, PhD, Department of Psychology, University of Kentucky, Lexington

Colin MacLeod, PhD, School of Psychology, University of Western Australia, Nedlands, Perth, Australia

Colin M. MacLeod, PhD, Department of Psychology, University of Waterloo, Ontario, Canada

Andrew Mathews, PhD, Medical Research Council, Cognition and Brain Sciences Unit, Cambridge, England

Richard J. McNally, PhD, Department of Psychology, Harvard University, Cambridge, MA

Henry L. Roediger III, PhD, Department of Psychology, Washington University, St. Louis, MO

David C. Rubin, PhD, Psychological and Brain Sciences, Duke University, Durham, NC

Amy Selvig, MS, Department of Psychology, University of Georgia, Athens

Amy Wenzel, PhD, Department of Psychology, University of Pennsylvania, Philadelphia

Jenny Yiend, PhD, Department of Psychiatry, University of Oxford, England

COGNITIVE METHODS

INTRODUCTION: APPLYING COGNITIVE METHODS WITH CLINICAL POPULATIONS

AMY WENZEL AND DAVID C. RUBIN

The past 20 years have witnessed an explosion of research examining cognitive biases in individuals with a variety of clinical diagnoses. This research was prompted in part by the growing study and use of cognitive behavior therapy and discourse pertaining to the theory underlying this intervention (cf. Beck, 1976; Beck & Emery, 1985). According to many cognitive theories of psychopathology, individuals suffering from emotional disorders are characterized by a maladaptive schema, or cognitive orientation, that drives them to process disorder-specific information differently than they process non-disorder-specific information. This pattern of biased information processing maintains and exacerbates psychopathology, as it prevents these individuals from making a more balanced, realistic appraisal of information in their environment. Today, this field is generally known as *cognitive psychopathology*, or the scientific study of cognitive processes that pertain to the etiology and maintenance of various clinical disorders.

Although cognitive theories of psychopathology outline the negative self-statements and other types of cognitive distortions that characterize various types of psychopathologies (e.g., Beck & Emery, 1985), their assumptions clearly suggest that individuals with these psychopathologies should attend to, interpret, and remember disorder-specific information to a maladaptive degree. In fact, a PsycINFO literature search reveals that much more empirical research has investigated the nature of information processing (e.g., attention, interpretation, memory) than the cognitive content (e.g., negative self-statements) that characterizes biased cognition in psychopathology. To examine information processing in individuals with various types of psychopathologies, clinical psychologists often adapt standard laboratory cognitive tasks, such as the Stroop task. A parallel trend has been for cognitive psychologists to use their standard laboratory tasks with clinical populations to extend their theories in clinically relevant directions and to subject their theories to tests not possible in other populations. However, clinical psychologists often have little background in cognitive psychology, and cognitive psychologists often have little training in conducting research with special populations. The proposed volume covers the popularly used cognitive tasks in applied research and, for each, provides the background necessary for readers to ground themselves in the basics and be directed to more detailed information that they might need. It is hoped that researchers who consult this volume will use the information to implement studies with the utmost experimental rigor.

Five common categories of tasks are highlighted in this volume: the Stroop, selective attention, implicit memory, directed forgetting, and autobiographical memory. The latter four areas focus on a particular area of cognition and can be measured using a variety of cognitive tasks. The Stroop, in contrast, is a specific cognitive task that, depending on the underlying theory one chooses to guide interpretation (see chap. 2, this volume), can measure several types of cognitive processes. A section on the Stroop task was included because this task was used in the earliest, seminal studies of cognitive psychopathology (e.g., Mathews & MacLeod, 1985) and continues to be used in more empirical studies on this topic than is any other cognitive task. The areas of selective attention, implicit memory, directed forgetting, and autobiographical memory were identified on the basis of a count of articles published in recent years in *Journal of Abnormal Psychology* and *Behaviour Research and Therapy* and because they were sufficiently bounded and defined to be carefully described.

There also are several categories of tasks that we chose *not* to include in this volume. In our original plan, we had intended to include a section on explicit memory to balance the section on implicit memory. The pool of studies that have investigated memory biases toward certain categories of stimuli, particularly with anxious participants (Coles & Heimberg, 2002), has yielded mixed explicit memory results that might be clarified with a more careful consideration of methodological variables. However, there really is no easily bounded corresponding contemporary "explicit memory" field of study in the cognitive psychology that could be brought together in one coherent chapter. A second task that we considered including in this book is the lexical decision task, as cognitive psychologists have used it in a number of capacities, particularly to measure speed of linguistic processing. But there is not necessarily a theoretical reason to examine linguistic processing in and of itself in most types of psychopathology. Some clinical psychology researchers have used lexical decision tasks, but usually with the intent to prime disorder-related and neutral stimuli in the context of implicit memory experiments (e.g., Bradley, Mogg, & Williams, 1995). There are other cognitive methods that have recently begun to be applied with clinical populations, such as the Deese–Roediger–McDermott false memory paradigm (Roediger & McDermott, 1995). Depending on the extent to which clinical researchers adopt them in the future, these additional cognitive methods also would benefit from the type of methodological analysis that is undertaken in this book.

We chose a format for the book that would offer full coverage of implementation of these methods from both cognitive and clinical psychology perspectives and would allow researchers from different backgrounds to easily find the information they needed. For each methodological area, there are two authors: a cognitive/experimental author and a clinical author. These two individuals (or sets of individuals) authored three chapters. First, each area has a brief opening chapter that includes (a) a description of the basic task or tasks used, (b) the theoretical reasons people use the task, (c) the basic procedure, and (d) general theoretical and methodological cautions. The two chapters that follow, one by the cognitive/experimental researcher and the other by the clinical researcher, include a "why use the task" theoretical part and a "how to do it" methodological part. These chapters point to good examples in the literature on which readers can base their work, more extensive literature reviews, common problems and ways to avoid them, theoretical positions, and controversies. The experimental chapters, which are placed before the clinical chapters, outline methodological variations on the basic task described in the introductory chapters and provide a historical development of the manner in which the task has been used. In fact, they provide state-of-the-art methodological suggestions for implementing the task that will be useful even for experimental researchers who do not wish to focus on applied issues. The clinical chapters concentrate on special populations, clinical issues, variables of interest in relevant studies that have been conducted to date, and, when applicable, the potential uses of the tasks for assessment and other forms of clinical usefulness. Overall, an experimental or clinical researcher reading these chapters should have a good idea how to proceed in testing an undergraduate or a clinical population, what conclusions they could reasonably draw from their results, and where they could look to answer detailed questions not in the brief coverage.

We focused on methods that have elicited *content-related* biases in the literature, many of which have been used primarily with samples of anxious or depressed participants. That is, each of these five categories of methods have been implemented in the clinical psychology literature with different categories of stimuli, such as positive, negative, and neutral stimuli in investigations of depression, or threat-related and neutral stimuli in investigations of anxiety disorders. There are also extensive literatures on general cognitive *deficits* associated with a variety of psychopathologies, such as schizophrenia and attention-deficit/hyperactivity disorder (ADHD), that, for the most part, are not included in this book (but see chap. 9, this volume, for an exception). In such studies, individuals with particular clinical disorders complete cognitive tasks comprising stimuli that are *not* necessarily related to their pathology (e.g., individuals with ADHD complete the standard Stroop task to measure the degree to which the names of colors interfere with identifying the colors in which words are presented). These studies generally are conducted because symptoms of these disorders are defined in terms of information-processing disruptions (e.g., inattention in ADHD). Results from studies examining deficits in clinical populations contribute to understanding nonspecific information-processing *disruption* rather than the *direction* of information processing that occurs within otherwise fairly normal limits. We are most interested in methods to examine the latter, as these studies are conducted to advance cognitive theories of psychopathology.

The chapters in this book are not exhaustive reviews of the literature. There are several existing reviews of information processing in psychopathology, the most comprehensive being Williams, Watts, MacLeod, and Mathews' (1997) seminal volume, *Cognitive Psychology and Emotional Disorders*, now in its second edition, and Dalgleish and Power's (1999) *Handbook of Cognition and Emotion*. Both of these books provide an excellent overview of the history and development of the field, important theoretical underpinnings, and similarities and differences among information-processing styles in various types of psychopathologies. In this volume, results from studies in the literature are discussed only in the context of specific methodological variables that drive particular patterns of results. As much as was possible, chapter authors included specific recommendations for the actual implementation of these cognitive tasks.

In many instances, chapter authors make suggestions for the norming of stimuli, length of stimulus presentation, and calculation of dependent variables. Having said that, we also make the interesting observation that, at times, it was quite difficult to make concrete recommendations for the implementation of these methodologies. We often pushed authors to specify the "optimal" number of trials, intertrial intervals, stimulus duration, and so on. And often their response to us was simply, "It depends on the purpose of the research." One take-home message from this compilation is that these are guidelines and recommendations, but that ultimately, researchers must understand what varying the parameters of a particular experiment means and decide what issues are important before settling on the specifics of an experimental design.

Some main themes emerged across the five sections. First, there is a tension in applied research between conducting experiments on analogue, or convenience, samples (of which there are often unlimited numbers) and difficult-to-find-and-recruit samples of individuals with a particular type of psychopathology. Yiend and Mathews point out that results from selective attention experiments are much "cleaner" in clinical samples than in samples of undergraduates who score high on anxiety questionnaires. McNally makes the sound suggestion to test out a new method with an analogue sample to "work out the bugs" and then use it with clinical samples after it has been refined. If a researcher has access to only an analogue sample, then it might be wise to follow Wenzel's suggestion and use more than one inventory of a construct related to psychopathology and select only those individuals who score in a high range on both of the measures.

Second, it is evident that many cognitive methods have yet to be applied systematically to examine clinical issues. For example, Rubin describes an involuntary autobiographical memory method that is useful in assessing unbidden memories that emerge with no conscious attempt at recollection. Such a method has obvious implications for the study of intrusive memories associated with posttraumatic stress disorder and has the potential to provide an ecologically valid view of the manner in which intrusive memories relate to subsequent distress. In addition, Cowan explains four classes of selective attention tasks. Although three types of tasks—cuing, visual search, and filtering—have been used extensively with clinical populations (see chap. 6, this volume), multiple task paradigms have not been implemented as frequently in the cognitive psychopathology literature. Cowan suggests that multiple task paradigms might be important to use with clinical populations to examine the extent to which attention narrows on pathology-related stimuli at the expense of other stimuli, such as stimuli that represent happiness or safety.

Third, subtle variations in experimental designs often make a profound impact on obtained results. For example, C. M. MacLeod points out that research participants rarely comprehend fully written instructions pertaining to cognitive tasks and expect to learn the procedure as they go along, which could bias results obtained in the first part of the experiment. To address this issue, he suggests that experimenters ask participants to relay the instructions in their own words before commencing the task. C. MacLeod warns that pathology-relevant stimuli could have different levels of personal relevance to clinical samples versus nonclinical samples, which has the potential to cloud the interpretation of any between-group differences that might be obtained. Moreover, several of the clinical psychology researchers indicated that pathology-relevant stimuli often form a coherent category (e.g., depression-related words), but neutral stimuli do not; thus, pathology-relevant stimuli might be processed more efficiently because of intracategory priming. To guard against this confound, many cognitive psychopathologists include neutral stimuli that form coherent categories, such as household items, into their cognitive tasks.

Fourth, there is a disproportionate focus on applying cognitive methods to samples of individuals with anxiety disorders as compared to individuals with other types of psychopathology. As referenced by C. MacLeod (chap. 3, this volume), the emotional Stroop task is the cognitive task that has been applied perhaps most broadly to various types of psychiatric distrubance. It is our hope that this book will provide a foundation for clinical researchers interested in types of pathology that have not yet been considered systematically in the cognitive psychopathology literature. Identifying particular types of cognitive biases associated with different domains of pathology has the potential to uncover the mechanisms that differentiate pathologies, increase diagnostic specificity, and hone the types of cognitive interventions that are implemented to reduce these distortions.

A clear message from the chapters authored by clinical psychology researchers is that it is well established that cognitive biases associated with psychopathology exist, but that the mechanism by which they develop and are causally related to distress remain unclear. Thus, although this literature has been developed to address issues of the mechanism and etiology of psychopathology, to date it is mainly descriptive in nature. Only recently has research attempted to manipulate cognitive biases and examine effects on distress. Yiend and Mathews describe a recent study conducted by MacLeod, Rutherford, Campbell, Ebsworthy, and Holker (2002), in which participants were trained to selectively attend to threat or neutral stimuli. Participants who were trained to attend selectively to threat stimuli, but not those who were trained to attend selectively to neutral stimuli, reported an increase in anxiety during the course of the experimental session. We expect that future researchers will make innovative adaptations to the standard cognitive paradigms described in this book in order to continue to investigate this issue. Other research has documented that cognitive biases toward pathology-related stimuli decrease in severity after a course of treatment is completed (e.g., Mattia, Heimberg, & Hope 1993; Williams, Teasdale, Segal, & Soulsby, 2000). In the future, it will be important to examine prospectively whether cognitive biases toward pathology-related stimuli predict the onset of emotional distress (cf. MacLeod & Hagan, 1992). Thus, at this point we know that cognitive biases are a correlate of psychopathology, but it is incumbent upon future researchers to document the mechanism by which they cause distress, the manner in which they predispose individuals to develop psychopathology or predict relapse, and the path by which they develop.

The examination of cognitive biases in clinical populations has resulted in a richly descriptive literature that has advanced theories of psychopathology. However, conducting such research requires an understanding of two disciplines within psychology: cognitive psychology and clinical psychology. A thorough understanding of theoretical and methodological assumptions from cognitive psychology will help clinical scientists to implement experimental designs in as rigorous and controlled a manner as possible. Moreover, a thorough understanding of theoretical and methodological assumptions from clinical psychology will help cognitive psychologists to formulate hypotheses about how information processing might be biased in special populations and to understand these biases in the broader context of emotional distress. We view this book as a first step in providing a forum for members of these two disciplines to learn from each other.

REFERENCES

Beck, A. T. (1976). *Cognitive therapy and emotional disorders*. New York: International Universities Press.

Beck, A. T., & Emery, G. (1985). *Anxiety disorders and phobias: A cognitive perspective*. New York: Basic Books.

Bradley, B. P., Mogg, K., & Williams, R. (1995). Implicit and explicit memory for emotion-congruent information in clinical depression and anxiety. *Behaviour Research and Therapy, 35*, 755–770.

Coles, M. E., & Heimberg, R. G. (2002). Memory biases in the anxiety disorders: Current status. *Clinical Psychology Review, 22*, 587–627.

Dalgleish, T., & Power, M. (Eds). (1999.) *Handbook of cognition and emotion*. Chichester, England: John Wiley and Sons.

MacLeod, C., & Hagan, R. (1992). Individual differences in the selective processing of threatening information and emotional responses to a stressful event. *Behaviour Research and Therapy, 30*, 151–161.

MacLeod, C., Rutherford, E., Campbell, L., Ebsworthy, G., & Holker, L. (2002). Selective attention and emotional vulnerability: Assessing the causal basis of their association through the experimental induction of attentional bias. *Journal of Abnormal Psychology, 111*, 107–123.

Mathews, A., & MacLeod, C. (1985). Selective processing of threat cues in anxiety states. *Behaviour Research and Therapy, 23*, 563–569.

Mattia, J. I., Heimberg, R. G., & Hope, D. A. (1993). The revised Stroop-color naming task in social phobics. *Behaviour Research and Therapy, 31*, 305–313.

Roediger, H. L., & McDermott, K. B. (1995). Creating false memories: Remembering words not presented in lists. *Journal of Experimental Psychology: Learning, Memory, and Cognition, 21*, 803–814.

Williams, J. M. G., Teasdale, J. D., Segal, Z. V., & Soulsby, J. (2000). Mindfulness-Based Cognitive Therapy reduces overgeneral autobiographical memory in formerly depressed patients. *Journal of Abnormal Psychology, 109*, 150–155.

Williams, J. M. G., Watts, F. N., MacLeod, C., & Mathews, A. (1997). *Cognitive psychology and emotional disorders* (2nd ed.). Chichester, England: John Wiley and Sons.

I

THE STROOP TASK

1

THE STROOP TASK: INDIRECTLY MEASURING CONCEPT ACTIVATION

COLIN MACLEOD AND COLIN MACLEOD

For well over a century, since the earliest days of the discipline, psychologists have sought to develop methods that permit them to uncover the current contents of mind. To oversimplify with a dichotomy, there are two intuitive ways to accomplish this goal. In the direct technique, psychologists can ask the individual what he or she is thinking, being entirely candid that this is what they are doing. Introspection relies on this explicit approach. In the indirect technique, psychologists can ask the individual to perform some seemingly unrelated task that they believe will reveal what he or she is thinking, without his or her awareness. Such psychoanalytic staples as free association and dream analysis rely on this implicit approach. Experimental psychologists and clinical psychologists have shown endless creativity in constructing many clever variants of these two approaches.

Imagine that you have come to believe that thoughts of suicide are dominating the thinking of a troubled teenager. You reason that if such

Order of authorship was determined alphabetically. Correspondence may be directed to either Colin MacLeod, one of whom is now at the Department of Psychology, University of Waterloo, Waterloo, Ontario, and the other of whom is at the Department of Psychology, University of Western Australia, Nedlands, Perth, Western Australia. Only we know which is which.

thoughts are dominant, then words related to suicide should be more highly activated than words not related to suicide. So you design a simple, quite direct test of speeded word reading. You ask that young person to read aloud— as quickly as possible—a series of words, some of which are neutral (i.e., unrelated to suicide), words such as *table* and *honesty*. But you also mix in words that are related to suicide, such as *death* and *sadness*. If the teenager's thoughts are dominated by suicide, you expect that his or her time to read these two sets of words aloud will be different. It might be slower to read the suicide-related words than the neutral words because he or she is defending against them; it might be faster to read the suicide-related words because these words and concepts are already in consciousness. Either finding would support your hypothesis and would influence how you interact with or treat this young person.

There are, of course, potential problems with this approach. The most obvious of these is that the person performing your test cannot help but notice the distinction between the suicide-related and the neutral words. After all, the person's attention is directed to and he or she is responding to the words. This could in turn influence the time to read the words for reasons other than those that led you to construct the test. The greater activation of the suicide-related words may result in those words being read more quickly. Or the person may start to explicitly search for the suicide-related words, slowing down when these words are detected. Or, guessing the rationale for the test, he or she might intentionally speed up or slow down when responding to the suicide-related words relative to the neutral words. How can you be certain that the pattern of reading times that you observe is uncontaminated by such strategic responding? It is for this very reason that the indirect approach has long been seen as offering certain advantages.

Change the procedure just described apparently only superficially and you have an indirect measure of what your troubled teenager is thinking. Print each of the words in color, such as *table* in red and *sadness* in yellow, and ask the person not to read the words but to name the colors in which they are printed as quickly as possible. Attention is now directed away from the words, despite the fact that the words are what you are interested in. Now if you find that the time to name the colors of suicide-related words is longer than the time to name the colors of neutral words, you have evidence that the suicide-related words are more activated and hence interfere with naming the colors in which they are printed more than do the neutral words. Because the person is not intentionally reading the words—indeed, he or she is explicitly told not to read them—this interference provides an indirect measure of concept activation.

It is really quite remarkable that at the height of behaviorism, with its abhorrence of all things mentalistic, this very task was created. In his dissertation, John Ridley Stroop (1935) presented participants with color words printed in color (e.g., *red* in green), instructing them either to read the word (say "red," the more natural, direct response) or to name its print color (say "green," indirectly measuring the interference from the word on the color). He showed that, compared with a suitable control item—reading a word in normal black ink in the case of reading, or naming a color patch without a word in the case of color naming—there was substantial interference in the color-naming task but none in the reading task. Since 1935, but primarily since the mid-1960s, many hundreds of studies have been done in the subdiscipline that we now call cognitive psychology in which the Stroop task was used to explore aspects of attention, learning, and memory (see MacLeod, 1991, for a review). This powerful interference effect has helped to disentangle numerous puzzles about the operation of mind.

The classic color–word Stroop task has more recently been adapted to incorporate noncolor words in place of the traditional color words. This modification has come to be called the *emotional Stroop task* because the response to the critical noncolor words, as in the suicide illustration just described, is seen as at least partly having to do with affect. Since the 1980s, there has been a rapidly increasing number of studies in clinical psychology in which this emotional Stroop task has been used to explore aspects of anxieties and clinical disorders (see Williams, Mathews, & MacLeod, 1996). This variation on the task has been useful in diagnosing problems and even in evaluating the efficacy of treatments.

In the two chapters that follow, we describe the cognitive and clinical perspectives on the Stroop task, with emphasis on the methods used to carry out these studies. It is all too easy to let the surface simplicity of this task lead one to assume that the construction of a good Stroop experiment is straightforward. That would be a mistake. There are rich complexities to this task, as reflection on its 69-year (and counting) history should make evident. In chapters 2 and 3, our primary goal is to bring these complexities under the light and to suggest ways in which they have been and can be handled, along the way discussing what we have learned from these studies.

We cannot preface here all of the issues that we consider in more detail in our two chapters. Instead, we just raise two issues as illustrating the complexity inherent in the Stroop task. The first is at the empirical core of the task: the composition of the neutral, control condition. What should be the nature of this condition? This may seem obvious, but we show in our chapters that it is not, and that it warrants substantial thought. The second issue that we emphasize here has in fact already been raised. It is a crucial conceptual issue. Investigators routinely, probably too routinely, treat the Stroop task as an indirect measure of the processing of the to-be-ignored words. The logic goes that because the participant must name the color and not read the word, then any influence of the word on the speed of color naming is necessarily indirect. We advise caution in accepting this logic uncritically. Participants may well notice the words and even attend to them as they name their colors. At what point does this attention to the words begin to move the task from indirect to direct? There is no easy answer to this question, but investigators using the task because of its perceived indirect advantages should always be alert for evidence that the participants may not be treating the task as indirect, even though the investigator is doing so.

We have raised these two issues not to suggest that it is impossible to construct good Stroop experiments from which useful interpretations can be drawn. On the contrary, our intention has been to suggest that, as always, good conclusions hinge on good experiments, which in turn are based on hypotheses derived from sound theories. We believe that a great deal can be learned about cognitive processes—normal and abnormal—with this tool that is so familiar to every psychologist. And we very much hope that our chapters will assist investigators in using the Stroop task to advance our understanding of these fundamental processes.

REFERENCES

MacLeod, C. M. (1991). Half a century of research on the Stroop effect: An integrative review. *Psychological Bulletin, 109,* 163–203.

Stroop, J. R. (1935). Studies of interference in serial verbal reactions. *Journal of Experimental Psychology, 18,* 643–662. (Reprinted in 1992 in the *Journal of Experimental Psychology: General, 121,* 15–23.)

Williams, J. M. G., Mathews, A., & MacLeod, C. (1996). The emotional Stroop task and psychopathology. *Psychological Bulletin, 120,* 3–24.

2

THE STROOP TASK
IN COGNITIVE RESEARCH

COLIN M. MACLEOD

The Stroop task is the one of the best known paradigms in cognitive psychology; it is also among cognitive psychology's most used contributions to clinical psychology. It is really quite extraordinary that a paradigm of such apparent simplicity has flourished as the discipline has grown and become more sophisticated. In fact, the Stroop task can trace its lineage directly to the origins of experimental psychology. In his dissertation, done under Wundt's supervision, Cattell (1886) made a fundamental observation. He measured response time to name a variety of stimuli and noted that it took longer to name objects (such as a picture of a horse) and properties of objects (such as their color) than it did to read the corresponding words. His explanation—that reading words was much more practiced than naming pictures or colors—introduced the concept of automaticity to psychology, a concept that has remained highly influential (see, e.g., Logan, 1988, 2002; Posner & Snyder, 1975; Shiffrin & Schneider, 1977).

My research cited in this chapter has been continuously supported by a discovery grant from the Natural Sciences and Engineering Research Council of Canada. I appreciate the helpful comments provided on the initial draft of this chapter by Uri Bibi, Ramona Bobocel, and Michael Dodd.

Almost 50 years later, working on his dissertation, John Ridley Stroop[1] (1935) combined word and color, creating a conflict situation. His first experiment contrasted reading color words in normal black ink on a white background (e.g., *green* in black, say "green": the control condition) with reading words in incongruent colors, ignoring the colors (e.g., *green* in red, say "green": the experimental condition). Stroop found little difference in oral word reading time, indicating that the incompatible ink colors were easily ignored during reading. It was his Experiment 2 that introduced the task that now goes by his name. The contrast here was between naming the colors of colored rectangles (e.g., for the green rectangle, say "green": the control condition) and naming the colors of incongruent color-word combinations (e.g., *red* in green, say "green": the experimental condition). Color naming was dramatically slower for the incompatible color words, and the Stroop effect was born.

Stroop accepted Cattell's differential practice account to explain the asymmetrical interference pattern between Experiments 1 and 2, augmenting it with the idea of his dissertation supervisor, Peterson (cf. Peterson, Lanier, & Walker, 1925), that words lead to a single reading response whereas colors lead to multiple reading responses. Stroop later put this idea to further experimental test (Stroop, 1938) and again concluded that it provided an adequate explanation. It is perhaps surprising that his task did not immediately catch on; for the next 30 years, use was limited, typically as a psychometric marker of attention (e.g., Thurstone, 1944).

A study by Klein (1964) opened the floodgates. Klein reasoned that the type of word that had to be ignored while color naming could be critical, suggesting that the word's meaning and its relation to the response of color naming were important in determining the size of the effect. To test this idea, he compared naming the colors (say, blue) of rows of asterisks (*****), nonwords (*evgjc*), low-frequency words (*helot*), high-frequency words (*heart*), color-related words (*grass*), color words not among the ink colors to be named (*black*), and incompatible color words in the response set (*green*). He found that interference increased across these conditions as the reading response to the item became stronger and more color-related. This study unleashed the potential of the Stroop effect as a research tool. Bibi and MacLeod (2004) have replicated the results of the classic Stroop and Klein studies using modern computerized presentation, providing contemporary benchmarks for these procedures.

Two more studies deserve places at the head table for their methodological innovations. Tecce and Dimartino (1965) introduced a tachisto-

---

[1]For a biographical sketch of John Ridley Stroop, see MacLeod (1991b). My Web site (http://www.arts.uwaterloo.ca/~cmacleod/Research/Stroopbiog.htm) contains an electronic version of this sketch and further pictures. Copies of my articles since 1991 can also be downloaded as PDF files from http://www.arts.uwaterloo.ca/~cmacleod/Research/Publications2.htm.

scopic version of the task. Instead of requiring the naming of the colors of multiple items on a single card, as Stroop (1935) and Klein (1964) had done, this new version presented single color-word trials for individual color-naming responses. To investigate this single item procedure more thoroughly, Dalrymple-Alford and Budayr (1966) introduced a new condition: They included congruent trials, in which the color and the word were compatible (e.g., *red* in red, say "red" to the color). Later studies demonstrated that this congruent condition often (but not always) resulted in faster responding than did the control condition—this effect is called Stroop facilitation—although the facilitation was virtually always much less than the interference (see pp. 174–175 in MacLeod, 1991a).[2] By this point, then, the standard ingredients were all in place, and the Stroop literature was just beginning to burgeon.

A number of review articles have since been published. Jensen and Rohwer (1966) reviewed the largely clinical and psychometric literature up to that point, emphasizing the utility of the task as a measure of attention in applied and clinical settings. Dyer (1973b) reviewed the early cognitive literature. MacLeod (1991a) provided an extensive review of the cognitive literature over the first 50-plus years of the task's existence. In 2000, MacLeod and MacDonald provided a sketch of the cognitive and especially the recent cognitive neuroscience research involving the Stroop task. All of these reviews are useful sources for pointers to and details about specific experimental questions that have been addressed.

In this chapter, my goal is to cover how Stroop experiments have been done in the past and how they are done now, with consideration of the many factors involved in conducting these experiments and in interpreting the data that they produce. I begin with the original paradigm and then move to contemporary procedures, along the way attempting to highlight issues especially relevant to the clinical researcher who uses variants of this task.

THE ORIGINAL MULTIPLE-ITEM CARD VERSION

In Stroop's (1935) original procedure, he used cards containing 100 items, arranged in 10 rows and 10 columns. In his Experiment 2, in which the task was color naming, the control card had 20 rectangles in each of five colors: red, blue, green, brown, and purple. He ensured that no color appeared more than twice in any row or column. For the incongruent card, he attempted the same arrangement, stating that no word or color was presented more than twice in any row or column. As it turns out, this is impossible:

---

[2] All references to "MacLeod" are to the work of Colin M. MacLeod, author of this chapter. All references to "C. MacLeod" refer to the work of Colin MacLeod, author of chapter 3.

Inspection of his original cards, on display at Vanderbilt University, confirms that he applied the constraint to the rows but not the columns. Each participant was given two cards in each condition, the second having the items in the reverse order from the first. Short practice sequences (10 items/card) prepared the participant for each condition. Although we do not know why Stroop did not use congruent cards, my guess is that he realized that, when the word and color agreed, participants would notice and switch to reading. As a result, the congruent condition would not necessarily involve the intended color-naming response and consequently would not be comparable to the other two conditions.

Stroop's instructions to participants were to respond as quickly as possible, leaving no error uncorrected. He started a stopwatch with the participant's first response and stopped it with his or her last response, obtaining one total time in seconds per card. The issue of how to handle errors is a significant one because errors are common, especially on the difficult incongruent cards. Requiring participants to correct errors results in two responses to those items. Thus, researchers often do not require error correction online which would ensure precisely 100 responses to all cards. Of course, more responses are errors on the incongruent card than on other cards, so there is a discrepancy across conditions regardless of the instructions concerning errors. Jensen (1965) discusses how to score the card version of the Stroop task.

The standard way to report data in the card version of the Stroop task is to sum the times for the (two) cards in a condition and then average them to provide a condition mean. The difference between the condition means on the control card and on the incongruent cards is taken to be a measure of interference, termed the *Stroop effect* or *Stroop interference*. The original data are highly replicable (cf. MacLeod, 1991a, pp. 164–165) in terms of both pattern and, remarkably, absolute times. In the card version, for with my data, it takes about 60 seconds to name the 100 control items and 102 seconds to name the 100 incongruent items. The 42-second difference constitutes an increase due to interference of about 70%, a truly huge increment when compared with virtually any other effect frequently investigated in the cognitive literature.

The card version has given way to the computerized version over the past 30 years. The card version does have disadvantages. First, errors are mixed in with correct responses because the single-card response time is a kind of "all in" measure. Second, previous or upcoming stimuli, which are visible simultaneously, can also influence processing of the current stimulus. Third, it is tedious to create multiple randomizations. Fourth, it is difficult to establish reliability, given limited numbers of observations per participant. Of course, the principal advantages of the card version are that it requires no equipment and is very portable.

THE MODERN SINGLE-ITEM COMPUTER VERSION

Today, cognitive psychologists conduct the vast majority of their studies under computer control. As a result, the single-item version of the Stroop task has supplanted the traditional multiple-item card version. Generally, the colored rectangle control used by Stroop has been replaced by a control item made up of keyboard characters (I discuss control items more in depth later in the chapter). In the single-item version, one item appears on each trial and is separately timed from its onset to the participant's response, which results in a time per trial in milliseconds. The single-item version allows error trials to be discarded, which solves one of the problems inherent in the card version of the task. The typical instructions for a cognitive response time task—"Respond as quickly as possible while avoiding errors"—are used despite their inherent ambiguity.

If one were to attempt to abstract a prototypical modern Stroop experiment, I believe that it would look something like this: There would be the standard four colors—red, blue, green, and yellow—and the corresponding words. Each of the 12 incongruent color-word combinations (given four colors) would be presented equally often. There would be at least two to three repetitions of the set, resulting in 24 to 36 trials. The control condition would be treated in the same way, although the precise control string (or strings) actually used varies widely. The trials from the incongruent and control conditions would be intermingled randomly. If a congruent condition was included, these trials would also be mixed in randomly. The congruent condition makes sense in the single-item procedure because, due to the random sequence, the participant cannot guess the condition and therefore cannot switch to a reading strategy on congruent trials. Note, however, that there would be only four congruent items, so they would be repeated more often than would individual incongruent items.

The total number of trials would range from 48 to 288, depending upon the number of conditions and the number of trials within each condition. Ordinarily, each participant would receive a unique random ordering of the trials. Administration of the task would take from 5 to 30 minutes, not counting initial instructions and practice trials. The number of practice trials varies, but 8 to 24 would not be uncommon (unless performance on initial trials is specifically of interest). The practice trials are especially important in the single-item procedure to acclimatize the participant to the display and especially to the response characteristics of the task.

Now consider a single trial. First, a blank screen would appear, perhaps lasting 500 ms and possibly broken into a fixation (e.g., ++++) and then a blank (250 ms each). Next, the color-word item would appear, usually centered on the screen in lower case (which is more like normal reading). The computer timing would be initiated with the item onset. The item would be removed and the timing would stop with the participant's response. Sometimes, the item is displayed for a fixed time (e.g., 150 ms) rather than having its offset contingent on the response. If scoring is done online, the temporal gap before the next trial might be a little variable due to the experimenter having to input a keypress to indicate accuracy. One can overcome this problem by programming a sufficiently long time between trials (e.g., 500 ms or more) to allow the experimenter to input accuracy easily within that interval.

Responding in the single-item procedure is done either vocally or manually (see pp. 182–183 in MacLeod, 1991a). Vocal responding into a microphone/voice key requires special circuitry to interface with the computer, but setting it up is not difficult.[3] When responding is via keypresses, often the index and middle fingers of each hand are used, with one color assigned to each finger. Common keys to use are "z", "x", ".", and "?". It is essential in manual responding to have a practice session to accustom the participant to the assignment of colors to keys. I recommend a minimum of 48 trials that perhaps use colored rows of asterisks (or the like) to conserve the word-based trials for the actual experiment. In light of the robustness of the task in the face of practice, though (see, e.g., MacLeod, 1998), it would do little harm to include actual word-based trials in practice. Keypress responses are typically slower than vocal responses, possibly because participants must translate a covert vocal response to an overt keypress.

Although keypresses are nonnatural responses to colors, with a little practice they work quite well. They have the advantage that no responses are lost due to not speaking loudly enough, or the like. Moreover, an experimenter need not be present during testing because accuracy can be scored by the computer; thus multiple participants can be tested simultaneously. Keypress responses have the disadvantage that the size of the Stroop effect is considerably smaller than with vocal responding (e.g., Redding & Gerjets, 1977), although it is still a large effect in comparison with other cognitive response time measures. It is worth noting that there is continuing debate about what processing differences underlie the response modality difference in effect size (Brown & Besner, 2001; Sharma & McKenna, 1998).

Vocal responding raises the issue of how to handle response errors. Options include tape-recording responses and retrospectively locating and marking errors or, more commonly, scoring responses online, which requires an experimenter to be present to record accuracy following each trial. It is important to realize that experimenters are also vulnerable to the Stroop effect, so they should simply record the participant's response without trying to judge its accuracy online; the computer can then make the necessary comparison. Note that there are at least two types of errors. Most obvious is making the wrong oral response, which usually means reading the word instead of

---

[3]Commercial experimental packages such as e-Prime (http://www.pstnet.com/) can provide both the software and the input hardware at a not-exorbitant cost.

naming the color (although occasionally a participant faced with *green* in red will respond "yellow" or "blue" and then look rather sheepish!). Recording actual responses on error trials, rather than just the fact that an error was made, also preserves the entire record of the participant's responses. The other main type of error is a voice key error, such as speaking too quietly on a trial or coughing or saying "uh" before the response. Participants should be instructed to speak in a quite loud voice and to be careful not to precede their response with any other sound. Such voice key errors are best scored with a different code than are true errors so that they can be differentiated and reported separately.

Reporting of data in the single-item version of the task is straightforward. First, all errors are removed and counted. It is important to report both error proportions and mean correct response times to expose any possible trade-off between speed and accuracy (cf. Pachella, 1974). Fortunately, response time and accuracy are usually positively correlated in the Stroop task, with most errors in the slow incongruent condition, so no trade-off clouds interpretation. The individual response times from each condition are then assembled. Often, investigators define upper and lower criteria to trim extreme response times, known as outliers, out of the data. There are quite a few techniques for this (see, e.g., Miller, 1991; Ratcliff, 1993; Ulrich & Miller, 1994; Van Selst & Jolicoeur, 1994), but the basic goal is to remove anticipations (less than, say, 300 ms) and lapses of attention (more than, say, 1,500 ms). The proportion of outliers removed should also be reported and ordinarily should not exceed 3% to 5%. At this point, the mean response time for each condition can be calculated; these values form the primary data. Trimmed means are much more common than are medians as central tendency measures in the Stroop literature, although both measures should produce the same qualitative data pattern.[4]

Data in the typical single-item Stroop task are rather different from data in the multiple-item version. Estimating the mean response time per item from the card version produces estimates of about 600 ms for the control condition and about 1,020 ms for the incongruent condition (based on the means in the previous section), which suggests 420 ms of interference. In fact, on the basis of data from my laboratory over the years (see, e.g., MacLeod, 1998), mean response times in the single-item version are on the order of 700 ms for the control condition and 820 ms for the incongruent condition, assuming vocal responding.[5] Thus, the interference effect is estimated here

---

[4]Researchers have occasionally reported transformed response time data, using a ratio (e.g., [Incongruent–Neutral]/Neutral), the log, speed, or the like. My position is that, unless there is a powerful, theory-driven reason to transform the data, response times are best left untransformed. In this way, the data represent actual processing time.

[5]A reasonable estimate of the congruent condition mean for the single-item procedure with vocal responding would be on the order of 680 ms, or about a 20-ms facilitation effect, although facilitation can be rather variable and is quite often not significant. Response times in the keypressing version of

at 120 ms. This represents a 17% increase as opposed to a 70% increase from the control to the incongruent condition. Why should the single-item method produce so much less interference? No doubt the ability to look ahead in the multiple-item version speeds overall responding (hence the low control condition estimate) but also permits more interference from nearby items, and the additional problem of recovering from errors slows total response time more in the multiple-item version. In this regard, Salo, Henik, and Robertson (2001) have begun the important job of directly comparing the two test formats.

STROOP VARIANTS AND OTHER INTERFERENCE TASKS

Methods other than vocal and keypress responding have been used to measure interference over the years, though much less frequently. Most prevalent among these is the card-sort method, in which individual color–word stimuli on cards are sorted into bins by color or by word, and sorting time for a deck of cards is the dependent measure (Chmiel, 1984; Tecce & Happ, 1964; see pp. 166–167 in MacLeod, 1991a). This method has been largely abandoned with the rise of computerized methods of conducting cognitive experiments, but still has potential value for settings (or individuals) where computerized testing is not possible.

There are also many other interference tasks, in which different types of materials are used. Most prevalent among these is the picture-word task (Glaser & Düngelhoff, 1984; Hentschel, 1973; see pp. 167–168 in MacLeod, 1991a), in which the participant names a line-drawing picture while ignoring the word typed within it. A version that is seeing more use, notably in the brain imaging literature, is the *counting Stroop task*, in which the participant counts the number of digits displayed, ignoring their identity (Bush et al., 1998; Windes, 1968). And, of course, there is the *emotional Stroop task* (Williams, Mathews, & C. MacLeod, 1996) considered at length in chapter 3. Numerous other interference tasks exist as well, as I have described elsewhere (pp. 168–170 in MacLeod, 1991a). Conceptual cousins are also common in the literature. These include the flanker task (Eriksen & Eriksen, 1974), in which a response-relevant target is surrounded by irrelevant but competing distracters, and the global-local task (Navon, 1977), in which a large letter is constructed from different smaller letters and the individual must attend to one of the sizes, ignoring the other. In my view, researchers are often too willing to refer to any task that involves interference as a Stroop task. The term *Stroop task* should probably be reserved for the color-word

---

the task depend on the amount of practice given with the color-key assignments before the experiment proper begins, so these are harder to estimate. With a little practice, control response times could be around 650 ms and incongruent times could be 700–720 ms, for interference of about 60 ms, half that of the vocal version but still quite a large and robust effect.

interference task, and the more superordinate term *interference task* should be used to designate the class of which the Stroop task is only one member.

THE THREE CONDITIONS

As already discussed, three conditions see frequent use in Stroop experiments: incongruent, congruent, and control. Although these conditions may appear straightforward, complexities lurk just beneath the surface, as so often is the case in experimental psychology. Consider the incongruent condition. How many words and colors should be included? What perceptual characteristics are important to take into consideration?

The typical number of colors and words is from three to five, although other quantities have been used (see p. 177 and pp. 183–184 in MacLeod, 1991a). Using only two colors/words can be problematic because participants can develop special strategies (e.g., in the incongruent condition, instead of naming the color, covertly read the word but respond aloud with the other word). Thus, I recommend always using more than two colors and words. Going beyond five words/colors begins to introduce potential hue discrimination problems, so the range three to five generally seems best. With odd numbers of color responses in the keypress situation, it may be best to have participants respond with one finger to multiple keys, rather than having an imbalanced key distribution across hands. The colors should be chosen to be readily discriminable, on the basis of careful pilot research. It may be useful to consult a set of color norms, such as those of Solso (1971). Klopfer (1996) has shown that interference, whether measured by response time or error rate, increases as the color–word similarity of individual items increases, something the investigator may wish to control.

In the incongruent condition, typically all of the combinations are used equally often, so for a set of four colors and the corresponding words, there are 12 possible incongruent items. Of course, for this same set of items, there are only four possible congruent items, where word and color coincide. It may be important that there are therefore fewer different congruent items than incongruent items; Melara and Mounts (1993) and Sabri, Melara, and Algom (2001) have begun to investigate this, focusing on the important topic of discriminability. Melara and Algom (2003) have in fact developed a theory of Stroop interference based on discriminability. The issue of number of different items may also apply to the control condition, depending on how it is constructed.

The most difficult decisions have to be made in constructing the control condition. Exactly what is to be controlled for, and what does this demand in terms of choosing the to-be-ignored word dimension? It has been quite common to use a string of characters as the control, such as ***** or xxxxx in red. This configuration uses a repeated keyboard character with no word-like properties to convey the color, so there should be no interference with color naming. Repeated character strings are closest to the colored rectangle that Stroop used with the goal of measuring pure (i.e., unidimensional) color naming while avoiding making the control condition too distinctive from the other conditions. Sometimes, a different letter string is constructed to correspond to each of the color words (e.g., www, xxxx, sssss, and mmmmmm, to correspond to red, blue, green, and yellow in length; see MacLeod & Hodder, 1998). Care should be taken not to use letters that are themselves the first letters of color words (even those not in the response set), as Regan (1978) has shown that the first letter of a color word (e.g., *g* in green, say "green") by itself causes substantial interference. Although letter strings do produce a small amount of interference relative to nonletter strings, these can all be treated as relatively pure estimates of color-naming time without verbal distraction.

When possible controls are considered, the next candidate is a to-be-ignored verbal item more like a word. Pronounceable nonwords (e.g., *dral*) cause measurable interference relative to unpronounceable nonwords (e.g., *hbnw*), which behave like letter strings (see Bibi & MacLeod, 2004; Dalrymple-Alford, 1972; Dalrymple-Alford & Azkoul, 1972; Klein, 1964). These might be suitable control items when verbal item pronounceability is of concern. When lexical status is considered crucial, switching to actual (noncolor) words as control items makes sense. There is some question as to whether the frequency of the word in the language is (Burt, 1999, 2002; Klein, 1964) or is not (Bibi & MacLeod, 2004; Monsell, Taylor, & Murphy, 2001) a factor. Although other control items could be and have been suggested (e.g., the color nonwords such as *blat* and *grend* of Besner, Stolz, & Boutilier, 1997, but these are problematic because they use the first few letters of color words), the standard ones are nonletter strings, letter strings, nonwords, and noncolor words.

And then there is the congruent condition (see pp. 174–175 in MacLeod, 1991a). The received view is that congruent trials produce facilitation for the same reason that incongruent trials produce interference, with the smaller effect size (on the order of 20 ms of facilitation vs. the 120 ms of interference) viewed as a consequence of it being more difficult to speed up a response than to slow it down (see MacLeod, 1998). However, MacLeod and MacDonald (2000) briefly describe research indicating that there may not be true facilitation, but rather that on some proportion of congruent trials participants slip and accidentally read the word instead of naming the color. Given the faster reading response (Cattell, 1886), there appears to be facilitation, but it is not true facilitation. This issue is not yet completely worked out, but unless a researcher has a particular reason for including congruent trials, I recommend omitting them. Of course, the congruent condition does not make sense in the context of noncolor-word experiments (e.g., there is no color with which *table* or *spider* is congruent or incongruent).

Sometimes, researchers compare the congruent and incongruent conditions directly, without a neutral control condition. In this case, the congruent condition is essentially treated as the control condition, according to the argument that the words and colors are the same in the two conditions and only congruency is manipulated. This argument has been made most strongly by Sabri et al. (2001) and by Melara and Algom (2003), who maintain that there is an advantage to having the same words in both the incongruent and the congruent/control condition, and that the difference score in this case can be meaningfully interpreted as the total effect of congruency/incongruency.

One more factor should be considered regarding conditions: the randomization of trials and conditions. Although fully randomized trial sequences are often used, some researchers prefer to program their experiments to prevent the occurrence of consecutive trials from the same condition or of the same entire item, or of the same color or word. Sequence effects do occur in the task (see pp. 177–178 in MacLeod, 1991a), and it may be desirable to avoid them. Of course, this rule could be relaxed slightly to allow runs of two or three but not longer, for example. The smaller the set of items, the more this issue becomes salient.

PRIMING IN THE STROOP TASK

In the same article in which they introduced the congruent condition, Dalrymple-Alford and Budayr (1966) also reported a new phenomenon hidden in the trial sequence. Imagine the following sequence of two trials: The first trial is the word *red* in green (respond "green") and the second is the word *yellow* in red (respond "red"). In this situation, the response "red" must be avoided on the first trial and then produced on the second trial. Dalrymple-Alford and Budayr reported an additional slowing of the response on the second trial in such a sequence, relative to sequences without repetition. This delay has come to be called *negative priming* and has been widely studied (see Fox, 1995; May, Kane, & Hasher, 1995, for reviews), although more recently it has usually been studied in contexts outside the Stroop task. It may be desirable under some circumstances to preclude or to systematically manipulate these ignored repetition trials that can be used to measure negative priming. The relation between the amounts of negative priming and Stroop interference observed within the paradigm should also be considered (see, e.g., Mari-Beffa, Estevez, & Danziger, 2000); changes in one can help in interpreting changes in the other.

The more standard priming procedure, so familiar in cognitive psychology, has also been used quite extensively in Stroop studies (see pp. 173–174 in MacLeod, 1991a). In the Stroop case, priming usually involves presenting one or a few words prior to the color-naming trial, varying the relation between the prime and the ignored item in the critical color-naming trial. However, in the priming work (unlike in standard Stroop studies) the words are noncolor words. This work originated with Warren (1972, 1974) and has continued in the studies of Henik, Friedrich, and Kellogg (1983), Whitney (1986; Whitney & Kellas, 1984), Burt (1994, 1999, 2002), MacLeod (1996), and others.

Warren (1972) originally showed greater interference when *aunt, uncle, cousin* preceded either *aunt* in red or *relative* in red (the response being to say "red" to the color) than when three unrelated words or the phrase "no list this trial" preceded the colored target. The intuitive idea that priming the word itself (called *repetition priming* or *identity priming*)—or its semantically related superordinate (called semantic priming)—would make it interfere more with color naming was supported. Warren (1974) obtained a similarly enhanced interference effect when the related word was a semantic associate. This pattern was later extended to the role of semantic context in sentences by Whitney and his colleagues (Whitney, 1986; Whitney & Kellas, 1984; Whitney, McKay, Kellas, & Emerson, 1985).

Burt (1994, 1999, 2002) has questioned whether the straightforward story that priming increases interference is as simple as was first believed. She has shown that identity/repetition priming actually tends to facilitate color naming, making it faster, a pattern that I have also repeatedly observed in unpublished research. Burt has argued that facilitation is, in fact, normal for identical words except when phonological activation of the word increases response competition. In contrast, non-identity priming tends to produce interference, as originally shown by Warren and others. Identity primes may allow the to-be-ignored word on the next color-naming trial to be more easily or more completely ignored, whereas related (but not identical) primes lead the individual to check back to determine the prime-target relation, which absorbs additional time and thereby appears to increase interference.

THE USE OF NONCOLOR WORDS

I noted that priming studies use noncolor words. Thus, these studies are not truly Stroop experiments, but rather use the color-naming task as a way to indirectly measure the activation of words and/or concepts. This use of priming is highly relevant, of course, to the applied domain. In clinical studies, the goal is generally to explore the state of activation of certain concepts relating to an individual's diagnosis or to the investigator's dimension of concern. The innovation in this work is in the type of words used. This innovation goes back to Ray (1979) who investigated test anxiety by using exam-related words as the to-be-ignored dimension. Shortly after Ray's study, other work began to explore anxiety (Mathews & C. MacLeod, 1985), phobias (Watts, McKenna, Sharrock, & Trezise, 1986), eating disorders (Ben-

Tovim, Walker, Fok, & Yap, 1989), and numerous other diagnosed disorders and dimensions of concern (for a review, see Williams et al., 1996). This clinical Stroop research has now become a very large domain of research.

In essence, the studies in the clinical literature that use what is now widely known as the emotional Stroop task also rely on priming. Their goal is to use color naming as an indirect (presumably nonstrategic) measure of the activation of a concept. Here, it is useful to make a distinction between acute (short-term, within-session) and chronic (long-term, extended over time) priming. The cognitive literature has examined acute priming from a just-presented prime that is related to the word whose color is to be named. In the clinical literature, in contrast, activation is assumed to be chronic because of the history and experience of the individual. There may be no within-experiment priming manipulation; instead, the manipulation is one of individual differences. This distinction has several important implications that will be considered in chapter 3; I consider only one here.

When priming is acute, one can either prime or not prime a given word. By way of illustration, the target word *table* in red could be preceded by a neutral prime (*****), an unrelated prime (*horse*), a related prime (*chair*), or an identity prime (*table*). This acute priming procedure permits tight experimental control in that each item serves as its own control, either within or across participants. Moreover, investigators can select as many different words as they need from a very large set in the language, controlling selected item characteristics. In contrast, in the chronic situation, the words must be relevant to the diagnosed disorder or dimension of concern, which limits the investigator to a small set of items that may not be easily balanced with respect to their properties. Furthermore, the concern-related words necessarily are the primed items, so the problem then becomes finding a suitable unprimed set. Words ordinarily cannot serve as their own controls in the clinical setting, except perhaps in the case where both a pretest and a posttest are used to determine whether a treatment has been effective in reducing a problem (cf. Watts et al., 1986). Even in that case, however, it may be best to use two counterbalanced sets, to avoid item repetition.

What should the control items be in the clinical setting? The answer hinges on the composition of the experimental item set. Consider an example in which the concern is eating. The experimental set consists of eating-related words, most likely including foods (*cake*), but also eating-related activities (*lunch*), body-shape-related terms (*obese*), and possibly instances of other eating-related categories. Creation of the control set now becomes complicated. One can begin by selecting items from the Thorndike and Lorge (1944) corpus, perhaps finding a length-matched word for each of the critical items. One can also control for category membership (using the Battig & Montague, 1969, norms), word frequency (using the Kučera & Francis, 1967, and Francis & Kučera, 1982, norms), and perhaps imageability (using the Paivio, Yuille, & Madigan, 1968, norms). Still, it is often difficult to find a suitable set, let alone to match the members of that set to the members of the critical set. Nonetheless, this is a very important aspect of the design of the experiment, given that the amount of interference—or even its presence—is based on the deviation of the experimental set from the control set. It is worth noting here that using a separate control group can help to solve this problem (e.g., spider phobics or normal controls should not show enhanced interference on words related to eating).

OTHER FACTORS IN EXPERIMENTAL DESIGN

Even a procedure as superficially uncomplicated as the Stroop paradigm has its intricacies when one reaches the concrete stage of actually setting up and programming the experiment. In addition to the stimuli and the response format, other elements must be selected and fine-tuned as well. Consider the instructions. Participants avoid reading (or even listening to) instructions, expecting to figure it out on the fly. In my laboratory, after giving the participants the opportunity to read the instructions, we ask them (without forewarning) to summarize the task. After they admit that they did not pay attention to the instructions, the experimenter explains the task and then again asks for a summary. We find that participants pay attention this second time, so the repetition is well worth doing. A few sample trials on large index cards are also useful to demonstrate stimulus format and the desired response. A series of practice trials—eight or more, depending on available time—is valuable as well.

When the participant is responding vocally, we usually follow the response with a brief blank screen and then the word "ready?" The participant is told that this provides a chance to ask for a short break, but in fact it allows the experimenter to input a keypress indicating the participant's response. It is worth noting that the time between a response to one trial and the onset of the next trial—the response-stimulus interval (RSI)—can be influential and should be taken into account. Sharma and McKenna (2001) have presented evidence that time pressure, achieved primarily with a short RSI, can substantially impact the amount of interference observed. Indeed, they found emotional interference only when there was time pressure.

One decision that may have to be made is whether to present the word in color—the integrated version—or to present the color separately from the word—the separated version (see pp. 175–176 in MacLeod, 1991a). Separation would be necessary, for example, if the two dimensions were to be presented simultaneously to different hemispheres (e.g., Dyer, 1973a; see pp. 185–186 in MacLeod, 1991a) or sequentially to investigate the time course of the effect (e.g., Glaser & Glaser, 1982; see pp. 179–180 in MacLeod, 1991a). Interference certainly declines with practice in the separated case (MacLeod, 1998), although the large interference seen in the integrated version appears to diminish even more quickly with practice. I have argued that, with practice, participants may learn to separate the two dimensions of the integrated stimulus.

In the separated case, not surprisingly, interference declines with distance of separation (Gatti & Egeth, 1978). When the first and second dimensions are presented sequentially, the time between their appearance is referred to as the stimulus onset asynchrony (or SOA; e.g., Glaser & Glaser, 1982; see pp. 179–180 in MacLeod, 1991a). Interference maximizes when the two dimensions appear within about 100 ms of each other and falls off sharply outside this window. It is very difficult to obtain a reverse Stroop effect, which occurs when an incongruent color interferes with reading the word, even when the color is given a substantial head start (Glaser & Glaser, 1982). With simultaneous exposure, Dunbar and MacLeod (1984) even showed that interference was almost identical for normally oriented words and for upside-down words, despite the dramatic slowing of word reading when words were upside down. The word exerts a powerful influence on color naming even when intuition—and reading time—might lead one to expect otherwise.

In discussing separation of word and color, it is worth noting that subliminal presentation of the word prior to the color has a checkered history in terms of whether interference occurs and, if so, under what conditions (e.g., Cheesman & Merikle, 1984, 1986; Severance & Dyer, 1973). Part of the difficulty is in defining the criteria for *subliminal*. Because this technique has been popular in the clinical literature (e.g., C. MacLeod & Rutherford, 1992; Mogg, Bradley, Williams, & Matthews, 1993; Mogg, Kentish, & Bradley, 1993)—it provides another way to reduce intentional or conscious processing—this important consideration is given more attention in Williams et al. (1996) and in chapter 3.

There are two additional somewhat related factors to weigh in constructing the trials in a Stroop experiment. First, it is well established that the probability of various trial types can affect the amount of interference observed (see pp. 176–177 in MacLeod, 1991a). Increasing the proportion of congruent trials (Lowe & Mitterer, 1982) or of neutral/control trials (Tzelgov, Henik, & Berger, 1992) leads to increased interference on incongruent trials, but interestingly does not appear to affect facilitation on congruent trials. It is most common to include equal proportions of trial types, but in some situations, deviation from this should be carefully considered, for both applied and theoretical reasons (see the argument made by Melara & Algom, 2003).

The second trial composition factor is repetition. In any Stroop-like experiment, the to-be-named colors are presented repeatedly across trials, given the limited set. In the traditional Stroop experiment, the words are also repeated because they are the corresponding color words. This repetition may actually heighten interference, given that the words are eligible responses and are being frequently presented across trials, so priming builds up. But what should be done when the words are not color words, as in studies of acute or chronic priming? This can be a critical question in clinical studies, in which the set of relevant words may be quite finite. My recommendation is to block repetitions, so that all words in the set are presented before any word is presented again. This blocking also permits analysis of changes in interference due to repetition across blocks, which may help to provide additional insight.

INDIVIDUAL DIFFERENCES IN INTERFERENCE

There have been fairly extensive studies of how certain individual differences affect Stroop interference. In my review (MacLeod, 1991a, pp. 184–187), I singled out three prominent differences: sex, age, and language. I concluded that sex differences were negligible; I have not seen evidence that would lead me to revise that conclusion. With regard to developmental trend, interference emerges with the onset of reading, rises in the early grades of school as reading skill develops, and then very slowly decreases over the adult years (Comalli, Wapner, & Werner, 1962). Comalli et al. also suggested that interference then rises again after age 60, but a meta-analysis by Verhaeghen and De Meersman (1998) suggests that this effect may result from overall cognitive slowing, not increased interference. As for the case of bilingualism, interference is almost as strong between languages as within language, although the dominant language tends to produce more interference (Chen & Ho, 1986; Dyer, 1971; Mägiste, 1984). I also included a subsection in my review article on a within-individual parameter—hemispheric differences; I concluded that the left hemisphere is subject to more interference, not surprising given its central role in language (MacLeod, 1991a, pp. 185–186). More clinically relevant individual differences were considered by Williams et al. (1996) and will be examined in chapter 3.

THEORY: WHAT CAUSES INTERFERENCE?

At the end of the day, what we are always aiming to do in cognitive experiments is to isolate and characterize the processes that underlie our routine information processing. In clinical studies, the goal is to characterize the disruption that occurs when processes are distorted, are replaced, or become altogether unavailable. We wish to understand the stream of processing that permits us to perform basic cognitive functions such as attending and remembering. So it is reasonable to ask: What does Stroop interference measure?

At the outset of this chapter, I mentioned several early accounts of interference. Cattell (1886) theorized that stimuli differ in the degree to which their processing has been practiced, with more practiced dimensions having greater automaticity. From this premise, one can derive the prediction that whenever the processing of one dimension is more practiced than that of another dimension, the more practiced dimension will be more likely to interfere with the less practiced one, and interference will be asymmetric. This is precisely what Stroop (1935) observed, and he adopted a differential practice account that was closely related to Cattell's theory. Efforts to directly control practice have also supported the automaticity account, as in the training experiments of MacLeod and Dunbar (1988). Using newly learned and practiced arbitrary shape-to-color-name connections, we observed a shift in interference over practice, such that the more practiced dimension did interfere more with the less practiced dimension. Automaticity explains these results and is readily extended to explain priming effects.

Stroop (1935) added the idea that greater practice led to less variance in the set of possible responses, and this may well be true, as automaticity becomes hyper-specific. Over the years, it became fairly standard to see the asymmetric interference of the Stroop effect as being due to a kind of horse race or speed-of-processing account, in which the faster-to-process dimension interfered with the slower-to-process dimension, and not vice versa (see Dyer, 1973b). This speed-of-processing is very intuitive, and is widely invoked in textbooks. But it is almost certainly wrong. Studies have shown that (a) the slower dimension can interfere with the faster to the same extent as the faster interferes with the slower (e.g., Dunbar & MacLeod, 1984), (b) giving the slower dimension a head start, even a substantial one, does not reverse the pattern of interference (Glaser & Glaser, 1982), and (c) dimensions that are processed at different speeds can nevertheless interfere with each other equivalently (MacLeod & Dunbar, 1988). Relative speed accounts cannot accommodate these results, and their reliance on a serial model of processing is now also seen as dated.

Instead, more contemporary explanatory ideas emphasize the strength of the disposition to make particular responses. They also move away from the older view of processing as involving the sequential queuing of processes, rather like a relay race (cf. Dyer, 1973b), and favor instead parallel processing occurring along multiple dimensions simultaneously. Thus, Logan (1980) painted the Stroop effect as the result of competition between ongoing processing of the word and the color dimensions at the same time, with differential rates of gain of evidence along the two dimensions. The strength idea grows out of automaticity and has been most explicitly realized in connectionist models, also known as parallel distributed processing models. Cohen, Dunbar, and McClelland (1990; see also Phaf, Van der Heijden, & Hudson, 1990) built a simple model that captured many of the results that

MacLeod (1991a) specified as pivotal for any account of the Stroop effect to explain. To account for interference, the Cohen et al. model relied on the buildup of practice for the word pathway being greater than that for the color pathway, a process tuned by attention. Like Logan's model, evidence accrual occurred in parallel along the two dimensions.

There are numerous other accounts of the Stroop effect (e.g., Virzi & Egeth, 1985), with new ones appearing regularly. Both Melara and Algom (2003) and Roelofs (2003) have presented powerful new theoretical frameworks. One conclusion that can be drawn on this basis is that assuming one of the existing accounts to be the correct one at this point is premature. For this reason, interpreting the results of Stroop experiments as evidence for a particular type of processing or for a particular process is suspect. One illustration of this principle is the concept of inhibition. Does the word have to be inhibited for the color to be named? This idea is widespread and quite intuitive, but the evidence in favor of it is not compelling. MacLeod, Dodd, Sheard, Wilson, and Bibi (2003) have tackled the question of inhibition in cognition more broadly and do not find strong support for inhibitory processing.[6] So it is important to devote considerable thought to the nature of the processing that is happening and not to assume a kind of one-to-one mapping between task and process, as is too often done.

CONCLUSION

In this chapter, I have set out how Stroop experiments are usually done, indicating along the way some of the methodological hurdles that are likely to be encountered. My goal has been to identify the important experimental parameters that should be considered in constructing a Stroop experiment. Such considerations are especially salient in the always complex realm of abnormal behavior. No experiment makes sense outside the context of theory, so I have also sketched out some of the theoretical ideas that have been proposed for explaining interference. My hope is that bringing these ideas together in one place will be helpful to researchers who wish to use the Stroop task as a tool for understanding attention, memory, and other basic cognitive processes, including their clinical ramifications. Studies of disrupted cognitive processing should inform our understanding of the normal operation of cognitive processing, just as the reverse should be true.

---

[6]As a consequence, I would prefer to banish the designation *Stroop inhibition* and always refer instead to the performance cost in the incongruent condition relative to the control condition as *Stroop interference*.

REFERENCES

Battig, W. F., & Montague, W. E. (1969). Category norms of verbal items in 56 categories: A replication and extension of the Connecticut category norms. *Journal of Experimental Psychology Monographs, 80*(3, Pt. 2), 1–46.

Ben-Tovim, D. I., Walker, M. K., Fok, D., & Yap, E. (1989). An adaptation of the Stroop Test for measuring shape and food concerns in eating disorders: A quantitative measure of psychopathology? *International Journal of Eating Disorders, 8*, 681–687.

Besner, D., Stolz, J. A., & Boutilier, C. (1997). The Stroop effect and the myth of automaticity. *Psychonomic Bulletin & Review, 4*, 221–225.

Bibi, U., & MacLeod, C. M. (2004.) *Stroop, Klein, and interference: Modern benchmarks for the color-word interference task.* Manuscript in preparation.

Brown, M., & Besner, D. (2001). On a variant of Stroop's paradigm: Which cognitions press your buttons? *Memory & Cognition, 29*, 903–904.

Burt, J. S. (1994). Identity primes produce facilitation in a colour naming task. *Quarterly Journal of Experimental Psychology, 47A*, 957–1000.

Burt, J. S. (1999). Associative priming in color naming: Interference and facilitation. *Memory & Cognition, 27*, 454–464.

Burt, J. S. (2002). Why do non-color words interfere with color naming? *Journal of Experimental Psychology: Human Perception and Performance, 28*, 1019–1038.

Bush, G., Whalen, P. J., Rosen, B. R., Jenike, M. A., McInerney, S. C., & Rauch, S. L. (1998). The Counting Stroop: An interference task specialized for functional neuroimaging: Validation study with functional MRI. *Human Brain Mapping, 6*, 270–282.

Cattell, J. M. (1886). The time it takes to see and name objects. *Mind, 11*, 63–65.

Cheesman, J., & Merikle, P. M. (1984). Priming with and without awareness. *Perception & Psychophysics, 36*, 387–395.

Cheesman, J., & Merikle, P. M. (1986). Distinguishing conscious from unconscious perceptual processes. *Canadian Journal of Psychology, 40*, 343–367.

Chen, H.-C., & Ho, C. (1986). Development of Stroop interference in Chinese-English bilinguals. *Journal of Experimental Psychology: Learning, Memory, and Cognition, 12*, 397–401.

Chmiel, N. (1984). Phonological recoding for reading: The effect of concurrent articulation in a Stroop task. *British Journal of Psychology, 75*, 213–220.

Cohen, J. D., Dunbar, K., & McClelland, J. L. (1990). On the control of automatic processes: A parallel distributed processing account of the Stroop effect. *Psychological Review, 97*, 332–361.

Comalli, P. E., Jr., Wapner, S., & Werner, H. (1962). Interference effects of Stroop color-word test in childhood, adulthood, and aging. *Journal of Genetic Psychology, 100*, 47–53.

Dalrymple-Alford, E. C. (1972). Associative facilitation and interference in the Stroop color-word task. *Perception & Psychophysics, 11*, 274–276.

Dalrymple-Alford, E. C., & Azkoul, J. (1972). The locus of interference in the Stroop and related tasks. *Perception & Psychophysics, 11*, 385–388.

Dalrymple-Alford, E. C., & Budayr, B. (1966). Examination of some aspects of the Stroop Color-Word Test. *Perceptual & Motor Skills, 23*, 1211–1214.

Dunbar, K., & MacLeod, C. M. (1984). A horse race of a different color: Stroop interference patterns with transformed words. *Journal of Experimental Psychology: Human Perception and Performance, 10*, 622–639.

Dyer, F. N. (1971). Color-naming interference in monolinguals and bilinguals. *Journal of Verbal Learning and Verbal Behavior, 10*, 297–302.

Dyer, F. N. (1973a). Interference and facilitation for color naming with separate bilateral presentations of the word and color. *Journal of Experimental Psychology, 99*, 314–317.

Dyer, F. N. (1973b). The Stroop phenomenon and its use in the study of perceptual, cognitive, and response processes. *Memory & Cognition, 1*, 106–120.

Eriksen, B. A., & Eriksen, C. W. (1974). Effects of noise letters upon the identification of a target letter in a nonsearch task. *Perception & Psychophysics, 16*, 143–149.

Fox, E. (1995). Negative priming from ignored distractors in visual selection: A review. *Psychonomic Bulletin & Review, 2*, 145–173.

Francis, W. N., & Kučera, H. (1982). *Frequency analysis of English usage: Lexicon and grammar*. Boston: Houghton Mifflin.

Gatti, S. V., & Egeth, H. E. (1978). Failure of spatial selectivity in vision. *Bulletin of the Psychonomic Society, 11*, 181–184.

Glaser, W. R., & Düngelhoff, F.-J. (1984). The time course of picture-word interference. *Journal of Experimental Psychology: Human Perception and Performance, 10*, 640–654.

Glaser, M. O., & Glaser, W. R. (1982). Time course analysis of the Stroop phenomenon. *Journal of Experimental Psychology: Human Perception and Performance, 8*, 875–894.

Henik, A., Friedrich, F. J., & Kellogg, W. A. (1983). The dependence of semantic relatedness effects upon prime processing. *Memory & Cognition, 11*, 366–373.

Hentschel, U. (1973). Two new interference tests compared to the Stroop Color-Word Test. *Psychological Research Bulletin, Lund University, 13*, 1–24.

Jensen, A. R. (1965). Scoring the Stroop test. *Acta Psychologica, 24*, 398–408.

Jensen, A. R., & Rohwer, W. D. (1966). The Stroop color-word test: A review. *Acta Psychologica, 25*, 36–93.

Klein, G. S. (1964). Semantic power measured through the interference of words with color-naming. *American Journal of Psychology, 77*, 576–588.

Klopfer, D. S. (1996). Stroop interference and color-word similarity. *Psychological Science, 7*, 150–157.

Kučera, H., & Francis, W. N. (1967). *Computational analysis of present-day American English*. Providence, RI: Brown University Press.

Logan, G. D. (1980). Attention and automaticity in Stroop and priming tasks: Theory and data. *Cognitive Psychology, 12*, 523–553.

Logan, G. D. (1988). Toward an instance theory of automatization. *Psychological Review, 95*, 492–527.

Logan, G. D. (2002). An instance theory of attention and memory. *Psychological Review, 109*, 376–400.

Lowe, D. G., & Mitterer, J. O. (1982). Selective and divided attention in a Stroop task. *Canadian Journal of Psychology, 36*, 684–700.

MacLeod, C., & Rutherford, E. M. (1992). Anxiety and the selective processing of emotional information: Mediating roles of awareness, trait and state variables, and personal relevance of stimulus materials. *Behaviour Research & Therapy, 30*, 479–491.

MacLeod, C. M. (1991a). Half a century of research on the Stroop effect: An integrative review. *Psychological Bulletin, 109*, 163–203.

MacLeod, C. M. (1991b). John Ridley Stroop: Creator of a landmark cognitive task. *Canadian Psychology, 32*, 521–524.

MacLeod, C. M. (1996). How priming affects two speeded implicit tests of remembering: Naming colors versus reading words. *Consciousness & Cognition, 5*, 73–90.

MacLeod, C. M. (1998). Training on integrated versus separated Stroop tasks: The progression of interference and facilitation. *Memory & Cognition, 26*, 201–211.

MacLeod, C. M., Dodd, M. D., Sheard, E. D., Wilson, D. E., & Bibi, U. (2003). In opposition to inhibition. In B. H. Ross (Ed.), *The Psychology of Learning and Motivation* (vol. 43, pp. 163–214). San Diego, CA: Academic Press.

MacLeod, C. M., & Dunbar, K. (1988). Training and Stroop-like interference: Evidence for a continuum of automaticity. *Journal of Experimental Psychology: Learning, Memory, and Cognition, 14*, 126–135.

MacLeod, C. M., & Hodder, S. L. (1998). Presenting two incongruent color words on a single trial does not alter Stroop interference. *Memory & Cognition, 26*, 212–219.

MacLeod, C. M., & MacDonald, P. A. (2000). Inter-dimensional interference in the Stroop effect: Uncovering the cognitive and neural anatomy of attention. *Trends in Cognitive Sciences, 4*, 383–391.

Mägiste, E. (1984). Stroop tasks and dichotic translation: The development of interference patterns in bilinguals. *Journal of Experimental Psychology: Learning, Memory, and Cognition, 10*, 304–315.

Mari-Beffa, P., Estevez, A. F., & Danziger, S. (2000). Stroop interference and negative priming: Problems with inferences from null results. *Psychonomic Bulletin & Review, 7*, 499–503.

Mathews, A., & MacLeod, C. (1985). Selective processing of threat cues in anxiety states. *Behaviour Research & Therapy, 23*, 563–569.

May, C. P., Kane, M. J., & Hasher, L. (1995). Determinants of negative priming. *Psychological Bulletin, 118*, 35–54.

Melara, R. D., & Algom, D. (2003). Driven by information: A tectonic theory of Stroop effects. *Psychological Review, 110,* 422–471.

Melara, R. D., & Mounts, J. R. (1993). Selective attention to Stroop dimensions: Effects of baseline discriminability, response mode, and practice. *Memory & Cognition, 21,* 627–645.

Miller, J. (1991). Reaction time analysis with outlier exclusion: Bias varies with sample size. *Quarterly Journal of Experimental Psychology, 43A,* 907–912.

Mogg, K., Bradley, B. P., Williams, R., & Mathews, A. M. (1993). Subliminal processing of emotional information in anxiety and depression. *Journal of Abnormal Psychology, 102,* 304–311.

Mogg, K., Kentish, J., & Bradley, B. P. (1993). Effects of anxiety and awareness on color identification latencies for emotional words. *Behaviour Research & Therapy, 31,* 559–567.

Monsell, S., Taylor, T. J., & Murphy, K. (2001). Naming the color of a word: Is it responses or task sets that compete? *Memory & Cognition, 29,* 137–151.

Navon, D. (1977). Forest before trees: The precedence of global features in visual perception. *Cognitive Psychology, 9,* 353–383.

Pachella, R. G. (1974). The interpretation of reaction time in information-processing research. In B. H. Kantowitz (Ed.), *Human information processing: Tutorials in performance and cognition* (pp. 41–82). Hillsdale, NJ: Erlbaum.

Paivio, A., Yuille, J. C., & Madigan, S. A. (1968). Concreteness, imagery, and meaningfulness values for 925 nouns. *Journal of Experimental Psychology Monographs, 76* (1, Pt. 2), 1–25.

Peterson, J., Lanier, L. H., & Walker, H. M. (1925). Comparisons of white and negro children in certain ingenuity and speed tests. *Journal of Comparative Psychology, 5,* 271–283.

Phaf, R. H., Van der Heijden, A. H. C., & Hudson, P. T. W. (1990). SLAM: A connectionist model for attention in visual selection tasks. *Cognitive Psychology, 22,* 273–341.

Posner, M. I., & Snyder, C. R. R. (1975). Attention and cognitive control. In R. L. Solso (Ed.), *Information processing and cognition: The Loyola symposium* (pp. 55–85). Hillsdale, NJ: Erlbaum.

Ratcliff, R. (1993). Methods for dealing with reaction time outliers. *Psychological Bulletin, 114,* 510–532.

Ray, C. (1979). Examination stress and performance on a color-word interference test. *Perceptual & Motor Skills, 49,* 400–402.

Redding, G. M., & Gerjets, D. A. (1977). Stroop effect: Interference and facilitation with verbal and manual responses. *Perceptual & Motor Skills, 45,* 11–17.

Regan, J. E. (1978). Involuntary automatic processing in color-naming tasks. *Perception & Psychophysics, 24,* 130–136.

Roelofs, A. (2003). Goal-referenced selection of verbal action: Modeling attentional control in the Stroop task. *Psychological Review, 110,* 88–125.

Sabri, M., Melara, R. D., & Algom, D. (2001). A confluence of contexts: Asymmetric versus global failures of selective attention to Stroop dimensions. *Journal of Experimental Psychology: Human Perception and Performance, 27*, 515–537.

Salo, R., Henik, A., & Robertson, L. C. (2001). Interpreting Stroop interference: An analysis of differences between task versions. *Neuropsychology, 15*, 462–471.

Severance, L. J., & Dyer, F. N. (1973). Failure of subliminal word presentations to generate interference to color naming. *Journal of Experimental Psychology, 101*, 186–189.

Sharma, D., & McKenna, F. P. (1998). Differential components of the manual and vocal Stroop tasks. *Memory & Cognition, 26*, 1033–1040.

Sharma, D., & McKenna, F. P. (2001). The role of time pressure on the emotional Stroop task. *British Journal of Psychology, 92*, 471–481.

Shiffrin, R. M., & Schneider, W. (1977). Controlled and automatic human information processing: II. Perceptual learning, automatic attending and a general theory. *Psychological Review, 84*, 127–190.

Solso, R. L. (1971). Meaningfulness of colors. *Psychonomic Science, 23*, 301–303.

Stroop, J. R. (1935). Studies of interference in serial verbal reactions. *Journal of Experimental Psychology, 18*, 643–662. (Reprinted in 1992 in the *Journal of Experimental Psychology: General, 121*, 15–23.)

Stroop, J. R. (1938). Factors affecting speed in serial verbal reactions. *Psychological Monographs, 50*, 38–48.

Tecce, J. J., & Dimartino, M. (1965). Effects of heightened drive (shock) on performance in a tachistoscopic color-word interference task. *Psychological Reports, 16*, 93–94.

Tecce, J. J., & Happ, S. J. (1964). Effects of shock-arousal on a card-sorting test of color-word interference. *Perceptual & Motor Skills, 19*, 905–906.

Thorndike, E. L., & Lorge, I. (1944). *The teacher's word book of 30,000 words.* New York: Columbia University, Teachers College Press.

Thurstone, L. L. (1944). *A factorial study of perception.* Chicago: University of Chicago Press.

Tzelgov, J., Henik, A., & Berger, J. (1992). Controlling Stroop effect by manipulating expectation for color related stimuli. *Memory & Cognition, 20*, 727–735.

Ulrich, R., & Miller, J. (1994). Effects of truncation on reaction time analysis. *Journal of Experimental Psychology: General, 123*, 34–80.

Van Selst, M., & Jolicoeur, P. (1994). A solution to the effect of sample size on outlier elimination. *Quarterly Journal of Experimental Psychology, 47A*, 631–650.

Verhaeghen, P., & De Meersman, L. (1998). Aging and the Stroop effect: A meta-analysis. *Psychology & Aging, 13*, 120–126.

Virzi, R. A., & Egeth, H. E. (1985). Toward a translational model of Stroop interference. *Memory & Cognition, 13*, 304–319.

Warren, R. E. (1972). Stimulus encoding and memory. *Journal of Experimental Psychology, 94*, 90–100.

Warren, R. E. (1974). Association, directionality, and stimulus encoding. *Journal of Experimental Psychology, 102*, 151–158.

Watts, F. N., McKenna, F. P., Sharrock, R., & Trezise, L. (1986). Colour naming of phobia-related words. *British Journal of Psychology, 77*, 97–108.

Whitney, P. (1986). Processing category terms in context: Instantiations as inferences. *Memory & Cognition, 14*, 39–48.

Whitney, P., & Kellas, G. (1984). Processing category terms in context: Instantiation and the structure of semantic categories. *Journal of Experimental Psychology: Learning, Memory, and Cognition, 10*, 95–103.

Whitney, P., McKay, T., Kellas, G., & Emerson, W. A. (1985). Semantic activation of noun concepts in context. *Journal of Experimental Psychology: Learning, Memory, and Cognition, 11*, 126–135.

Williams, J. M. G., Mathews, A., & MacLeod, C. (1996). The emotional Stroop task and psychopathology. *Psychological Bulletin, 120*, 3–24.

Windes, J. D. (1968). Reaction time for numerical coding and naming of numerals. *Journal of Experimental Psychology, 78*, 318–322.

3

THE STROOP TASK
IN CLINICAL RESEARCH

COLIN MACLEOD

Across recent years, the idea that automatic biases in selective attention might causally underpin the symptoms of psychological dysfunction has become a core premise shared by a wide spectrum of explanatory models, put forward to account for a diverse array of clinical conditions. Without doubt, such accounts have enjoyed their greatest popularity as potential explanations for various types of emotional pathology (cf. MacLeod & Rutherford, 2004; Mathews & MacLeod, 1994). In addition to the common hypothesis that clinical depression results, at least in part, from an automatic attentional bias toward emotionally negative information (McCabe & Gotlib, 1993; Westra & Kuiper, 1997), it frequently has been postulated that the various anxiety disorders also reflect automatic biases in the allocation of selective attention toward information concerning threat and danger (Ehrenreich & Gross, 2002; Logan & Goetsch, 1993).

Although the present review focuses principally upon the ways in which variations of the Stroop task have been employed to empirically address such

My research cited in this article has been continuously supported by a discovery grant from the Australian Research Council.

attentional hypotheses concerning emotional vulnerability, it should be noted that biased attention has been similarly implicated in the mediation of many other types of psychological disorder. For example, clinical theorists have suggested that attentional bias toward particular classes of information may characterize patients who suffer from delusions (Bentall & Kaney, 1989), mania (Murphy et al., 1999), hypochondriasis (Pauli, Schwenzer, Brody, & Rau, 1993), addictions (Ehrman et al., 2002; Stetter, Ackermann, Bizer, & Straube, 1995), psychogenic amnesia (Merckelbach & Van den Hout, 1993), eating disorders (Faunce, 2002; Williamson, 1996), morbid jealousy (Intili & Tarrier, 1998), and borderline personality disorder (Ceumern-Lindenstjerna, Brunner, Parzer, Fiedler, & Resch, 2002). Many researchers have employed Stroop task variants to test predictions derived from such accounts. However, the basic methodological issues associated with the use of Stroop task variants to assess attentional bias remain similar in all cases and can be illustrated by drawing upon the concentrated body of literature that has accumulated within the field of emotion research.

ADAPTING THE STROOP TASK TO ASSESS ATTENTIONAL BIAS IN PSYCHOPATHOLOGY

Stroop's (1935) original finding, that the time taken to name a word's ink color is delayed when the content of the word is a conflicting color name, served to establish that color-naming latency can index the processing of word content without requiring participants to explicitly report this content. Later task variants, some reviewed in MacLeod (see chap. 2, this volume), have demonstrated that when words other than color names are presented, then manipulations likely to encourage the processing of a word's content, such as semantic priming (Warren, 1972) or situational relevance (Geller & Shaver, 1976), also slow the naming of its ink color. Therefore, it follows that one might infer the degree to which participants selectively process the content of differing words by recording the speed with which they can name the ink colors in which such items are presented. Many researchers have indeed addressed hypotheses concerning emotionally linked attentional bias by examining the speed with which anxious and depressed participants could color-name affectively toned words. It has become conventional to use the term *emotional Stroop task* to describe this methodology (Jones, Jones, Blundell, & Bruce, 2002; McKenna & Sharma, 1995; Williams, Mathews, & MacLeod, 1996; Williams, Watts, MacLeod, & Mathews, 1997) and, despite some differences, there are close procedural parallels between the traditional Stroop task and this emotional variant. For example, both have been delivered either by using multiple-item presentation within a card-based approach or by presenting single items individually for color naming.

The Multiple-Item Card Version of the Emotional Stroop Task

A number of clinical investigators have opted to deliver the emotional Stroop task using the card-based approach employed to administer the original color conflict task by Stroop (1935) himself and by other early cognitive-experimentalists such as Comalli, Wapner, and Werner (1962) and Preston and Lambert (1969). Aside from the obvious difference in stimulus word identity, procedural aspects of the approach remain characteristic of this earlier research. For example, Mathews and MacLeod (1985) presented four such cards to patients suffering from generalized anxiety disorder and to nonanxious control participants. One card contained 12 physically threatening words (such as *disease* and *injury*) and another contained 12 socially threatening words (such as *foolish* and *lonely*), while the remaining two cards contained length- and frequency-matched neutral control words. On each card, words appeared variously in red, green, blue, or yellow ink, and every item was repeated eight times to yield 96 colored words per card, arranged in an array 8 words wide and 12 words deep. Participants were instructed to color-name each word in turn, and the time taken to complete the color naming of each entire card was recorded. Whereas control participants took an almost identical time on cards displaying threat words and neutral words, the generalized anxiety disorder patients took almost five seconds longer to complete the color naming of the threat word cards compared with the neutral word cards.

Using similar card-based approaches, many other researchers have replicated this finding that generalized anxiety disorder patients are disproportionately slow to complete the color naming of cards that contain threat words (Golombok et al., 1991; Mathews, Mogg, Kentish, & Eysenck, 1995). This slowing to color-name threat words likewise has been demonstrated, with such card-based variants of the emotional Stroop task, in patients suffering from a wide range of other anxiety disorders, including specific phobias (Martin, Horder, & Jones, 1992; Watts, Trezise, & Sharrock, 1986b), social phobia (Becker, Rinck, Margraf, & Roth, 2001; Hope, Rapee, Heimberg, & Dombeck, 1990), obsessive compulsive disorder (Lavy, van Oppen, & van den Hout, 1994; Unoki, Kasuga, Matsushima, Ohta, & Doi, 2000), panic disorder (Ehlers, Margraf, Davies, & Roth, 1988; Quero, Banos, & Botella, 2000), and posttraumatic stress disorder (McNally, Amir, & Lipke, 1996; McNally, Kaspi, Riemann, & Zeitlin, 1990a). On a similar card-based version of the emotional Stroop task, Williams and Nulty (1986) also observed that depressed individuals demonstrated disproportionate slowing of color naming on cards that contained generally negative words, though this effect has not consistently been replicated by other researchers who have tested depressives (Carter, Maddock, & Magliozzi, 1992; Hill & Knowles, 1991).

The Single-Item Version of the Emotional Stroop Task

Aside from word content, the procedures adopted to deliver this alternative version of the emotional Stroop task closely parallel those associated with the modern version of the color-conflict Stroop, described in MacLeod (see chap. 2, this volume). Emotionally toned words repeatedly are exposed individually, in differing ink colors, and participants are required to identify the color of each item while attempting to ignore the word's meaning. In most studies, these individual stimuli are delivered on a computer monitor (McNally, Riemann, & Kim, 1990b), but in some experiments they have been presented by tachistoscope (Gotlib & Cane, 1987) or slide projection (Klieger & Cordner, 1990). Usually, each stimulus word remains visible until the participant's response is detected, although in some task variants, to be described shortly, the word can be exposed more briefly. In most experiments, the response involves naming each color aloud and is detected by voice key (Segal, Gemar, Truchon, Guirguis, & Horowitz, 1995; Stewart, Conrod, Gignac, & Pihl, 1998), although in a number of studies keypresses have been employed to register color identity (Mogg, Kentish, & Bradley, 1993b; Richards, French, Johnson, Naparstek, & Williams, 1992). In either case, the critical response latency is the interval between stimulus word onset and detection of the color identification response. In general, results from studies employing this single-item variant of the emotional Stroop task have served to confirm that emotional pathology is associated with increased color-naming interference on emotionally negative stimulus words.

A wide range of studies employing this single-item version of the emotional Stroop task have demonstrated that color naming of individual negatively toned stimulus words is retarded in emotionally disturbed patients. This finding has been observed in patients suffering from a wide range of anxiety disorders, including specific phobias (Kindt & Brosschot, 1997; Lavy et al., 1994), social phobia (Amir, Freshman, & Foa, 2002; Holle, Neely, & Heimberg, 1997), generalized anxiety disorder (Bradley, Mogg, Millar, & White, 1995a; Mogg et al., 1993b), posttraumatic stress disorder (Beck, Freeman, Shipherd, Hamblen, & Lackner, 2001; Foa, Rothbaum, Riggs, & Murdock, 1991), panic disorder (Buckley, Blanchard, & Hickling, 2002; McNally, Riemann, Louro, Lukach, & Kim, 1992), and obsessive compulsive disorder (Foa, Ilai, McCarthy, & Shoyer, 1993; McNeil, Tucker, Miranda, Lewin, & Nordgren, 1999). Likewise, when presented with this single-item task variant, clinically depressed patients also have been found to display delayed color naming on emotionally negative words, under certain conditions (Segal et al., 1995). However, using the same task, a number of other researchers have failed to obtain evidence of such an effect in depressives (Doost, Taghavi, Moradi, Yule, & Dalgleish, 1997; Mogg et al., 1993b).

The great majority of studies employing Stroop task variants to address hypotheses concerning the patterns of attentional bias associated within psychopathology have adopted either of these two main methodological approaches, regardless of whether such hypotheses have concerned the selective processing of emotionally toned information in anxiety and depression, or the selective processing of alternative categories of information in quite different clinical conditions. For example, similar variants of the Stroop task have served to establish that patients suffering from delusions are slow to color-name words associated with delusional content (Kinderman, 1994), those suffering from eating disorders demonstrate increased color-naming times on words related to food and weight (McManus, Waller, & Chadwick, 1996), manic patients show delays when color-naming words related to mania (Murphy et al., 1999), smokers display retarded color-naming latencies on words associated with cigarettes (Wertz & Sayette, 2001), and patients dependent on alcohol or cocaine are slow to name the colors of words related to their addictions (Cox, Hogan, Kristian, & Race, 2002; Franken, Kroon, Wiers, & Jansen, 2000). In all cases, the findings have been taken as evidence of an attentional bias toward these classes of information in such disorders.

CATEGORICAL VERSUS DIMENSIONAL APPROACHES TO CLINICAL STROOP RESEARCH

As the studies already cited have demonstrated, both clinically anxious and clinically depressed individuals have been found to show delayed color naming of emotionally negative words. However, on conventional questionnaire instruments clinically anxious and clinically depressed patients each characteristically report elevated levels of both depression and anxiety. Thus, the observation that both categories of clinical patients display slowed color naming of negative words tells us nothing about which emotional dimension is associated with this effect. In fact, when correlational analyses have been carried out, it has been found that slowed color naming of negative words, relative to neutral words, tends to be associated with questionnaire measures of anxiety, rather than with questionnaire measures of depression, in clinical patients (Mathews & MacLeod, 1985; Mogg, Mathews, & Weinman, 1989), even when their primary emotional symptom is depression (Williams & Nulty, 1986).

Failure to ensure that experimental designs are driven by a clearly formulated position concerning the categorical or dimensional nature of those individual differences under scrutiny also at times has undermined researchers' conclusions that certain types of attentional bias are characteristic of other forms of clinical pathology. For example, there is little doubt that patients suffering from eating disorders display slowed color naming of food and weight words (Lovell, Williams, & Hill, 1997). Many of the studies demonstrating this effect have compared eating-disordered patients with control participants who report no restriction of food intake (Jones-Chesters, Monsell, & Cooper, 1998), yet the observed group differences have led to the proposal that retarded color naming of food and weight words may represent a feature of eating pathology (Fairburn, Cooper, Cooper, & McKenna, 1991). However, this methodological approach confounds the categorical distinction of clinical status with individual differences on the dimension of eating restraint. When investigators have contrasted eating-disordered patients with nonclinical populations also engaged in dietary restraint, then they typically have found these groups to demonstrate equivalent patterns of color naming (Perpina, Hemsley, Treasure, & de Silva, 1993), as delayed color naming of food and weight words appears to be associated with dietary restraint within the normal population (Stewart & Samoluk, 1997). This finding has led researchers to conclude that the phenomenon is not a distinctive feature of clinical pathology (Black, Wilson, Labouvie, & Heffernan, 1997; Huon, 1995), although it may represent a marker of vulnerability to eating disorders (Cooper & Fairburn, 1992).

Similar confounds between clinical status and participant variations on normal dimensions of individual difference also have characterized many studies that have used Stroop task variants to investigate the association between emotional pathology and attentional bias to negative information. Typically, such experiments have compared the performance of participants suffering from emotional disorders with that of nonclinical control participants, who differ not only in clinical status but also on those dimensions of state and trait emotion that vary within the normal population. Yet investigators employing correlational analyses often have found that the magnitude of the clinical patients' slowing to color-name threat words is associated with their reported levels of either trait anxiety (Lundh, Wikstrom, Westerlund, & Öst, 1999) or state anxiety (Brosschot, de Ruiter, & Kindt, 1999). Furthermore, within nonclinical populations it also has been observed that trait and/or state anxiety elevations are associated with heightened color-naming interference on threat words (Richards & Millwood, 1989; Riemann & McNally, 1995). The fact that attentional bias to threat, as assessed with the emotional Stroop task, appears to be associated with trait and state anxiety variations within the normal population does not preclude the possibility that certain distinctive features of this attentional bias might be uniquely associated with clinical pathology. However, experiments designed to test such hypotheses should avoid confounding the categorical group differences associated with clinical status with dimensions of individual difference that are not definitive of clinical pathology. The most appropriate choice of participants always will always depend critically upon the precise theoretical hypothesis concerning attentional bias that the researcher wishes to address. Similarly, selection of stimulus materials must also be closely guided by the researcher's specific hypothesis, with the aim of eliminating undesired confounds.

STIMULUS SPECIFICITY EFFECTS ON
CLINICAL STROOP TASK VARIANTS

Virtually all of the early studies that employed the emotional Stroop task to address the hypothesis that emotional pathology is associated with an attentional bias toward negative information contrasted color-naming latencies on negative and neutral words. Therefore the observed pattern of effects might reflect a tendency for anxiety patients to display slowed color naming of emotional words in general, rather than of negative words in particular. Using a card-based version of the emotional Stroop task, Martin, Williams, and Clark (1991) compared the color-naming latencies of clinical anxiety patients and nonanxious control participants on neutral words, emotionally negative words, and emotionally positive words. These researchers found that, compared with control participants, the anxiety patients displayed a selective slowing to color-name both categories of emotional words; this result led the researchers to propose that anxiety is associated with an attentional bias toward all emotional information, regardless of its valence.

Despite serving to illustrate the importance of avoiding unintended confounds between alternative stimulus dimensions, Martin et al.'s (1991) findings have not replicated consistently. Some researchers who have employed negative, positive, and neutral words within the emotional Stroop task have likewise observed that anxious individuals are slow to color-name both the negative and positive items (Mogg & Marden, 1990). However, other investigators using very similar sets of materials have observed that anxiety patients display evidence of retarded color naming only on negative words, and not on positive words (Bryant & Harvey, 1995; Kaspi, McNally, & Amir, 1995; Mogg, Bradley, Williams, & Mathews, 1993a). A variety of explanations have been offered to account for the discrepant findings. Rutherford, MacLeod, and Campbell (in press) contend that these two classes of effects each are associated with different dimensions of anxiety. In contrast, Mathews and Klug (1993) assert that the presence or absence of such interference effects on positive materials depends upon their relevance to participants' personal concerns, which has varied across studies.

This possibility that color-naming interference effects may be restricted to specific domains of emotional information, directly associated with clinical patients' personal concerns, actually has received considerable experimental support. For example, the greatest level of color-naming interference has been found on suicide-related words for depressed suicide attemptors (Becker, Strohbach, & Rinck, 1999; Williams & Broadbent, 1986), on social threat words for social phobics (Hope et al., 1990; Lundh & Öst, 1996), on physical threat words for panic disorder patients (Buckley et al., 2002; Ehlers et al., 1988), on spider-relevant words for spider phobics (Thorpe & Salkovskis, 1997; Watts, McKenna, Sharrock, & Trezise, 1986a), on trauma-related words for posttraumatic stress disorder patients (Kaspi et al., 1995;

Vrana, Roodman, & Beckham, 1995), and on words associated with obsessional concerns in patients suffering from obsessive compulsive disorder (Foa et al., 1993; Lavy et al., 1994). Nevertheless, interpretation of such effects once again is compromised by the likely presence of particular confounds within the stimulus sets that have been employed.

It has been common to interpret such findings as evidence that the attentional bias toward negative stimuli demonstrated by emotionally disordered individuals is restricted to personally relevant information. However, an alternative possibility is that emotional negativity commonly has been confounded with personal relevance. Take, for example, Muris, Merckelbach, and de Jongh's (1995) finding that, compared with control participants, dental phobics show the greatest slowing of color naming on words associated with dental procedures (such as hole or tooth). It seems likely that such terms would be negatively valenced only for the phobic individuals. This confound within the stimulus set, between subjective negativity and relevance to personal concern, means that one cannot determine whether the specificity effect represents something other than a valence effect. Personally relevant threat stimuli may simply be disproportionately threatening.

To determine whether any given patient group's slowing to color-name emotionally negative words is influenced by the personal relevance of stimuli, researchers must endeavor to ensure that patients and controls are exposed to negative words that differ in terms of their personal relevance, but not in terms of their subjective emotional valence. This methodological goal can be pursued through the careful collection of stimulus ratings. Some researchers go so far as to advocate the use of stimulus materials individually selected for each participant. For example, when McNally et al. (1994) contrasted panic disorder patients and control participants to examine the specificity of color-naming interference on negative words, they commenced their experimental session by having each participant rate the subjective emotional valence of many stimulus words, drawn from pools intended to represent panic-relevant threat (e.g., *collapse*), general threat (e.g., *violence*), positive items (e.g., *confident*), and neutral items (e.g., *button*). For each participant, only five words then were selected from each set for use within the emotional Stroop task. Word selection was based on the ratings provided, which permitted the researchers to reduce the problematic confound between emotional negativity and personal relevance. Whereas the control participants displayed equivalent color-naming latencies across all four classes of stimulus words, McNally et al. found that their panic disorder patients were disproportionately slow to color-name both classes of threat words.

The general methodological principle here is straightforward. To provide an adequate test of hypotheses stating that one stimulus dimension, rather than another, modifies the magnitude of color-naming interference, the investigator must ensure that no confound exists between these alternative dimensions within the stimulus set. The above examples represent only a brief illustration of such potential confounds; the full range of possibilities is very great indeed. Other researchers have, for instance, worried that slowing to color-name emotionally negative words relative to control words might reflect the fact that the former stimuli typically are selected from a semantically more homogenous category than the latter. These researchers have eliminated this confound (without modifying observed effects) by employing semantically categorized sets of neutral stimuli (Doost et al., 1997; Foa et al., 1993; Mathews & Sebastian, 1993). As always, the specific manifestations of this methodological issue and the best ways to overcome the particular problems it presents will depend upon the precise theoretical hypotheses under investigation.

DISTINGUISHING AUTOMATIC AND STRATEGIC CONTRIBUTIONS TO ATTENTIONAL BIAS

Cognitive psychologists characteristically draw a distinction between automatic and strategic processes, construing the former as cognitive operations that proceed without intention and require no conscious mediation, and the latter as intentionally executed processes that depend upon conscious awareness (Hasher & Zacks, 1979; Posner & Snyder, 1975). Influential models of selective processing in psychopathology often attribute such effects to automatic biases in attention (e.g., Beck, 1976; Beck, Emery, & Greenberg, 1985; Williams, Watts, MacLeod, & Mathews, 1988; Williams et al., 1997), although most cognitive therapies that have been developed to therapeutically ameliorate biases in selective processing appear to rely upon the strategic modification of cognition. It should come as little surprise, then, that clinical researchers have created variants of the Stroop task designed to distinguish automatic and strategic contributions to the patterns of attentional bias associated with psychopathology (cf. MacLeod & Rutherford, 1998).

For this purpose, researchers have used the backward masking procedure (cf. Turvey, 1973), which involves exposing a stimulus word very briefly before replacing it with a meaningless pattern, often composed of rotated and inverted letter fragments. Although such presentation conditions can eliminate participants' capacity to report a stimulus word, there is evidence that the word's content nevertheless undergoes semantic processing (cf. MacLeod, 1998; Marcel, 1983). Thus, if an attentional bias effect is truly automatic, then associated patterns of color-naming interference may continue to be observed on variants of the emotional Stroop task that render the content of stimulus words unreportable through the use of this exposure condition.

Emotional pathology is indeed associated with selective slowing to color-name particular categories of stimulus words even when backward masking successfully precludes the reporting of word content. In a typical implementation of this methodological approach, Mogg et al. (1993a) presented generalized anxiety patients and nonanxious control participants with an individual-item version of the emotional Stroop task. On each trial, a single word was presented on a background patch of color, which could be red, green, blue, or yellow. In the unmasked condition, this display remained onscreen until the color identification response was detected. However, in the masked condition, the word was replaced after only 14 ms[1] with a meaningless string of characters. This presentation procedure was designed to obscure the identity of the word, without compromising perception of the patch color. The order of masked and unmasked trials was randomized, and participants were required only to indicate the patch color on each trial by pressing the appropriate response key. The efficacy of the masking procedure was confirmed by the observation that performance was at chance levels on an awareness test, which involved presenting words on half of the trials under such exposure conditions and requiring participants to guess whether a word appeared on each trial. Nevertheless, despite this inability to report the presence of the backward masked words, Mogg et al. (1993a) observed that, relative to the controls, their generalized anxiety patients displayed an equivalent selective slowing of color naming in the presence of negative words under both masked and unmasked exposure conditions.

The finding that generalized anxiety disorder patients are slow to color-name masked threat words has proven to be a replicable one (Mogg, Bradley, Millar, & White, 1995). It also has been demonstrated that phobics show retarded color naming of masked fear-relevant words (van den Hout, Tenney, Huygens, & de Jong, 1997) and that patients suffering from posttraumatic stress disorder take disproportionately long to color-name masked trauma-relevant words (Harvey, Bryant, & Rapee, 1996). However, automaticity of attentional bias to threat is not exclusive to patients suffering from clinical anxiety disorders. Nonclinical individuals who report high levels of trait anger also display disproportionate slowing to color-name anger-related words under both masked and unmasked exposure conditions (van Honk et al., 1999). It also has been observed that elevated anxiety levels within the normal population are associated with slowing to color-name threat words rendered unreportable by backward masking (Lundh, Wikstroem, & Westerlund, 2001; MacLeod & Hagan, 1992; MacLeod & Rutherford, 1992). Nevertheless, the profiles of effects may not be equivalent for clinically anxious patients and for nonclinical individuals who report elevated levels of trait anxiety.

Clinically anxious participants reliably demonstrate retarded color naming of negative words presented under both masked and unmasked exposure

---

[1]The minimum possible onset asynchrony between the initial stimulus and the pattern mask is constrained by the screen refresh rate, which varies according to the specifications of the computer monitor. In backward masking studies of this type, it is common to separate these stimuli by a single screen refresh, as was the case in this present experiment.

conditions (e.g., Bradley, Mogg, & Williams, 1995b; Harvey et al., 1996; Mogg et al., 1993a; van den Hout et al., 1997). However, in contrast, nonclinical participants reporting high levels of trait anxiety commonly have been found to display color-naming interference on negative words only when these are masked, and not when they are unmasked (e.g., MacLeod & Hagan, 1992; MacLeod & Rutherford, 1992; Mogg et al., 1993b; van den Hout, Tenney, Huygens, & Merckelbach, 1995). This pattern of observed similarities and differences between clinically anxious patients and high-trait anxious normals has led to speculation concerning the attentional characteristics that are shared by such populations, and those characteristics that might serve as distinctive markers of clinical pathology. Some researchers contend that, whereas general vulnerability to anxiety is caused by an automatic attentional bias to threatening information, the inability to strategically override this bias may underpin the development of clinical anxiety disorders (MacLeod & Rutherford, 1998; Mathews & MacLeod, 1994). Although such a proposal remains speculative at this stage, it illustrates that our future capacity to fully understand the attentional characteristics of psychopathology may well be enhanced by the use of Stroop task variants designed in ways that make them differentially sensitive to automatic and strategic aspects of selective information processing.

SOME KEY ISSUES FOR FUTURE CLINICAL RESEARCH WITH THE STROOP APPROACH

This brief review necessarily has been selective, as it is beyond the scope of a single chapter to comprehensively summarize the wealth of clinical research studies that have used Stroop task variants. It appears certain that task variations will continue to proliferate, as clinical researchers identify the specific methodologies best suited to answering their chosen questions. However, it also seems likely that these questions will converge around a number of key themes. In particular, it will be important to refine understanding of the precise mechanisms that underpin the interference effects demonstrated by clinical populations, to establish the causal nature of observed associations between these effects and clinical symptomatology, and to effectively exploit the potential clinical applications of this research approach.

In regard to the mechanisms that give rise to the impaired color naming of certain word categories by clinically disordered participants, it must be recognized that such effects cannot be taken as conclusive evidence of an attentional bias toward the semantic content of these words. For example, one alternative possible reason for the slowed color naming of threat words by anxiety patients may be that such terms simply have a higher subjective frequency within this population. Word sets typically are matched for frequency using conventional norms. However, it does not seem improbable that a spider phobic, for instance, might personally employ (or think about) spider-related terms with unusually high frequency. Another possibility is that color-naming interference effects could result not from increased selective processing of particular word content, but from unusually intense emotional reactivity to such content. For example, it has been suggested that generalized anxiety disorder patients and control participants may access the semantic content of threat words to the same degree, but that this information could elicit a more intense anxiety response in the former population, which interferes with their color-naming responses (MacLeod, Mathews, & Tata, 1986).

One major limitation of the Stroop task is that although researchers can confidently determine when color information is not processed efficiently, they can only speculate about the information that may enjoy preferential processing. The fact that color information receives inadequate attention does not require the conclusion that attention is diverted instead to the processing of word content. Indeed, the tendency to selectively divert attention away from the stimulus item altogether would also serve to impair such color-naming performance. Adding empirical weight to this concern, Lavy and van den Hout (1994) demonstrated that when participants were directly instructed to selectively avoid processing information associated with the content of certain emotionally neutral stimulus words, their color-naming latencies on such words increased significantly. In view of such alternative possible explanations, it always is prudent to ensure that firm conclusions concerning the patterns of selective attention associated with clinical pathology are based upon converging evidence, provided by a variety of experimental paradigms. Attentional bias also can be assessed in other ways, such as through the use of speeded probe detection tasks (MacLeod et al., 1986), priming techniques (McNally, Hornig, Otto, & Pollack, 1997), visual search approaches (Freeman, Garety, & Phillips, 2000), and eye-movement methodologies (Mogg, Miller, & Bradley, 2000). Although such alternatives typically involve fairly complex experimental procedures, lacking the convenience and simplicity of Stroop task variants, it is reassuring to note that all of these approaches have yielded converging support for the existence of an attentional bias toward threat information in anxious populations. It remains to be seen whether the same is true for each of the various candidate attentional biases that researchers have identified, using adaptations of the Stroop task, across differing clinical populations.

Of course, the confirmation that patients suffering from a clinical disorder do indeed display a genuine attentional bias toward a particular category of information cannot serve to establish that such a bias contributes causally to their symptomatology. To address this hypothesis, investigators must incorporate their Stroop task variants into appropriate experimental designs, as some have done to appraise whether attentional bias makes a causal contribution to anxiety (cf. Campbell, MacLeod, & Rutherford, 2004).

For example, investigators have employed longitudinal designs to determine whether early measures of color-naming interference predict later individual differences in emotional reactivity to subsequent stressful life events. The results of such research have lent encouraging support to the idea that attentional bias may indeed play a causal role in the mediation of emotional experience. For example, MacLeod and Hagan (1992) found that an early measure of color-naming interference on threat words predicted later variations in the intensity of negative emotional reactions to a subsequent diagnosis of cervical pathology better than did any of their questionnaire measures of emotional vulnerability. Similarly, MacLeod and Rutherford (1998) reported a study in which degree of color-naming interference on threat words, shown by high school graduates, proved to be the most powerful predictor of their subsequent state anxiety elevation when they commenced university studies some weeks later. This capacity to predict future emotional experience on the basis of slowing to color-name negative words within the emotional Stroop task has been confirmed by other researchers (Lundh et al., 2001; van den Hout et al., 1995).

In addition to supporting the possibility that attentional bias might causally mediate emotional reactivity, such findings also highlight the potential value that Stroop task variants may have as clinical assessment tools. Furthermore, they suggest that the attentional bias to threat, revealed by anxiety patients' performance on the emotional Stroop task, may represent an important target of therapeutic change in the treatment of such conditions. Motivated by this possibility, researchers have recently worked to develop cognitive-experimental procedures designed to directly modify attentional responses to threatening stimuli, some of which represent training adaptations of the emotional Stroop task itself (Campbell, 2001; Masia, McNeil, Cohn, & Hope, 1999; Mathews & MacLeod, 2002). The direct manipulation of attentional bias, using cognitive-experimental training approaches, not only has been found to modify emotional vulnerability within the laboratory (MacLeod, Rutherford, Campbell, Ebsworthy, & Holker, 2002), but now also has been shown to attenuate symptom severity in clinically anxious patients (Amir, Selvig, Elias, & Rousseau, 2002; Vasey, Hazen, & Schmidt, 2002). Such findings provide grounds for optimism that variants of the Stroop task not only will advance theoretical understanding of the attentional anomalies that characterize alternative manifestations of psychopathology, but also may contribute to the enhanced assessment, and perhaps even the remediation, of such clinical conditions.

CONCLUSION

In the previous chapter, it was observed to be quite remarkable that a paradigm as simple as the Stroop task has recruited increasing experimental attention while the discipline of cognitive psychology has steadily grown more sophisticated. Precisely the same observation can be made with respect to the burgeoning use of Stroop task variants within the field of clinical psychology, especially across the past decade or so. Undoubtedly, the very simplicity of the procedure contributes to the explanation of its popularity. However, this chapter has illustrated that the ease with which such tasks can be delivered may obscure a number of methodological complexities. It is extremely important, yet not always easy, to ensure that populations to be contrasted by means of this task differ only on those dimensions of theoretical importance or, failing this, to employ statistical approaches capable of discerning the association between observed interference effects and alternative dimensions of individual difference. Care also must be taken to select word sets that are differentiated only by the theoretically critical distinctions, and to employ presentation methods appropriately suited to the particular questions being addressed.

Alternative explanations of color-naming interference effects always must be entertained, and conclusions concerning the attentional correlates of psychopathology ideally will be based upon converging evidence from differing experimental approaches. Nevertheless, it is quite clear that, when used with due diligence, variants of the Stroop task are likely to long retain their present position of importance within the arsenal of techniques employed by clinical researchers to investigate the attentional characteristics of psychopathology. Indeed, it seems possible that John Ridley Stroop's inadvertent contribution to clinical psychology may well be further extended across the coming years in ways that promise to increase the power of clinical assessment, and perhaps also to yield novel procedures for achieving therapeutic change.

REFERENCES

Amir, N., Freshman, M., & Foa, E. B. (2002). Enhanced Stroop interference for threat in social phobia. *Journal of Anxiety Disorders, 16,* 1–9.

Amir, N., Selvig, A., Elias, J., & Rousseau, G. (2002, November). *Manipulation of information processing bias in anxiety: Malleability of attention and interpretation biases.* Paper presented at the 36th American Association of Behavior Therapy annual convention, Reno, NV.

Beck, A. T. (1976). *Cognitive therapy and the emotional disorders.* New York: International Universities Press.

Beck, A., Emery, G., & Greenberg, R. L. (1985). *Anxiety disorders and phobias: A cognitive perspective.* New York: Basic Books.

Beck, J. G., Freeman, J. B., Shipherd, J. C., Hamblen, J. L., & Lackner, J. M. (2001). Specificity of Stroop interference in patients with pain and PTSD. *Journal of Abnormal Psychology, 110,* 536–543.

Becker, E. S., Rinck, M., Margraf, J., & Roth, W. T. (2001). The emotional Stroop effect in anxiety disorders: General emotionality or disorder specificity? *Journal of Anxiety Disorders, 15*, 147–159.

Becker, E. S., Strohbach, D., & Rinck, M. (1999). A specific attentional bias in suicide attempters. *Journal of Nervous and Mental Disease, 187*, 730–735.

Bentall, R. P., & Kaney, S. (1989). Content specific information processing and persecutory delusions: An investigation using the emotional Stroop test. *British Journal of Medical Psychology, 62*, 355–364.

Black, C. M. D., Wilson, G. T., Labouvie, E., & Heffernan, K. (1997). Selective processing of eating disorder relevant stimuli: Does the Stroop Test provide an objective measure of bulimia nervosa? *International Journal of Eating Disorders, 22*, 329–333.

Bradley, B. P., Mogg, K., Millar, N., & White, J. (1995a). Selective processing of negative information: Effects of clinical anxiety, concurrent depression, and awareness. *Journal of Abnormal Psychology, 104*, 532–536.

Bradley, B. P., Mogg, K., & Williams, R. (1995b). Implicit and explicit memory for emotion-congruent information in clinical depression and anxiety. *Behaviour Research and Therapy, 33*, 755–770.

Brosschot, J. F., de Ruiter, C., & Kindt, M. (1999). Processing bias in anxious subjects and repressors, measured by emotional Stroop interference and attentional allocation. *Personality and Individual Differences, 26*, 777–793.

Bryant, R. A., & Harvey, A. G. (1995). Processing threatening information in post-traumatic stress disorder. *Journal of Abnormal Psychology, 104*, 537–541.

Buckley, T. C., Blanchard, E. B., & Hickling, E. J. (2002). Automatic and strategic processing of threat stimuli: A comparison between PTSD, panic disorder, and nonanxiety controls. *Cognitive Therapy and Research, 26*, 97–115.

Campbell, L. W. (2001). *An investigation of the causal association between attentional bias and anxiety vulnerability*. Unpublished doctoral dissertation, University of Western Australia, Perth.

Campbell, L. W., MacLeod, C., & Rutherford, E. M. (2004). *Appraising the causal role of attentional bias in the mediation of anxiety vulnerability: A critical review*. Manuscript submitted for publication.

Carter, C. S., Maddock, R. J., & Magliozzi, J. (1992). Patterns of abnormal processing of emotional information in panic disorder and major depression. *Psychopathology, 25*, 65–70.

Ceumern-Lindenstjerna, I.-A., Brunner, R., Parzer, P., Fiedler, P., & Resch, F. (2002). Borderline-Steorung un verzerrungen der aufmerksamket: theoretische modelle und empirische befunde [Borderline personality disorder and attentional biases: Theoretical models and empirical findings]. *Fortschritte der Neurologie-Psychiatrie, 70*, 321–330.

Comalli, P. E., Jr., Wapner, S., & Werner, H. (1962). Interference effects of Stroop color–word test in childhood, adulthood, and aging. *Journal of Genetic Psychology, 100*, 47–53.

Cooper, M. J., & Fairburn, C. G. (1992). Selective processing of eating, weight and shape related words in patients with eating disorders and dieters. *British Journal of Clinical Psychology, 31*, 363–365.

Cox, W. M., Hogan, L. M., Kristian, M. R., & Race, J. H. (2002). Alcohol attentional bias as a predictor of alcohol abusers' treatment outcome. *Drug and Alcohol Dependence, 68*, 237–243.

Doost, H. T. N., Taghavi, M. R., Moradi, A. R., Yule, W., & Dalgleish, T. (1997). The performance of clinically depressed children and adolescents on the modified Stroop paradigm. *Personality and Individual Differences, 23*, 753–759.

Ehlers, A., Margraf, J., Davies, S., & Roth, W. T. (1988). Selective processing of threat cues in subjects with panic attacks. *Cognition & Emotion, 2*, 201–219.

Ehrenreich, J. T., & Gross, A. M. (2002). Biased attentional behavior in childhood anxiety: A review of theory and current empirical investigation. *Clinical Psychology Review, 22*, 991–1008.

Ehrman, R. N., Robbins, S. J., Bromwell, M. A., Lankford, M. E., Monterosso, J. R., & O'Brien, C. P. (2002). Comparing attentional bias to smoking cues in current smokers, former smokers, and non-smokers using a dot-probe task. *Drug and Alcohol Dependence, 67*, 185–191.

Fairburn, C. G., Cooper, P. J., Cooper, M. J., & McKenna, F. P. (1991). Selective information processing in bulimia nervosa. *International Journal of Eating Disorders, 10*, 415–422.

Faunce, G. J. (2002). Eating disorders and attentional bias: A review. *Eating Disorders: the Journal of Treatment and Prevention, 10*, 125–139.

Foa, E. B., Ilai, D., McCarthy, P. R., & Shoyer, B. (1993). Information processing in obsessive-compulsive disorder. *Cognitive Therapy and Research, 17*, 173–189.

Foa, E. B., Rothbaum, B. O., Riggs, D. S., & Murdock, T. B. (1991). Treatment of posttraumatic stress disorder in rape victims: A comparison between cognitive-behavioral procedures and counseling. *Journal of Consulting and Clinical Psychology, 59*, 715–723.

Franken, I. H. A., Kroon, L. Y., Wiers, R. W., & Jansen, A. (2000). Selective cognitive processing of drug cues in heroin dependence. *Journal of Psychopharmacology, 14*, 395–400.

Freeman, D., Garety, P. A., & Phillips, M. L. (2000). The examination of hypervigilance for external threat in individuals with generalized anxiety disorder and individuals with persecutory delusions using visual scan paths. *The Quarterly Journal of Experimental Psychology, 53A*, 549–567.

Geller, V., & Shaver, P. (1976). Cognitive consequences of self-awareness. *Journal of Experimental Psychology, 12*, 99–108.

Golombok, S., Stavrou, A., Bonn, J., Mogg, K., Critchlow, F., & Rust, J. (1991). The effects of diazepam on anxiety-related cognition. *Cognitive Therapy and Research, 15*, 459–467.

Gotlib, I. H., & Cane, D. B. (1987). Construct accessibility and clinical depression: A longitudinal investigation. *Journal of Abnormal Psychology, 96*, 199–204.

Harvey, A. G., Bryant, R. A., & Rapee, R. M. (1996). Preconscious processing of threat in posttraumatic stress disorder. *Cognitive Therapy and Research, 20,* 613–623.

Hasher, L., & Zacks, R. T. (1979). Automatic and effortful processes in memory. *Journal of Experimental Psychology: General, 108,* 356–388.

Hill, A. B., & Knowles, T. H. (1991). Depression and the "emotional" Stroop effect. *Personality and Individual Differences, 12,* 481–485.

Holle, C., Neely, J. H., & Heimberg, R. G. (1997). The effects of blocked versus random presentation and semantic relatedness of stimulus words on response to a modified Stroop Task among social phobics. *Cognitive Therapy and Research, 21,* 681–697.

Hope, D. A., Rapee, R. M., Heimberg, R. G., & Dombeck, M. J. (1990). Representations of the self in social phobia: Vulnerability to social threat. *Cognitive Therapy and Research, 14,* 177–189.

Huon, G. F. (1995). The Stroop Color-Naming Task in eating disorders: A review of the research. *Eating Disorders: The Journal of Treatment and Prevention, 3,* 124–132.

Intili, R., & Tarrier, N. (1998). Attentional bias in morbid jealousy. *Behavioural and Cognitive Psychotherapy, 26,* 323–338.

Jones, B. C., Jones, B. T., Blundell, L., & Bruce, G. (2002). Social users of alcohol and cannabis who detect substance-related changes in a change blindness paradigm report higher levels of use than those detecting substance-neutral changes. *Psychopharmacology, 165,* 93–96.

Jones-Chesters, M. H., Monsell, S., & Cooper, P. J. (1998). The disorder-salient Stroop effect as a measure of psychopathology in eating disorders. *International Journal of Eating Disorders, 24,* 65–82.

Kaspi, S. P., McNally, R. J., & Amir, N. (1995). Cognitive processing of emotional information in posttraumatic stress disorder. *Cognitive Therapy and Research, 19,* 433–444.

Kinderman, P. (1994). Attentional bias, persecutory delusions and the self-concept. *British Journal of Medical Psychology, 67,* 53–66.

Kindt, M., & Brosschot, J. F. (1997). Phobia-related cognitive bias for pictorial and linguistic stimuli. *Journal of Abnormal Psychology, 106,* 644–648.

Klieger, D. M., & Cordner, M. D. (1990). The Stroop task as a measure of construct accessibility in depression. *Personality and Individual Differences, 11,* 19–27.

Lavy, E. H., & van den Hout, M. A. (1994). Cognitive avoidance and attentional bias: Causal relationships. *Cognitive Therapy and Research, 18,* 179–191.

Lavy, E. H., van den Hout, M., & Arntz, A. (1993). Attentional bias and spider phobia: Conceptual and clinical issues. *Behaviour Research and Therapy, 31,* 17–24.

Lavy, E. H., van Oppen, P., & van den Hout, M. A. (1994). Selective processing of emotional information in obsessive compulsive disorder. *Behaviour Research and Therapy, 32,* 243–246.

Logan, A. C., & Goetsch, V. L. (1993). Attention to external threat cues in anxiety states. *Clinical Psychology Review, 13,* 541–559.

Lovell, D. M., Williams, J. M. G., & Hill, A. B. (1997). Selective processing of shape-related words in women with eating disorders, and those who have recovered. *British Journal of Clinical Psychology, 36,* 421–432.

Lundh, L.-G., & Öst, L.-G. (1996). Recognition bias for critical faces in social phobics. *Behaviour Research and Therapy, 34,* 787–794.

Lundh, L.-G., Wikstroem, J., & Westerlund, J. (2001). Cognitive bias, emotion, and somatic complaints in a normal sample. *Cognition & Emotion, 15,* 249–277.

Lundh, L.-G., Wikstrom, J., Westerlund, J., & Öst, L.-G. (1999). Preattentive bias for emotional information in panic disorder with agoraphobia. *Journal of Abnormal Psychology, 108,* 222–232.

MacLeod, C. (1998). Implicit perception: Perceptual processing without awareness. In K. Kirsner & C. Speelman (Eds.), *Implicit and explicit mental processes* (pp. 57–78). Mahwah, NJ: Erlbaum.

MacLeod, C., & Hagan, R. (1992). Individual differences in the selective processing of threatening information, and emotional responses to a stressful life event. *Behaviour Research and Therapy, 30,* 151–161.

MacLeod, C., Mathews, A., & Tata, P. (1986). Attentional bias in emotional disorders. *Journal of Abnormal Psychology, 95,* 15–20.

MacLeod, C., & Rutherford, E. M. (1992). Anxiety and the selective processing of emotional information: Mediating roles of awareness, trait and state variables, and personal relevance of stimulus materials. *Behaviour Research and Therapy, 30,* 479–491.

MacLeod, C., & Rutherford, E. M. (1998). Automatic and strategic cognitive biases in anxiety and depression. In K. Kirsner & C. Speelman (Ed.), *Implicit and explicit mental processes* (pp. 233–254). Mahwah, NJ: Erlbaum.

MacLeod, C., & Rutherford, E. M. (2004). Information processing approaches to generalized anxiety disorder: Assessing the selective functioning of attention, interpretation, and retrieval in GAD patients. In R. G. Heimberg, C. L. Turk, & D. S. Mennin (Eds.), *Generalized anxiety disorder: Advances in research and practice* (pp. 109–142). New York: Guilford Press.

MacLeod, C., Rutherford, E. M., Campbell, L., Ebsworthy, G., & Holker, L. (2002). Selective attention and emotional vulnerability: Assessing the causal basis of their association through the experimental manipulation of attentional bias. *Journal of Abnormal Psychology, 111,* 107–123.

Marcel, A. J. (1983). Conscious and unconscious perception: Experiments on visual masking and word recognition. *Cognitive Psychology, 15,* 197–237.

Martin, M., Horder, P., & Jones, G. V. (1992). Integral bias in naming of phobia-related words. *Cognition & Emotion, 6,* 479–486.

Martin, M., Williams, R. M., & Clark, D. M. (1991). Does anxiety lead to selective processing of threat-related information? *Behaviour Research and Therapy, 29,* 147–160.

Masia, C. L., McNeil, D. W., Cohn, L. G., & Hope, D. A. (1999). Exposure to social anxiety words: Treatment for social phobia based on the Stroop paradigm. *Cognitive and Behavioral Practice, 6*, 248–258.

Mathews, A., & Klug, F. (1993). Emotionality and interference with color-naming in anxiety. *Behaviour Research and Therapy, 31*, 57–62.

Mathews, A., & MacLeod, C. (1985). Selective processing of threat cues in anxiety states. *Behaviour Research and Therapy, 23*, 563–569.

Mathews, A., & MacLeod, C. (1994). Cognitive approaches to emotion and emotional disorders. *Annual Review of Psychology, 45*, 25–50.

Mathews, A., & MacLeod, C. (2002). Induced emotional biases have causal effects on anxiety. *Cognition & Emotion, 16*, 310–315.

Mathews, A., Mogg, K., Kentish, J., & Eysenck, M. (1995). Effect of psychological treatment on cognitive bias in generalized anxiety disorder. *Behaviour Research and Therapy, 33*, 293–303.

Mathews, A. M., & Sebastian, S. (1993). Suppression of emotional Stroop effects by fear-arousal. *Cognition & Emotion, 7*, 517–530.

McCabe, S. B., & Gotlib, I. H. (1993). Attentional processing in clinically depressed subjects: A longitudinal investigation. *Cognitive Therapy and Research, 17*, 359–377.

McKenna, F. P., & Sharma, D. (1995). Intrusive cognitions: An investigation of the emotional Stroop task. *Journal of Experimental Psychology: Learning, Memory, and Cognition, 21*, 1595–1607.

McManus, F., Waller, G., & Chadwick, P. (1996). Biases in the processing of different forms of threat in bulimic and comparison women. *Journal of Nervous and Mental Disease, 184*, 547–554.

McNally, R. J., Amir, N., & Lipke, H. J. (1996). Subliminal processing of threat cues in posttraumatic stress disorder? *Journal of Anxiety Disorders, 10*, 115–128.

McNally, R. J., Amir, N., Louro, C. E., Lukach, B. M., Riemann, B. C., & Calamari, J. E. (1994). Cognitive processing of idiographic emotional information in panic disorder. *Behaviour Research and Therapy, 32*, 119–122.

McNally, R. J., Hornig, C. D., Otto, M. W., & Pollack, M. H. (1997). Selective encoding of threat in panic disorder: Application of a dual priming paradigm. *Journal of Behavior Research and Therapy, 35*, 543–549.

McNally, R. J., Kaspi, S. P., Riemann, B. C., & Zeitlin, S. B. (1990a). Selective processing of threat cues in post-traumatic stress disorder. *Journal of Abnormal Psychology, 99*, 398–402.

McNally, R. J., Riemann, B. C., & Kim, E. (1990b). Selective processing of threat cues in Panic Disorder. *Behaviour Research and Therapy, 28*, 407–412.

McNally, R. J., Riemann, B. C., Louro, C. E., Lukach, B. M., & Kim, E. (1992). Cognitive processing of emotional information in panic disorder. *Behaviour Research and Therapy, 30*, 143–149.

McNeil, D. W., Tucker, P., Miranda, R., Jr., Lewin, M. R., & Nordgren, J. C. (1999). Response to depression and anxiety Stroop stimuli in posttraumatic stress disorder, obsessive-compulsive disorder, and major depressive disorder. *Journal of Nervous and Mental Disease, 187*, 512–516.

Merckelbach, H., & van den Hout, M. A. (1993). Trauma, herinnering en amnesie: Een notitie ouer de experimentele analyse van psychogene amnesie [Trauma, remembering and amnesia: An experimental analysis of psychogenic amnesia]. *Gedragstherapie, 26*, 3–19.

Mogg, K., Bradley, B. P., Millar, N., & White, J. (1995). A follow-up study of cognitive bias in generalized anxiety disorder. *Behaviour Research and Therapy, 33*, 927–935.

Mogg, K., Bradley, B. P., Williams, R., & Mathews, A. (1993a). Subliminal processing of emotional information in anxiety and depression. *Journal of Abnormal Psychology, 102*, 304–311.

Mogg, K., Kentish, J., & Bradley, B. P. (1993b). Effects of anxiety and awareness on colour-identification latencies for emotional words. *Behaviour Research and Therapy, 31*, 559–567.

Mogg, K., & Marden, B. (1990). Processing of emotional information in anxious subjects. *British Journal of Clinical Psychology, 29*, 227–229.

Mogg, K., Mathews, A., & Weinman, J. (1989). Selective processing of threat cues in anxiety states: A replication. *Behaviour Research and Therapy, 27*, 317–323.

Mogg, K., Miller, N., & Bradley, B. P. (2000). Biases in eye movements to threatening facial expressions in generalised anxiety disorder and depressive disorder. *Journal of Abnormal Psychology, 109*, 695–704.

Muris, P., Merckelbach, H., & de Jongh, A. (1995). Colour-naming of dentist-related words: Role of coping style, dental anxiety, and trait anxiety. *Personality and Individual Differences, 18*, 685–688.

Murphy, F. C., Sahakian, B. J., Rubinsztein, J. S., Michael, A., Rogers, R. D., Robbins, T. W., & Paykel, E. S. (1999). Emotional bias and inhibitory control processes in mania and depression. *Psychological Medicine, 29*, 1307–1321.

Pauli, P., Schwenzer, M., Brody, S., & Rau, H. (1993). Hypochondriacal attitudes, pain sensitivity, and attentional bias. *Journal of Psychosomatic Research, 37*, 745–752.

Perpina, C., Hemsley, D., Treasure, J., & de Silva, P. (1993). Is the selective information processing of food and body words specific to patients with eating disorders? *International Journal of Eating Disorders, 14*, 359–366.

Posner, M. I., & Snyder, C. R. R. (1975). Attention and cognitive control. In R. L. Solso (Ed.), *Information processing and cognition: The Loyola Symposium* (pp. 55–85). Hillsdale, NJ: Erlbaum.

Preston, M. S., & Lambert, W. E. (1969). Interlingual interference in a bilingual version of the Stroop color–word task. *Journal of Verbal Learning and Verbal Behavior, 8*, 295–301.

Quero, S., Banos, R. M., & Botella, C. (2000). Sesgos cognivitos en el trastorno de panico: Comparacion entre el Stroop computerizado y con tarjetas [Cognitive biases in panic disorder: A comparison between computerized and card Stroop task]. *Psicothema, 12*, 165–170.

Richards, A., French, C. C., Johnson, W., Naparstek, J., & Williams, J. (1992). Effects of mood manipulation and anxiety on performance of an emotional Stroop task. *British Journal of Psychology, 83,* 479–491.

Richards, A., & Millwood, B. (1989). Colour-identification of differentially valenced words in anxiety. *Cognition & Emotion, 3,* 171–176.

Riemann, B. C., & McNally, R. J. (1995). Cognitive processing of personally relevant information. *Cognition & Emotion, 9,* 325–340.

Rutherford, E. M., MacLeod, C., & Campbell, L. W. (in press). Negative selectivity effects and emotional selectivity effects in anxiety: Differential attentional correlates of state and trait variables. *Cognition & Emotion.*

Segal, Z. V., Gemar, M., Truchon, C., Guirguis, M., & Horowitz, L. M. (1995). A priming methodology for studying self-representation in major depressive disorder. *Journal of Abnormal Psychology, 104,* 205–213.

Stetter, F., Ackermann, K., Bizer, A., & Straube, E. R. (1995). Effects of disease-related cues in alcoholic inpatients: Results of a controlled "Alcohol Stroop" study. *Alcoholism: Clinical and Experimental Research, 19,* 593–599.

Stewart, S. H., Conrod, P. J., Gignac, M. L., & Pihl, R. O. (1998). Selective processing biases in anxiety-sensitive men and women. *Cognition & Emotion, 12,* 105–133.

Stewart, S. H., & Samoluk, S. B. (1997). Effects of short-term food deprivation and chronic dietary restraint on the selective processing of appetitive-related cues. *International Journal of Eating Disorders, 21,* 129–135.

Stroop, J. R. (1935). Studies of interference in serial verbal reactions. *Journal of Experimental Psychology, 18,* 643–662. (Reprinted in 1992 in the *Journal of Experimental Psychology: General, 121,* 15–23.)

Thorpe, S. J., & Salkovskis, P. M. (1997). Information processing in spider phobics: The Stroop colour naming task may indicate strategic but not automatic attentional bias. *Behaviour Research and Therapy, 35,* 131–144.

Turvey, M. T. (1973). On peripheral and central processes in vision: Inferences from an information-processing analysis of masking with patterned stimuli. *Psychological Review, 80,* 1–52.

Unoki, K., Kasuga, T., Matsushima, E., Ohta, K., & Doi, N. (2000). Attentional process of emotional information: Comparison between clinical and nonclinical obsessive-compulsive disorder. [Japanese]. *Seishin Igaku (Clinical Psychiatry), 42,* 273–280.

van den Hout, M., Tenney, N., Huygens, K., & de Jong, P. (1997). Preconscious processing bias in specific phobia. *Behaviour Research and Therapy, 35,* 29–34.

van den Hout, M., Tenney, N., Huygens, K., & Merckelbach, H. (1995). Responding to subliminal threat cues is related to trait anxiety and emotional vulnerability: A successful replication of MacLeod and Hagan (1992). *Behaviour Research and Therapy, 33,* 451–454.

van Honk, J., Tuiten, A., Verbaten, R., van den Hout, M., Koppeschaar, H., Thijssen, J., & de Haan, E. (1999). Correlations among salivary testosterone, mood, and selective attention to threat in humans. *Hormones and Behavior, 36,* 17–24.

Vasey, M. W., Hazen, R., & Schmidt, N. B. (2002, November). *Attentional retraining for chronic worry and GAD*. Paper presented at the 36th American Association of Behavior Therapy annual convention, Reno, NV.

Vrana, S. R., Roodman, A., & Beckham, J. C. (1995). Selective processing of trauma-relevant words in posttraumatic stress disorder. *Journal of Anxiety Disorders, 9,* 515–530.

Warren, R. E. (1972). Stimulus encoding and memory. *Journal of Experimental Psychology, 94,* 90–100.

Watts, F. N., McKenna, F. P., Sharrock, R., & Trezise, L. (1986a). Colour naming of phobia-related words. *British Journal of Psychology, 77,* 97–108.

Watts, F. N., Trezise, L., & Sharrock, R. (1986b). Processing of phobic stimuli. *British Journal of Clinical Psychology, 25,* 253–261.

Wertz, J. M., & Sayette, M. A. (2001). Effects of smoking opportunity on attentional bias in smokers. *Psychology of Addictive Behaviors, 15,* 268–271.

Westra, H. A., & Kuiper, N. A. (1997). Cognitive content specificity in selective attention across four domains of maladjustment. *Behaviour Research and Therapy, 35,* 349–365.

Williams, J. M., & Broadbent, K. (1986). Autobiographical memory in suicide attempters. *Journal of Abnormal Psychology, 95,* 144–149.

Williams, J. M. G., Mathews, A., & MacLeod, C. (1996). The emotional Stroop task and psychopathology. *Psychological Bulletin, 120,* 3–24.

Williams, J. M. G., & Nulty, D. D. (1986). Construct accessibility depression and the emotional Stroop task: Transient mood or stable structure? *Personality and Individual Differences, 7,* 485–491.

Williams, J. M. G., Watts, F. N., MacLeod, C., & Mathews, A. (1988). *Cognitive psychology and emotional disorders.* Chichester, UK: Wiley.

Williams, J. M. G., Watts, F. N., MacLeod, C., & Mathews, A. (1997). *Cognitive psychology and emotional disorders.* (2nd ed.). Chichester, UK: Wiley.

Williamson, D. A. (1996). Body image disturbances in eating disorders: A form of cognitive bias? *Eating Disorders: The Journal of Treatment and Prevention, 4,* 47–58.

II

SELECTIVE
ATTENTION TASKS

4

SELECTIVE ATTENTION TASKS IN CLINICAL AND COGNITIVE RESEARCH

JENNY YIEND, ANDREW MATHEWS, AND NELSON COWAN

Look around, and you cannot help but become aware that the external world contains far more information than can be taken in at any one instant. The concept of selective attention is the psychologist's attempt to explain how one's limited-capacity processing system deals with this overload of information. As psychologists, we assume that selective attention starts with competition between possible inputs (both internal and external), resulting in a selection of what is important together with a rejection of the remainder. The precise point at which this selection occurs is one topic that we discuss in chapter 5.

The use of the phrase *selective attention*, however, can create the misleading impression that because there is one word, there is also one process. On the contrary, when one source of information is to be selected at the expense of another, various processes could be used to achieve this. For example, one might maintain visual focus on a particular location; search through items, looking for one and ignoring others; or elect to perform one entire task rather than another, more habitual, one. All require selection but may recruit different cognitive and neural processes. Together with most psychologists, we view performance in such situations as being a variable com-

TABLE 4.1
Framework Describing Selective Attentional Studies

Category	Method	Putative mechanisms	Key cognitive studies	Key clinical studies	Populations studied
Single Cueing	Location Cueing	Spatial Shifting, Engagement, Disengagement	Posner (1980)	Fox et al. (2001); Yiend and Mathews (2001)	Analogue Non-Clinical Only
Double Cueing	Deployment of Attention Task (DOAT)	Pre-Emptive Recruitment of Attention by Significant Stimulus		Gotlib et al. (1988); McCabe and Toman (2000)	Analogue Non-Clinical; Depressed, GAD
	Attentional (Dot) Probe	Spatial Engagement, Shifting, Disengagement		MacLeod et al. (1986); Mogg and Bradley (1999)	Analogue Non-Clinical; Most Clinical
Search	Target Among Distractors (e.g., Face-in-the-Crowd)	Serial/Parallel Search; Spatial Engagement; Distractor Suppression	Shiffrin and Schneider (1977); Treisman & Gelade (1980)	Byrne and Eysenck (1995); Fox et al. (2000)	Unselected; Analogue Non-Clinical; Social Anxiety
	Eye Movement Monitoring	Attention – Switching, Engagement, Disengagement	Rayner (1998)	Matthews and Antes (1992); Mogg et al. (2000)	Analogue Non-Clinical; GAD, Spider Phobics
Filtering	Stroop	Spatial and Non-Spatial Interference; Distractor Suppression	Stroop (1935); Elliott et al. (1998); MacLeod (1991)	Mathews and MacLeod (1985); Williams et al. (1996)	Analogue Non-Clinical; Most Clinical
	Dichotic Stimuli With Selective Listening	Distractor Suppression; Auditory Attention	Cherry (1953); Moray (1959); Conway et al. (2001)	Mathews and MacLeod (1986)	GAD; PTSD
	Flanker Task	Distractor Suppression	Eriksen and Eriksen (1974)	Mathews et al. (1990)	Analogue Non-Clinical; GAD

Multiple Tasks	Attentional Blink	Pre-Emptive Recruitment of Attention by Significant Stimulus	Raymond et al. (1992); Reeves and Sperling, (1986)	Barnard and Ramponi (personal communication); Mackintosh et al. (personal communication)
	Dichotic Stimuli With Dual Monitoring	Need for Attention-Switching	Broadbent (1957)	
	Inattentional Blindness	Limit in Capacity of Attentional Focus	Cowan (2001); Rensink (2002) Simons (2000)	
	Multi-Object Tracking	Limit in Capacity of Visual Attention	Pylyshyn and Storm (1988)	

posite of bottom-up and top-down processes. Thus, the capture of perceptual resources by a sensory event, such as the appearance of an object, may be influenced by higher control systems, which can to some extent determine the outcome of competition arising from multiple inputs (e.g., Desimone & Duncan, 1995).

An interesting point raised toward the end of chapter 5 is that this capacity to effortfully screen out unwanted information varies across people. Individuals with high working memory capacity may be better able to inhibit unwanted information from capturing attention. Clearly variation in capacity is also relevant to clinical research, where resources are often depleted, perhaps because of preoccupations with worrisome thoughts. Some of the findings regarding attention to emotional distracters may therefore represent inhibition failure due to reduced resources and impaired attentional control (Derryberry & Reed, 2002; Eysenck & Calvo, 1992) as well as the specific content of emotional distractors.

The impetus to develop methods of assessing attention in clinical populations grew out of the intuition that people with particular emotional disorders deploy their attention in distinctive ways and that this finding may be a factor in maintaining that disorder. Some clinical researchers (e.g., Beck, 1976) have long argued that emotional disorders are caused by maladaptive cognitive processes or schemata that influence how emotional information is encoded. Data showing that anxious patients, relative to control groups, attended more to threatening cues (e.g. Williams, Watts, MacLeod, & Mathews, 1997) have been taken as support for this general view. Additional data suggesting that cues related to individual worries or concerns were particularly likely to capture attention were taken as further evidence that measures of attentional deployment may be useful for diagnostic purposes, or as a means of investigating etiological differences.

In chapter 5, we explore the range of methods most commonly used within cognitive psychology to assess selective attention. For clarity, these methods are categorized into cuing, search, filtering, and multiple task paradigms. Cuing tasks include methods in which a stimulus or event attracts attention to a particular location(s) and is followed by a target to be detected, with attention usually measured by the speed of participants' response. This method also happens to be one that has been widely adopted by clinical researchers. Discussion of it thus forms a large part of chapter 6, which focuses on the application of selective attention tasks to clinical populations.

In search tasks, participants must find and report on a particular target in an array of distractors. A specific example of such a task is the face-in-the-crowd method, again discussed at length in our clinical chapter, in which angry faces are easier to find than those with neutral expressions. Filtering tasks involve presenting targets and distractors together, testing participants' ability to suppress or ignore the latter. The Stroop task (or the emotional

Stroop when applied to clinical populations) is perhaps the most obvious example of this (see chap. 1, this volume, for a discussion of the Stroop task).

Finally, in multiple tasks, people must allocate their limited processing capacity to meet more than one demand, as when having to report two sequential targets, in the *attentional blink* method. Attending to one target takes time, meaning that another arriving too soon afterward is often missed. We touch on this method only briefly in the clinical chapter, as work on its application to emotional processing is only just beginning.

In Table 4.1 we attempt to summarize the methods discussed in our two chapters into a single framework. It is hoped that this table will provide the reader with both an overview of the chapters themselves and a guide for easy future reference.

We end this introduction by emphasizing the point made in both chapters—that specific variations of method can often have powerful effects on results. This variance can be understood only from a sound knowledge of the many factors, theoretical and methodological, that influence attention and its interaction with emotion. We hope that together our chapters will assist the researcher in developing this understanding and will focus future work into domains of optimum theoretical and clinical relevance.

REFERENCES

Beck, A. T. (1976). *Cognitive therapy and the emotional disorders*. New York: International Universities Press.

Broadbent, D. E. (1957). Immediate memory and simultaneous stimuli. *Quarterly Journal of Experimental Psychology, 9*, 1–11.

Byrne, A., & Eysenck, M. W. (1995). Trait anxiety, anxious mood and threat detection. *Cognition and Emotion, 9*, 549–562.

Cherry, E. C. (1953). Some experiments on the recognition of speech, with one and with two ears. *The Journal of the Acoustical Society of America, 25*, 975–979.

Conway, R. A., Cowan, N., & Bunting, M. F. (2001). The cocktail party phenomenon revisited: The importance of working memory capacity. *Psychonomic Bulletin & Review, 8*, 331–335.

Cowan, N. (2001). The magical number 4 in short-term memory: A reconsideration of mental storage capacity. *Behavioral and Brain Sciences, 24*, 87–185.

Derryberry, D., & Reed, M. A. (2002). Anxiety-related attentional biases and their regulation by attentional control. *Journal of Abnormal Psychology, 111*, 225–236.

Desimone, R., & Duncan, J. (1995). Neural mechanisms of selective visual attention. *Annual Review of Neuroscience, 18*, 193–222.

Elliott, E. M., Cowan, N., & Valle-Inclan, F. (1998). The nature of cross-modal, color–word interference effects. *Perception & Psychophysics, 60*, 761–767.

Eriksen, B. A., & Eriksen, C. W. (1974). Effects of noise letters on the identification of a target in a non search task. *Perception & Psychophysics, 16,* 143–149.

Eysenck, M. W., & Calvo, M. G. (1992). Anxiety and performance: The processing efficiency theory. *Cognition & Emotion, 6,* 409–434.

Fox, E., Lester, V., Russo, R., Bowles, R. J., Pichler, A., & Dutton, K. (2000). Facial expressions of emotion: Are angry faces detected more efficiently? *Cognition & Emotion, 14,* 61–92.

Fox, E., Russo, R., Bowles, R., & Dutton, K. (2001). Do threatening stimuli draw or hold visual attention in subclinical anxiety? *Journal of Experimental Psychology-General, 130,* 681–700.

Gotlib, I. H., McLachlan, A. L., & Katz, A. N. (1988). Biases in visual attention in depressed and non-depressed individuals. *Cognition & Emotion, 2,* 185–200.

MacLeod, C., Mathews, A., & Tata, P. (1986). Attentional bias in emotional disorders. *Journal of Abnormal Psychology, 95,* 15–20.

MacLeod, C. M. (1991). Half a century of research on the Stroop effect: An integrative review. *Psychological Bulletin, 109,* 163–203.

Mathews, A., & MacLeod, C. (1985). Selective processing of threat cues in anxiety states. *Behaviour Research and Therapy, 23,* 563–569.

Mathews, A., & MacLeod, C. (1986). Discrimination of threat cues without awareness in anxiety states. *Journal of Abnormal Psychology, 95,* 131–138.

Mathews, A., May, J., Mogg, K., & Eysenck, M. (1990). Attentional bias in anxiety: Selective search or defective filtering. *Journal of Abnormal Psychology, 99,* 166–173.

Matthews, G. R., & Antes, J. R. (1992). Visual attention and depression: Cognitive biases in the eye fixations of the dysphoric and the nondepressed. *Cognitive Therapy and Research, 16,* 359–371.

McCabe, S. B., & Toman, P. E. (2000). Stimulus exposure duration in a deployment-of-attention task: Effects on dysphoric, recently dysphoric, and nondysphoric individuals. *Cognition & Emotion, 14,* 125–142.

Mogg, K., & Bradley, B. P. (1999). Some methodological issues in assessing attentional biases for threatening faces in anxiety: A replication study using a modified version of the probe detection task. *Behaviour Research and Therapy, 37,* 595–604.

Mogg, K., Millar, N., & Bradley, B. P. (2000). Biases in eye movements to threatening facial expressions in generalized anxiety disorder and depressive disorder. *Journal of Abnormal Psychology, 109,* 695–704.

Moray, N. (1959). Attention in dichotic listening: Affective cues and the influence of instructions. *Quarterly Journal of Experimental Psychology, 11,* 56–60.

Posner, M. I. (1980). Orienting of attention. *Quarterly Journal of Experimental Psychology, 32,* 3–25.

Pylyshyn, Z. W., & Storm, R. W. (1988). Tracking multiple independent targets: Evidence for a parallel tracking mechanism. *Spatial Vision, 3,* 179–197.

Raymond, J. E., Shapiro, K. L., & Arnell, K. M. (1992). Temporary suppression of visual processing in an RSVP task: An attentional blink? *Journal of Experimental Psychology: Human Perception and Performance, 18*, 849–860.

Rayner, K. (1998). Eye movements in reading and information processing: 20 years of research. *Psychological Bulletin, 124*, 372–422.

Reeves, A., & Sperling, G. (1986). Attention gating in short term visual memory. *Psychological Review, 93*, 180–206.

Rensink, R. A. (2002). Change detection. *Annual Review of Psychology, 53*, 245–277.

Shiffrin, R. M., & Schneider, W. (1977). Controlled and automatic human information processing: II. Perceptual learning, automatic attending, and a general theory. *Psychological Review, 84*, 127–190.

Simons, D. J. (2000). Attentional capture and inattentional blindness. *Trends in Cognitive Sciences, 4*, 147–155.

Stroop, J. R. (1935). Studies of interference in serial verbal reactions. *Journal of Experimental Psychology, 18*, 643–662. (Reprinted in 1992 in the *Journal of Experimental Psychology: General, 121*, 15–23.)

Treisman, A. M., & Gelade, G. (1980). A feature integration theory of attention. *Cognitive Psychology, 12*, 97–136.

Williams, J. M. G., Mathews, A., & MacLeod, C. (1996). The emotional Stroop task and psychopathology. *Psychological Bulletin, 120*, 3–24.

Williams, J. M. G., Watts, F. N., MacLeod, C., & Mathews, A. (1997). *Cognitive psychology and emotional disorders* (2nd ed.). Chichester, England: Wiley.

Yiend, J., & Mathews, A. (2001). Anxiety and attention to threatening pictures. *The Quarterly Journal of Experimental Psychology, 54A*, 665–681.

5

SELECTIVE ATTENTION TASKS IN COGNITIVE RESEARCH

NELSON COWAN

The goal of this chapter is to use research on selective attention within the field of cognitive psychology to provide a background that could guide researchers of clinical populations. The corpus of research on attention is huge but my policy nevertheless is to interpret the concept of attention broadly enough to make clear the rich interconnections between attention and other mental functions including perception, memory, and thought, and to point out the many options available if one is interested in studying attention.

Many essays on attention begin with a quote from the chapter on attention within William James' (1890) *Principles of Psychology*, in which he asserts, "Every one knows what attention is. It is the taking possession by the mind, in clear and vivid form, of one out of what seem several simultaneously possible objects or trains of thought." Although this statement is true, it seems equally telling that people do not often find similar quotes about how everyone knows what habit is, what memory is, what reasoning is, and so on. Perhaps more than most other aspects of the mind, there is a paradoxical difference between our ready folk knowledge of the concept of attention and

This chapter was written with support from National Institute of Health Grant R01 HD-21338.

the difficulty of understanding it, or even recognizing it, in clear and definite terms. For example, it is not as if, by looking at another person, one can consistently tell whether he or she is paying attention. In an episode of the cartoon strip *Dave* (by David Miller), our tongue-tied hero sits with his girlfriend, who is torturing him with a conversation about their relationship and is gazing intently at him while he silently muses, "How do I know that there is a god . . . and he's a guy? Because listening intently and zoning out look exactly the same!" On the whole, attention is known as a concept that is difficult to pin down and operationalize. I suspect that many a researcher has started a talk on some aspect of attention, only to be interrupted by a member of the audience who asks for a definition of what is meant by attention, perhaps mischievously expecting that the speaker will not be able to answer in a satisfactory manner. But life, and lectures, must go on despite the difficulty of defining attention.

The present chapter differs from most others in this book in that the topic is broader; attention is not a specific type of method as is, say, the Stroop effect, and it probably covers even more ground than do other relevant phenomena such as, say, autobiographical memory. Indeed, the deployment of attention affects almost everything humans do, and numerous methods have been developed to study it. The method must be shaped by the aspect of attention that is of interest and the starting assumptions that one is willing to make about how it operates. The floor plan for the present chapter consequently is as follows. First, I take stock of reasons why clinicians might be interested in seriously studying attention. Second, because a chapter cannot do justice to the broad topic of research on attention, some of the available book references are discussed. Third, a taxonomy of tasks that have been used to study attention are offered briefly, with a few examples and illustrations. Fourth, a key substantive question that can be addressed on the basis of such tasks—namely the question of what factors appear to cause attention or inattention—is discussed. Fifth, and finally, a more in-depth description of one line of attentional research, from the author's laboratory and collaborations, is presented to illustrate the methodological issues that must be taken into account in order to carry out a study of an aspect of attention.

WHY A CLINICIAN MIGHT STUDY ATTENTION

Why might a clinician or clinical researcher be interested in attention despite such difficulties? Perhaps because it is a key concept in understanding the human mind. It has been clear at least since James (1890), and almost certainly earlier, that there is a limit to how much information a human being can deal with at once, or within a limited period. I can think of at least three ways in which this human predicament is likely to be clinically relevant.

1. In abnormal individuals, there might be an abnormal attentional profile of diagnostic relevance. People with psychopathologies often attend to stimuli related to certain domains of clinically relevant interest (e.g., sex, violence, or emotional dependence) more than do normal individuals. Yiend and Mathews (see chap. 6, this volume) discuss this type of mechanism in detail. Conversely, it is theoretically possible that there could sometimes be a tendency to avoid such stimuli and therefore to focus attention on competing stimuli, or perhaps on no stimuli at all. In either case, an abnormal profile of attention might provide information about the topics of special concern to the patient, about the degree of severity of abnormality, and perhaps about the correct diagnosis. Yiend and Mathews offer numerous examples of different clinical populations (e.g., depressed versus anxious patients) responding differently in the same attention tasks.

2. An obsession with particular thoughts or types of thoughts can prevent attention from operating flexibly and normally. This kind of attentional abnormality can be very debilitating in its own right and warrants treatment. Of course, knowledge of research on attention is necessary for an effective treatment to be developed.

3. Some types of psychopathology (e.g., schizophrenia or attention-deficit/hyperactivity disorder) may physiologically cause cognitive impairment, including a debilitating deficit in the control of attention. Here, the treatments might differ from the case in which attentional deficits result indirectly, as a secondary consequence of obsessive thoughts.

EXTENSIVE SUMMARIES OF ATTENTION RESEARCH

In an important recent review of research in attention, Luck and Vecera (2002) stated, "The term *attention* has been used in the title or abstract of over 40,000 journal articles, books, and book chapters in the past 30 years. This greatly exceeds the 8,300 works that have used the term *emotion*, and it almost equals the 48,000 works that have used the term *memory*." Given the breadth of the topic of attention, it is best to start by describing a few resources that would allow the in-depth investigator to find out about a wider variety of experimental procedures and results than can be discussed in this chapter. Styles (1997) has written a short, general text on attention that is fairly accessible and Pashler (1998a) has written a longer but still-accessible one. A number of special, edited volumes on attention research also are worthwhile (e.g., Baddeley & Weiskrantz, 1994; Pashler, 1998b; Shapiro, 2001).

The book reporting proceedings from the regular *Attention and Performance* conference series has many useful entries, and the *Annual Review of Psychology* (Pashler, Johnston, & Ruthruff, 2000; Rensink, 2002) includes two recent summaries that are of relevance. Cowan (1995) summarized evidence of the interrelatedness of attention and memory. For historical insight regarding the development of the attention concept, one could read the chapter on attention by James (1890) and then the seminal book by Broadbent (1958). Shiffrin (1988) gives a comprehensive overview of aspects of attention research, including research on automatization of processes, that greatly increased the sophistication of researchers' understanding. Näätänen (1992) gives an in-depth summary of procedures that were used to examine the brain representation of attention, and that field has been growing rapidly (e.g., Braun, Koch, & Davis, 2001; Humphreys, Duncan, & Treisman, 1999; Parasuraman, 1998). Davies and Parasuraman (1982) and Hancock and Desmond (2001) give in-depth coverage of sustained attention, or vigilance, and practical aspects of it. There is enough overlap among these sources that it is not necessary to read all of them to gain a useful, working knowledge of research on attention. They do, however, reveal a range of theoretical perspectives and emphases as well as a great deal of empirical research.

MAJOR VARIETIES OF ATTENTION TASKS

There are various ways in which authors have classified the many different tasks that typically have been used to examine attention. Luck and Vecera (2002) provided a useful classification that distinguished between cuing paradigms, search paradigms, filtering paradigms, and dual-task paradigms and that classification will be followed here. Before that, however, a word on dependent measures is in order.

Dependent Measures in Attention Tasks

Within each category of task, some procedures measure the proportion of trials in which a correct response is given, or the difference that the direction of attention makes for the correctness of a response. Such procedures can involve very rapid presentations in order to make the task sufficiently difficult to discriminate between conditions or between individuals. Other procedures focus upon the reaction time to make a correct response. Ideally, both the reaction times and accuracy of responses must be taken into consideration in some way because there can be tradeoffs between the two. Specifically, some participants might answer more slowly so as to be sure to answer correctly, whereas others might take a greater risk of making incorrect or inaccurate responses in order to respond more quickly. This emphasis on accuracy versus speed falls along a continuum and can be modified with task instructions.

As a further complication, one can imagine tasks in which accuracy itself falls along a continuum. Such tasks are not very common in the laboratory but might be critical in real life, as for soldiers or police officers in a gun battle. Whereas either too slow or too inaccurate a firing upon a threatening attacker may mean death for the officer as a result of return fire, hitting the attacker just slightly off-target, that is, in an unintended anatomical location, still can have big consequences for either party but is not as risky for the officer as is missing the target completely. In a less life-threatening but still important example, a clinician has to respond to a statement by a patient within a relatively short time window but too hasty a response can throw the therapy onto the wrong track. People probably differ in their typical, overall tendency to be impulsive or reflective in responding in a particular situation.

Finally, in some tasks it is not just the correctness of responding that is at issue, but the particular response that is given. Sometimes the nature of erroneous responses is at issue (in error analysis) and other times there may be no correct answer or multiple possible correct answers, each of which has a different significance to the experimenter. All of these possibilities can be found in cuing, search, filtering, and dual-task procedures, although the emphasis is most often upon the pattern of proportion correct and reaction times across different conditions.

Cuing Paradigms

In cuing paradigms, as Luck and Vecera (2002, p. 240) put it, "a stimulus or an instruction is used to lead subjects to expect a specific source of inputs, and then the processing of this source of inputs is compared with the processing of other inputs." A well-known example is the procedure of Posner (1980) in which a participant is informed with a visual cue as to whether a target will appear on the left or right of visual fixation. The task is to respond with a buttonpress indicating which side of the screen the target is on, as quickly as possible. When a directional cue appears the cue usually (80% of the time) points to the correct location but on other trials (20% of the time) it is misleading, pointing to the incorrect location. On still other, control trials, there is no directional cue. For example, in some experiments the cue was a central arrow pointing left or right or a plus sign. This type of procedure produces an advantage for a correctly cued location and a disadvantage when attention is sent to the side opposite from the target. Investigators have drawn a distinction between *peripheral* or *exogenous* cues that appear at the location where the target probably will appear, which recruit attention to their locations rather involuntarily, and *central* or *endogenous* cues, such as the central arrow pointing to one side, which draw attention to the center but then allow the participant to move attention voluntarily in the direction in which the target is to be expected.

The value of cuing paradigms is that one can examine factors that recruit attention or allow attention to be shifted voluntarily, the speed and timing of these attention-shifting mechanisms, the difficulty of returning attention to a region that was recently attended, and other aspects of attention-shifting. Attention-shifting to a peripheral cue occurs automatically and, in fact, takes effort to suppress. Attention-shifting away from a central arrow toward the direction in which it points takes effort because the automatic tendency to direct attention to the arrow itself must be overcome. In this type of procedure one can usefully measure the response reaction time for trials with valid, invalid, and neutral cues and also eye movements to the cues. Given that the real-world application of attention often involves a shifting of attention to understand rapidly emerging threats and crises, cuing procedures can be quite informative. In clinical work, one could make a distinction between, say, an automatic aversion to threatening stimuli versus difficulty in using effortful processing to direct attention to threatening stimuli (see chap. 6, this volume). These mechanisms have different psychological implications. It is perhaps easier to combat a tendency that occurs with effort and voluntary processing than one that occurs automatically because the effortful processing is more visible to consciousness (e.g., Shiffrin, 1988).

Search Paradigms

In search paradigms, one item or several from a target set are to be found as quickly as possible within an array of items presented in the visual field (or, in principle at least, within a field of stimuli presented in any sensory modality or even across modalities). In a *memory search* procedure, there is just a single probe item to be examined but one searches through a memory representation to determine whether that probe was present within a previously learned or encountered set of items (Sternberg, 1966). In contrast, in a simple *visual search* procedure, there is only one item in memory, and it must be compared with a larger array of items in the visual field. Memory search and visual search also can be combined in the same experiment by having participants search for multiple possible targets, held in memory, within a multi-item array (e.g., Schneider & Shiffrin, 1977).

One benefit of search paradigms is that one can examine what factors influence the ability to use attention to find things in the environment or within a mental representation of a stimulus set. One also can examine the pattern of search times or accuracy as a function of how many items there are to be searched. For very rapid searches or searches in which items are processed in parallel, little time should be added to the reaction time for each additional item in the set to be searched. When searches must be made in a method in which only a small portion of the processing can be completed at once, say one item at a time, then each additional item in the set to be searched increases the reaction time substantially.

A key example is the visual search procedure used by Treisman and Gelade (1980). They distinguished between feature searches and conjunction searches. In an example of a feature search, a screen of dots might be presented, and one would have to press a button indicating if a red dot is present (among a field of blue dots). If a single red item is detected anywhere in the array, one can immediately ascertain that the target is present. The feature search might also involve, say, finding a triangle among circles. The reaction time for such a search does not increase much as a function of the number of objects in the display. In a conjunction search, one might be looking for a red circle among a set of items that includes at least two types of distractors: red triangles and blue circles. It is not enough to determine if the target features are present; one must carefully search to determine if they are present in the right combination. In this case, search time generally increases linearly as a function of the number of items in the display. Moreover, the slope of increase is twice as high when the target that one is searching for is absent from the display than when it is present. That is because one must search all items in a display to determine that a target is absent whereas, when a target is present, on average one finds it after searching through half of the items in the display. This type of procedure could be used to determine what the units of perception are. Clinically, we could speculate that certain objects of one's obsessions or concerns tend to be treated as features rather than conjunctions although to my knowledge there is no such research as yet.

Filtering Paradigms

In filtering paradigms, instructions given before a stimulus field indicate which part of the stimuli are to be attended and which others are to be ignored. One of the oldest examples of this type of paradigm is the selective-listening procedure in which competing spoken messages are presented to the two ears (Broadbent, 1958; Cherry, 1953). In Cherry's procedure, for example, one hears a message in one ear and a different message in the other ear and must quickly repeat (or *shadow*) everything that is said in one ear. It is clear that people can do a reasonably good job of processing only one coherent speech message at a time and that very little of the other message(s) is subsequently recalled, presumably because it could not be processed.

Filtering paradigms are useful because it is possible to learn the conditions under which distractions can or cannot be excluded from processing and the ways in which processing is impaired as a result. Learning all of this has considerable real-world application inasmuch as we live in a world with multiple concurrent stimuli and, much of the time, must exert effort to stay on task. Yiend and Mathews (see chap. 6, this volume) briefly mention early clinical work in which an emotional item is embedded within the ignored message in selective listening. To the extent that the subject's processing system is tuned to the issue of the emotional item, the item may tend to be noticed, resulting in a disruption of attention and revealing some of the subject's mental properties. An even older filtering procedure is the task by Stroop (1935/1992) discussed in previous chapters within this volume. When a color word is printed in a conflicting color of ink, people cannot name the color of the ink without massive interference from the printed color word, provided that they know how to read it. Also commonly used is the flankers task, in which the participant is to respond to a central target but not to distractors placed on the left and right of the target (see the review by Eriksen, 1995).

We have thus examined both auditory and visual filtering procedures. Although visual filtering studies traditionally have been easier to conduct with simple equipment, it is not clear that this is still the case with modern computers. In one way at least, auditory tests are especially useful: They allow ignored and attended stimuli to be presented at the same level of sensory acuity (because humans cannot close or redirect their ears). In contrast, ignored visual information tends to be perceived out of focus or peripherally, with less sensory acuity than the attended items, which can be focused with high acuity on the fovea and the closely surrounding regions of the retina. The uniform acuity found in audition makes it easier to avoid confounding sensory and attentional processes.

There are two ways in which a distractor can interfere with behavior. First, the control of the focus of attention may not be fine-grained enough to include the target and still exclude the distractors. Doing so depends on the precision of attention, the similarity of the features among target and distractors, and their spatial proximity. Second, some aspects of distractors may be processed automatically, without the need for attention. Nevertheless, this automatic processing may disrupt performance in one way or another. It may recruit attention away from processing of the target (as when a loud noise occurs in the unattended channel in selective listening) or it may contaminate the response-planning process (as in the Stroop effect). Variations on the filtering procedure are quite helpful in investigating the means whereby processing is disrupted.

A key type of evidence that ongoing processing has been disrupted is the orienting response (Sokolov, 1963), in which a shift of attention from one stimulus to another is accompanied by motor slowing and physiological signs such as heart-rate slowing, accompanied by privileged processing of the item that caused the orienting. Novel, abrupt stimuli tend to cause orienting, whereas repeated stimuli result in a habituation of orienting (see Cowan, 1995, for a review). Sokolov's theory stated that one builds a neural model of stimuli that are repeated, and there is evidence that this neural model can help a person to ignore the repeated stimuli and pay attention to something else (e.g., Cowan, 1995; Elliott & Cowan, 2001; Waters, McDonald, & Koresko, 1977). Thus, the switching of attention from one event to another is partly, but not entirely, under one's own voluntary control. If a very loud noise is unexpectedly heard, for example, attention will invariably shift from the ongoing activities to the noise. One can be internally conflicted, as when a student needs to pay attention to a boring lecture for the sake of a grade but finds it nearly impossible to do so, and attention often is a struggle between voluntary and involuntary processes. Of particular interest for clinical research, stimuli of special significance to the participant can cause continued orienting even when repeated (see Cowan, 1995).

Multiple-Task Paradigms

The final category of attentional paradigm described by Luck and Vecera (2002) was the dual-task paradigm, but we can talk more generally about multiple-task paradigms. When two or more tasks are to be accomplished at the same time, one can ask whether they all draw upon the same attentional processes or *resources*. To the extent that they do, improved performance in one task can be accomplished only at the expense of poorer performance in the other task or tasks. My own specialty in this regard is getting lost if driving to a rarely visited location while holding a discussion with a passenger, as several of my colleagues can attest (e.g., Monica Fabiani, personal communication, March 10, 2000). Broadbent (1957) described a prototypical dual-task procedure. Two different lists of three items were spoken simultaneously, with one list presented to the left ear and the other to the right ear, and then all six items were to be recalled. Recall was superior when the required order of recall was first one ear, and then the other, as opposed to an order in which the first, second, and third items in each ear were recalled in temporal order by alternating between left- and right-ear stimuli. The presumed reason is that sensory memory was used to hold the items that had not yet been recalled, and it was easiest to access one ear's representation at a time, without switching attention back and forth.

A particular dual task may have been groundbreaking in fostering the realization that human perception is fallible. As Boring (1957) has described, in Greenwich in 1796, an astronomer (Maskelyne) fired his assistant (Kinnebrook) because the two of them consistently produced results that were very different from one another. The task was one in which a metronome had to be used to time the movement of a star across hairlines in the telescope. Another forward-thinking astronomer, Bessel, from Königsberg, realized that the assistant may not have been at fault. Visiting various astronomers across Europe, he found that each one gave a different measurement but with an impressive amount of stability in judgment within an individual. Boring attributed the individual differences to the *law of prior entry*, which states that when two sensory impressions arrive concurrently, it is possible to allocate attention more to one or the other and that the attended sensory impression will seem to have arrived sooner than the initially unattended one. Differences in the style of attending to the telescope versus the metronome could have caused the astronomers to differ in their judgments.

Attention may have to be divided across time, across space, or both. It must be divided across time in the currently popular attentional blink procedure (Raymond, Shapiro, & Arnell, 1992; based on earlier, similar findings not using that nomenclature, by Broadbent & Broadbent, 1987; Reeves & Sperling, 1986; Weichselgartner & Sperling, 1987). In the attentional blink procedure, a stream of items is presented rapidly on the computer screen (e.g., 10 items per second), with one item replacing the next at the same spatial location. The participant must search for two targets, sometimes on different bases, and make two responses after the stream of characters ends. For example, the participant might be asked to search for the occurrence of two digits among letters, and then report the digits. The finding is that there is a period after the first target during which recognition of the second target is poor. If there are no items between the two targets, this *attentional blink* is not found. However, there is a period in which an occurrence of the second target will tend not to be noticed, which produces a scallop in the performance function for that target. Performance may be 50% down from its peak when there are 100 to 200 ms between targets and it returns to normal when there are about 500 to 600 ms between them.

One might worry that an attentional blink could occur because of an actual eye blink after the first target, but the data seem to rule out such an interpretation. For example, event-related brain potential recordings show that a second target that is not reported because of the attentional blink still elicits electrical components corresponding to sensory processing (P1 and N1 components) and semantic analysis (N400) but that a component corresponding to the updating of working memory (P3) is missing (Vogel, Luck, & Shapiro, 1998).

Another popular procedure in which attention is divided across time is the psychological refractory period procedure (e.g., see Ruthruff & Pashler, 2001). In that procedure, two stimuli requiring responses again are placed near one another with a variable interstimulus interval. However, here the dependent measure is not the accuracy of stimulus perception but, rather, the reaction times to the two stimuli. Again it is supposed that the allocation of attention to the first stimulus uses up some resource that may not yet be available again when the second stimulus arrives. The benefit of procedures in which attention is divided across time is that one can gain powerful indices of the time course of various types of processing that cannot be carried out for two stimuli at once.

In other procedures, attention must be divided over space instead of time. For example, in a dichotic listening experiment, such as the one by Broadbent (1957) described above, different left- and right-ear stimuli are presented at the same time and therefore have to be encoded concurrently. However, it has been assumed that we have a vivid but short-lived sensory memory that can outlast the actual stimuli (for reviews, see Cowan, 1988, 1995). It is therefore possible to complete the process of perceiving and identifying an item on the basis of its sensory memory. In essence, a simultaneous presentation of stimuli can be transformed by the participant into a sequential task in which items are processed, either directly or on the basis of the sensory memory trace, one by one. Therefore, concurrent presentation of stimuli may not yield such precise information about the time course of attentional processes. Researchers typically cannot tell which perceptual processes are delayed and then completed on the basis of a sensory memory or afterimage. This problem generally does not arise if stimuli are presented sequentially because each stimulus overwrites the sensory memory of previous ones.

In sequential presentations, one examines the consequences of pressuring the processing system in a temporal manner. The analogous possibility for simultaneous presentations is to examine the consequences of pressuring the processing system spatially, by presenting far more information than a participant possibly can deal with (even by offloading information to a short-lived sensory memory). That presumably is the situation leading to a phenomenon known as inattentional blindness (for reviews see Rensink, 2002; Simons, 2000). In this phenomenon, one finds that participants often are oblivious to very large changes in the environment, so long as an abrupt change within a single visual fixation is avoided. For example, a videotape with a visual scene of people at a table in a restaurant may cut to a very brief outdoor scene and then back to the restaurant scene, but water glasses appearing in the original scene may have disappeared and a pitcher of water may appear instead. Most participants do not notice such changes. Data and theorization in this area seem to suggest that people are able to keep in the focus of attention only a handful of independent aspects from an ongoing event. People are dependent on the external events themselves, and on logical coherence within the external scene, to perceive the stimulus bombardment that occurs at any one time.

Consistent with this suggestion of an attentional limitation, Cowan (2001) reviewed the limits on how many concurrent items can be held in the focus of attention at once. Across many different types of procedure, adult humans seem to be limited on average to about three or four independent items in the focus of attention at a time (although individual participants may yield estimates as low as two or as high as six). This limit may also be viewed as a fundamental working-memory limit, and so the relation between working memory and selective attention is a close one indeed (Cowan, 1995). Engle, Kane, and Tuholski (1999) explain how working-memory capacity on a variety of tests is related to the ability to control one's allocation and deployment of attention.

When one is confronted with a series of items one at a time, the typical finding is that people can remember and immediately repeat about seven items, give or take a few (Miller, 1956). However, Miller discussed the manner in which such immediate-memory estimates probably result from some amount of grouping together of items, or *chunking*, in memory. For example, it is difficult to recall nine random letters but easy to recall the nine letters FBI-CIA-IBM. In this example, for American readers at least, the nine letters have been transformed in memory into three well-known acronyms, each of which becomes a single chunk. Processes of covert rehearsal (e.g., Baddeley, 1986) may be useful in achieving such chunking transformations even when the stimuli do not contain already-known groups. That is probably why telephone numbers are presented as groups of three and four digits. Cowan (2001) found that, in a large variety of studies in which it is reasonable to assume that grouping and rehearsal processes have been prevented, the limit is three or four items in adults, much as in cases of concurrent stimulus presentation. Perhaps the largest current question is whether this is a central limit for stimuli presented in all modalities (presumably, a limit in the capacity of the focus of attention) or whether there are separate, albeit similar, limits for stimuli in different modalities or different types of perceptual code.

Although many of the multitask procedures have a heavy memory requirement, one also can find multitask procedures with no memory requirement, which is useful in distinguishing between memory and attention. For example, Pylyshyn and Storm (1988) developed a procedure in which a display of objects (e.g., dots) is presented and a certain number of the objects flash. They then stop flashing, and all of the objects begin to wander around the screen randomly and independently. When they stop, the required response is to indicate whether a particular object had been flashing at the beginning of the trial. Thus, this task requires multiobject tracking. It can be accomplished well by adults when there are, on average, four or fewer objects to be tracked, but certainly no more. Thus, attention must be divided between the target (previously flashing) objects throughout the trial.

A potential clinical benefit of multitask procedures is that one can examine differences in the quantity of what is attended. For example, an obsession could narrow the focus of attention as well as make the individual unable to shift the focus of attention. A narrowed attentional focus would show up in terms of fewer tasks or stimuli that could be perceived at the same time or recalled from a single stimulus array.

CAUSES OF ATTENTION AND INATTENTION AND CONSEQUENT CHOICES BETWEEN PARADIGMS

To determine which of the many attentional procedures is the right one to use for a particular experiment, one must first be explicit about which

kinds of attentional mechanisms are of interest. One can point to two funda-
mentally different reasons why an individual might be attentive to some
stimuli but inattentive to others, which can be called *processing limitations*
and *processing motives*. In both cases, some types of information are said to be
processed automatically, and other types of information are said to be processed only if sufficient attention of limited capacity is allocated. There also
are situations in which processing limitations and processing motivations are
combined. Processing limitations, processing motivation, automaticity, and
the combination of processing limitations with motivations are discussed in
turn below.

Processing Limitations

The first reason for attention and inattention, which can be found in
the writings of William James (1890), is that there is a limit on how much
information an individual is able to process at one time (i.e., a processing
limitation). That type of mechanism, known as an attentional capacity limit,
was one of the bases of the field of cognitive psychology as explained, for
example, by Broadbent (1958) and Neisser (1967), and it remains a major
topic of research. A practical situation that concerned Broadbent early on in
the history of the field was the predicament of military pilots trying to hear
instructions over the radio mixed in with instructions to other pilots. Another common example is the inability to process all conversations at once
at a party, the widely discussed *cocktail party phenomenon*. Given the impossi-
bility of processing everything in the environment, an individual must make
some kind of strategic choice as to which stimuli are most important to
process.

It is possible to adapt any of the types of attentional procedure to the
study of processing limitations and, for that matter, to examine whether they
are affected by clinical conditions or threatening situations that might drain
attention away from the task. In a cuing procedure (e.g., the cue-validity
procedure of Posner, 1980), one can study whether the attentional system is
capable of exerting attention to make good use of endogenous cues (central
arrows pointing to one side or another) to turn attention in a way that goes
against the natural urge to focus on that central arrow itself. One might expect that a participant preoccupied with personal concerns would have fewer
free resources to devote to the task and thus would do relatively poorly on
endogenous cues. In a search procedure (e.g., the feature and conjunction
search procedure of Treisman & Gelade, 1980), one can determine whether
the increase in reaction time to find a particular feature conjunction, as a
function of the display set size, is normal or slower than normal. In a filtering
procedure (e.g., the selective-listening procedure of Cherry, 1953), one can
examine how complex a stimulus stream can be processed and how well attention can be focused as a function of the degree of similarity between the

messages to be attended versus ignored. Finally, in a multiple-task procedure (e.g., the multiobject tracking procedure of Pylyshyn & Storm, 1988) one can ask how many items can be kept in attention at once.

Processing Motivation

Even if the individual has enough of the necessary mental resources to process multiple stimuli, there may be cases in which he or she would prefer not to process certain stimuli because they are emotionally painful or because they would disrupt other mental processes, interfering with ongoing task performance or social interactions. This idea of motivated inattention can be traced back to Sigmund Freud. For example, Freud (1915/1990, p. 428) said, "Psychoanalysis has taught us that the essence of the process of repression lies, not in abrogating or annihilating the ideational representation of an instinct, but in withholding it from becoming conscious." If we accept that attention to an idea is the means by which it becomes part of conscious experience, then it follows that inattention can result from a motivation not to become aware of something. Anderson and Green (2001) showed that it is possible to simulate this process experimentally through instructions to inhibit the thoughts of words (e.g., "when you see *bear*, avoid thinking of *dish*"). In such instances, participants later find it more difficult to recall the second word in the pair than in conditions without any such inhibition instructions. Of course, as Yiend and Mathews (chap. 6, this volume) discuss, the opposite can occur and a person can be biased toward processing a certain type of emotion-laden stimulus, even if processing that stimulus reduces the person's feeling of well-being.

All of the types of procedures can, once again, be adapted to the study of processing motivation or bias. Cuing procedures (e.g., Posner, 1980) can be used to determine whether it is easier or more difficult to draw attention toward an object that matches a certain emotional or semantic bias than it is to draw attention toward a neutral object. Search procedures (e.g., Treisman & Gelade, 1980) can be used to determine whether one can spot an emotionally laden object among a crowd of objects (e.g., faces; see Yiend & Mathews [chap. 6, this volume]) more quickly than one can spot a neutral target object. Filtering procedures (e.g., Cherry, 1953) can be used to determine whether one can ignore an emotional element presented to the unattended channel. Finally, multiple-task procedures (e.g., the multiobject tracking procedure of Pylyshyn & Storm, 1988) could be used to determine if emotional objects could be tracked more easily than other objects, although this adaptation has not been tried.

In the area of attention, a plethora of procedures have overlapping aims and are relevant to highly overlapping issues. How, then, should one pick a procedure to use in a clinical experiment? A key point is that each procedure has many intricacies inasmuch as there are multiple strategies that participants can use to carry out the task. Therefore, an acceptable general method of picking a procedure would be as follows: (a) find a few experiments with results that one particularly likes and that seem to demonstrate a specific process in attention; (b) try to ensure that the procedure or procedures are not the center of an active debate concerning what fundamental processes are used to carry out those procedures; (c) get to know a tightly knit body of literature regarding that procedure; and (d) stick with the procedure for a while, changing just one thing at a time until a new point of interest can be established. This process seems better than hopping between procedures too quickly, given the investment of time and effort that is needed to learn valuable things from each procedure. Yiend and Mathews (see chap. 6, this volume) appear to illustrate this process in clinical research. Some potential pitfalls of a method are illustrated later in this chapter in a discussion of recent selective-listening studies with normal adults.

Now, however, the point about understanding how an attentional method works is explored with respect to one basic issue that distinguishes procedures from one another. Specifically, some procedures index automatic selection of an object from a multiobject field and others index effortful, attention-demanding processing. It is especially important to determine how to tell them apart.

Consequences of Automatic Versus Attention-Demanding Processing

Automaticity and Processing Limitation

Both the common conception of a processing limit and the concept of processing motives include the assumption that some processing takes place even without attention. This is termed *automatic processing*, which typically is not easily controlled and may occur even against the participant's wishes. Within the notion of a processing limit, for example, consider a seminal, selective-listening study by Cherry (1953) that influenced Broadbent (1958). Cherry presented different spoken messages to the two ears through headphones and required that the participant repeat concurrently, or *shadow*, one of the messages. This shadowing led to an almost total inability to recall anything that had been presented in the nonshadowed message. However, if the message changed in a basic physical quality (from a male voice to a female voice), this was invariably noticed. The voice quality must have been processed automatically at some level of the nervous system, even though the nonshadowed channel did not receive enough attention for processing of the message content.

The assumption of automatic processing of simple physical features of stimuli in selective listening is reinforced by the work of Johnston and Heinz (1978). They used selective-listening procedures in which two word lists, spoken concurrently, could differ in terms of voice quality or only in terms of the message topic. (There were also single-stream control conditions.) Participants could learn to listen to one list of spoken words while ignoring another. Depending on the experiment, the task was to respond to comprehension questions after the list, respond by shadowing the message, or search for particular target words in the list. In any case, there also were occasional flashes of light during the sentences, and the secondary task was to respond to the light flash with a buttonpress as quickly as possible, without interrupting the selective-listening task. The rationale behind that experimental design is that, the more attention-demanding the listening task is, the slower the responses to the light will be on average. These experiments showed that the reactions to the light flashes were much slower when they accompanied the task of selective listening on the basis of semantic differences than they were when they accompanied the task of selective listening on the basis of voice differences. The data suggested that listening on the basis of voice differences consumes little, if any, attention; the nontarget voice could be excluded from processing relatively automatically, without withdrawing attention from the tasks of interpreting the target message and waiting for the light flash. In contrast, the nontarget semantic content could be identified and excluded only at the expense of slower performance in the reaction-time task. Thus, only the physical features were processed automatically.

Although some types of automatic processing (such as the processing of basic physical features of the environment) may be intact from birth or may develop as an inevitable consequence of normal childhood development, other types of automatic processing develop through habit. For example, James (1890) discussed an instance in which he went upstairs to change into dinner clothes and, his thoughts being preoccupied, he accidentally changed into bedclothes instead. Schneider and Shiffrin (1977) and Shiffrin and Schneider (1977) showed that habit leads to an automatization even of perceptual processes. They did this in a seminal, elaborate set of experiments in which they compared two types of search condition referred to as a consistent mapping and a varied mapping. The task was one in which a field of characters was to be searched for an item from a set of targets. For example, in one experiment (Schneider & Shiffrin, Experiment 2), a participant might have to search for the presence of either an E or an H among a visual array that included the letters F, B, H, and X (in which case the correct response would be to push the computer key indicating "yes" as quickly as possible because the H is present in the array). On each trial, the target set was given, followed by the array to be searched for the presence of any of the targets. The target set (items to be found) could include 1, 2, or 4 characters and, as well, the visual array to be searched could include 1, 2, or 4 characters. There never was more than one of the targets within a particular array. In the consistent mapping condition, target characters were drawn from the same set on every trial. For example, if the presence of an F would warrant a "yes" response on one trial, it would warrant a "yes" response whenever it occurred within that session. (It would occur in the array only if it also had been part of the target set on that trial.) In the varied mapping condition, in contrast, a particular character could serve as a target on one trial and as a distractor, or nontarget in the visual array, on another trial. For example, one might have to search for an H or S on trial n but, on trial n+x, either H or S or both could be present within an array for which one was to search instead for certain other letters. In that case, the correct answer on trial n+x would be "yes" only if those other, target letters were present, regardless of whether H or S were present (as distractors on this trial).

Practice succeeded in establishing an automatic perceptual process in the case of consistent mapping only. At first, reaction times were much slower for trials in which the memory set contained more items, and also for trials in which the array was larger. Presumably, searches had to take place a little bit at a time; searching processes could not cover the entire memory set or the entire visual array at once, at least not without interference between items. However, over many trials of consistent mapping, participants could learn to search arrays for a particular set of target characters. As a consequence, after a while it did not much matter how large the memory set was or how large the array was. In contrast, such learning never could take place in the varied mapping situation; the skill of searching for a new set of characters on each trial did not become automatized. Other experiments demonstrated the same thing by varying the duration of the array and measuring the proportion correct, which was reduced if the array was presented too quickly for the search process to be completed successfully.

In daily life, our considerable experience has divided items into different categories that can be used for automatic perceptual processing without specifically practicing for that purpose. For example, it is relatively easy to search for a digit among letters and relatively difficult to search for a letter among other letters or a digit among digits. The difficulty that can occur in searching for characters (e.g., a letter among other letters) occurs only if one is searching for an object that does not stand out on a physical basis. When one searches for basic physical features, they seem to pop out from the background and can be seen easily. For example, it is easy to search for a single red item among a field of items that are colored blue, or for a single triangle among circles. It is difficult to search when one needs to check the particular conjunction of features, such as searching for a single red circle in a field containing red triangles and blue circles, so that neither the color nor the shape is unique to the target items (Treisman & Gelade, 1980).

The automaticity of a perceptual process could play a role in performance in several ways: (a) If task-relevant items have come to be automatically perceived, the perception of these items can take place more efficiently. Automatization of the target set in the procedures of Shiffrin and Schneider exemplify that possibility. (b) If task-irrelevant distractors have come to be automatically perceived, and these distractors are clearly unlike the targets, this situation can prevent harmful attention to the distractors that otherwise would occur at the expense of the target processing. (c) In addition, though, if task-irrelevant distractors elicit the same response category as the targets, there may be some confusion that is *increased* after automaticity of the distractors because the response system is contaminated. There are examples of all of these possibilities in the research literature.

It has long been understood that when a process becomes automatic, it can be completed without attracting one's attention. That is one benefit of automaticity. For example, walking behavior has become relatively automatic so that one can walk and hold a conversation at the same time. Driving a car is also generally automatic except that an emergency on the road will interrupt the conversation. Recent research suggests that holding conversations through a cell phone, even one that does not have to be handheld, dangerously interferes with emergency coping within driving behavior (Strayer & Johnston, 2001).

Given that automatic behavior does not require one's attention, it often has been speculated that the memory system can be addressed and updated automatically, which results in unconscious perception and memory storage. Holender (1986) has reviewed a large number and range of studies purporting to demonstrate this automatic access and updating, and has cautioned that most of them are problematic in that one cannot be sure of the direction of participants' attention during testing.

Mechanisms Working Together

It is possible for both processing limitations and motivations, and their automatizations, to operate at the same time to control performance. Demonstrating this, Motley, Camden, and Baars (1982) examined slips of the tongue, which presumably reflect thoughts that were automatically formed and were converted to speech without being adequately monitored or suppressed. They set up a situation in which slips would occur more frequently than they do in daily life. In one example, after reading aloud numerous word pairs beginning with the letters f__ p__, as in *federal privilege, future payment*, and so on, participants were given a word pair with the opposite letter arrangement, p__ f__, such as *past fashion*. Participants often would incorrectly read this pair as *fast passion*, fitting the pattern of the previous pairs. Thus, the processing system was unable to prevent recently established automatic processes (the f__ p__ pattern) from dominating the response. The processing motivation also proved to be relevant. Participants who had been placed in a sexualized situation made more errors on sexual word pairs (e.g., *past fashion* misread as *fast passion*), whereas those placed under threat of shock made more errors on word pairs related to electricity (e.g., *worst cottage* misread as *cursed wattage*).

AN EXAMPLE OF A LINE OF RESEARCH ON
CENTRAL ISSUES OF ATTENTION

One must consider various confounding and complicating factors in order to make progress in understanding the role of attention in any domain. One line of research illustrating these confounding and complicating factors examines whether attention filters out information after physical features have been processed (an early filter) or only after semantic features also have been processed (a later filter). Participants in our studies were to shadow the spoken message presented to one ear, a procedure that allows one to examine how well the attentional set is maintained. After Cherry (1953) found that people can recall very little of the information that occurs in an unattended channel in selective listening except for the basic physical features, Moray (1959) challenged this approach with the finding that people could sometimes notice and recall their own names having been presented in the unattended channel. (This, along with the difficulty of perceiving much else in an unattended channel, is the cocktail party phenomenon.) However, even though Moray's finding is commonly used in cognitive textbooks, it was only a pilot study that was never replicated. Moray tested 12 individuals and 4 of them noticed their names. Even these four might be accounted for on the grounds that each participant's name had to be spliced into the audiotape with the rest of the unattended message, which could have created subtle acoustic irregularities that could have recruited attention.

We thought of replicating Moray's experiment as a consequence of some experimental results on sensory memory. Cowan, Lichty, and Grove (1990) had participants read a novel silently or in a whisper while hearing meaningless syllables through headphones. There was no response to most of the syllables but, occasionally, the participant would receive a cue to stop reading and recall the last spoken syllable. This last syllable occurred 1, 5, or 10 s before the recall cue. Memory for unattended speech declined dramatically as a function of the retention interval. However, it also was found that the slightest redirection of attention to the spoken channel at the time of the speech presentation resulted in an enormous improvement in memory for speech, suggesting an early filter.

Wood and Cowan (1995a) replicated a condition from Cherry (1953): a change in the unattended message from forward speech to backward speech and then back to forward speech again 30 s later. Shadowing responses were tape-recorded to enable examination of the direction of attention. After the shadowing session, participants were quizzed about whether they had noticed anything unusual in the unattended channel and, if so, what it was. About half of the participants reported noticing something unusual. In those who did notice, the shadowing record showed pauses and errors mounting within the first 15 s of backward speech. Subjects who did not report anything unusual in the unattended channel showed no such shifting of attention. Thus, noticing the change in the channel that was supposed to be unattended was accompanied by a shift in attention. Wood and Cowan (1995b) used a similar procedure to reexamine whether people noticed their name in an unattended channel. We improved upon Moray's (1959) procedure by (a) using a larger number of participants, (b) carefully analyzing the shadowing response for pauses and errors that could reflect attention shifts, (c) using only subjects' first names in the recording and restricting the sample to subjects with monosyllabic first names mixed with other monosyllabic words to avoid acoustic differences, (d) using computer digitization techniques to eliminate any acoustic cues from splicing audiotapes to insert the names, and (e) using yoked pairs of participants who each received both names in the acoustic channel, so that each participant was tested on his or her own name and a control name. No participant ever notice the yoked control's name, whereas 33% of the participants noticed their own names, which replicated Moray's finding surprisingly well. Those who noticed their names showed a large shift of attention away from shadowing just after the name, which did not occur in the other participants.

The verdict from Wood and Cowan (1995a, 1995b) appeared to be that names in the unattended channel are automatically processed, though this processing clearly then recruited attention away from shadowing. A final study illustrates, however, how difficult it can be to determine what is automatic. Conway, Cowan, and Bunting (2001) asked *which* participants noticed the names in the unattended channels. One possibility was that those with better working memory would be able to shadow one channel while monitoring the other channel at the same time, and thus would notice their names. Alternatively, though, participants with better working-memory spans might be better at inhibiting distraction and therefore *less* likely to notice their names than would lower-span individuals.

The results strongly favored the inhibition view. Of participants in the highest quartile of working-memory span, only 20% noticed their names, whereas of participants in the lowest quartile, 65% noticed their names. This finding is rather consistent with an early-filter view. The supposedly unattended channel could not be monitored or perceived without a drop in shadowing performance. Low-span individuals apparently distributed attention across channels rather than focusing it more exclusively on the assigned task, the channel to be shadowed.

It is noteworthy that the interpretation based on Conway et al. (2001) is just the opposite from what one would think based on Wood and Cowan (1995b) and numerous related studies (Holender, 1986). This discrepancy between conclusions underscores the point that one cannot rely on a convergence of results from multiple studies if those studies share some hidden logical flaw. A single study that identifies the flaw is worth more.

Another lesson is the importance of assessing the processing abilities of the participants one wishes to study clinically. Suppose one is comparing anxious and normal individuals on an attention task. It could be important to make sure that these two groups are equated on working-memory abilities. One could imagine that part of the anxiety that some participants face is an indirect consequence of trying to manage scholastic work with a relatively low working-memory ability.

In a single laboratory, it may be preferable to stick with one good procedure for a long time, until the many possible bugs can be worked out, rather than to hop from one attractive procedure to another. At the same time, one must be aware that typically multiple procedures need to be interpreted. For example, the case of attending to one's name has been looked at in visual studies of the attentional blink (Shapiro, Caldwell, & Sorensen, 1997) and repetition blindness (Arnell, Shapiro, & Sorensen, 1999) and these studies still need to be reconciled with that of Conway et al. (2001). Perhaps the answer is that there are both early and late filtering mechanisms (Johnston & Heinz, 1978) or filtering in a leaky manner that lets some semantic processing proceed in an attenuated form (Cowan, 1988, 1995; Treisman, 1964). In any case, this presentation of research in its unfinished state illustrates how experimental procedures can be used, with caution, to explore the deployment of attention in various situations that relate to clinical experiences and outcomes.

REFERENCES

Anderson, M. C., & Green, C. (2001). Suppressing unwanted memories by executive control. *Nature, 410*, 366–369.

Arnell, K. M., Shapiro, K. L., & Sorensen, R. E. (1999). Reduced repetition blindness for one's own name. *Visual Cognition, 6*, 609–635.

Baddeley, A. D. (1986). *Working memory*. Oxford Psychology Series, No. 11. Oxford, England: Clarendon Press.

Baddeley, A. D., & Weiskrantz, L. (Eds.). (1994). *Attention: Selection, awareness, and control: A tribute to Donald Broadbent*. New York: Oxford University Press.

Boring, E. G. (1957). *A history of experimental psychology* (2nd ed.). Englewood Cliffs, NJ: Prentice-Hall.

Braun, J., Koch, C., & Davis, J. L. (Eds.). (2001). *Visual attention and cortical circuits*. Cambridge, MA: MIT Press.

Broadbent, D. E. (1957). Immediate memory and simultaneous stimuli. *Quarterly Journal of Experimental Psychology, 9*, 1–11.

Broadbent, D. E. (1958). *Perception and communication*. New York: Pergamon Press.

Broadbent, D. E., & Broadbent, M. H. P. (1987). From detection to identification: Response to multiple targets in rapid serial visual presentation. *Perception & Psychophysics, 42*, 105–113.

Cherry, E. C. (1953). Some experiments on the recognition of speech, with one and with two ears. *The Journal of the Acoustical Society of America, 25*, 975–979.

Conway, R. A., Cowan, N., & Bunting, M. F. (2001). The cocktail party phenomenon revisited: The importance of working memory capacity. *Psychonomic Bulletin & Review, 8,* 331–335.

Cowan, N. (1988). Evolving conceptions of memory storage, selective attention, and their mutual constraints within the human information processing system. *Psychological Bulletin, 104,* 163–191.

Cowan, N. (1995). *Attention and memory: An integrated framework.* Oxford Psychology Series, No. 26. New York: Oxford University Press.

Cowan, N. (2001). The magical number 4 in short-term memory: A reconsideration of mental storage capacity. *Behavioral and Brain Sciences, 24,* 87–185.

Cowan, N., Lichty, W., & Grove, T. R. (1990). Properties of memory for unattended spoken syllables. *Journal of Experimental Psychology: Learning, Memory, and Cognition, 16,* 258–269.

Davies, D. R., & Parasuraman, R. (1982). *The psychology of vigilance.* New York: Academic Press.

Elliott, E. M., & Cowan, N. (2001). Habituation to auditory distractors in a cross-modal, color–word interference task. *Journal of Experimental Psychology: Learning, Memory, and Cognition, 27,* 654–667.

Engle, R. W., Kane, M. J., & Tuholski, S. W. (1999). Individual differences in working memory capacity and what they tell us about controlled attention, general fluid intelligence and functions of the prefrontal cortex. In A. Miyake & P. Shah (Eds.), *Models of working memory: Mechanisms of active maintenance and executive control* (pp. 102–134). Cambridge, England: Cambridge University Press.

Eriksen, C. W. (1995). The flankers task and response competition: A useful tool for investigating a variety of cognitive problems. *Visual Cognition, 2,* 101–118.

Freud, S. (1990). The unconscious (C. M. Baines, Trans). In M. J. Adler (Ed.), *Great books of the western world* (Vol. 54, pp. 428–443). Chicago: Encyclopedia Britannica. (Original work published 1915)

Hancock, P. A., & Desmond, P. A. (Eds.). (2001). *Stress, workload, and fatigue.* Mahwah, NJ: Erlbaum.

Holender, D. (1986). Semantic activation without conscious identification in dichotic listening, parafoveal vision, and visual masking: A survey and appraisal. *Behavioral & Brain Sciences, 9,* 1–66.

Humphreys, G. W., Duncan, J., & Treisman, A. (Eds.). (1999). *Attention, space, and action: Studies in cognitive neuroscience.* New York: Oxford University Press.

James, W. (1890). *The principles of psychology.* New York: Holt.

Johnston, W. A., & Heinz, S. P. (1978). Flexibility and capacity demands of attention. *Journal of Experimental Psychology: General, 107,* 420–435.

Luck, S. J., & Vecera, S. P. (2002). Attention. In H. Pashler & S. Yantis (Eds.), *Steven's handbook of experimental psychology* (3rd ed., pp. 235–286). New York: Wiley.

Miller, G. A. (1956). The magical number seven, plus or minus two: Some limits on our capacity for processing information. *Psychological Review, 63,* 81–97.

Moray, N. (1959). Attention in dichotic listening: Affective cues and the influence of instructions. *Quarterly Journal of Experimental Psychology, 11,* 56–60.

Motley, M. T., Camden, C. T., & Baars, B. J. (1982). Covert formulation and editing of anomalies in speech production: Evidence from experimentally elicited slips of the tongue. *Journal of Verbal Learning and Verbal Behavior, 21,* 578–594.

Näätänen, R. (1992). *Attention and brain function.* Hillsdale, NJ: Erlbaum.

Neisser, U. (1967). *Cognitive psychology.* New York: Appleton-Century-Crofts.

Parasuraman, R. (Ed.). (1998). *The attentive brain.* Cambridge, MA: MIT Press.

Pashler, H. E. (1998a). *The psychology of attention.* Cambridge, MA: MIT Press.

Pashler, H. (Ed.). (1998b). *Attention.* Hove, England: Psychology Press.

Pashler, H., Johnston, J. C., & Ruthruff, E. (2000). Attention and performance. *Annual Review of Psychology, 52,* 629–651.

Posner, M. I. (1980). Orienting of attention. *Quarterly Journal of Experimental Psychology, 32,* 3–25.

Pylyshyn, Z. W., & Storm, R. W. (1988). Tracking multiple independent targets: Evidence for a parallel tracking mechanism. *Spatial Vision, 3,* 179–197.

Raymond, J. E., Shapiro, K. L., & Arnell, K. M. (1992). Temporary suppression of visual processing in an RSVP task: An attentional blink? *Journal of Experimental Psychology: Human Perception and Performance, 18,* 849–860.

Reeves, A., & Sperling, G. (1986). Attention gating in short term visual memory. *Psychological Review, 93,* 180–206.

Rensink, R. A. (2002). Change detection. *Annual Review of Psychology, 53,* 245–277.

Ruthruff, E., & Pashler, H. E. (2001). Perceptual and central interference in dual-task performance. In K. Shapiro (Ed.), *The limits of attention: Temporal constraints in human information processing* (pp. 100–123). New York: Oxford University Press.

Schneider, W., & Shiffrin, R. M. (1977). Controlled and automatic human information processing: I. Detection, search, and attention. *Psychological Review, 84,* 1–66.

Shapiro, K. (Ed.) (2001). *The limits of attention: Temporal constraints in human information processing.* New York: Oxford University Press.

Shapiro, K. L., Caldwell, J., & Sorensen, R. E. (1997). Personal names and the attentional blink: A visual "cocktail party" effect. *Journal of Experimental Psychology: Human Perception and Performance, 23,* 504–514.

Shiffrin, R. M. (1988). Attention. In R. C. Atkinson, R. J. Herrnstein, G. Lindzey, & R. D. Luce (Eds.), *Stevens' handbook of experimental psychology* (Vol. 2., pp. 739–811). New York: Wiley.

Shiffrin, R. M., & Schneider, W. (1977). Controlled and automatic human information processing: II. Perceptual learning, automatic attending, and a general theory. *Psychological Review, 84,* 127–190.

Simons, D. J. (2000). Attentional capture and inattentional blindness. *Trends in Cognitive Sciences, 4,* 147–155.

Sokolov, E. N. (1963). *Perception and the conditioned reflex*. New York: Pergamon Press.

Sternberg, S. (1966). High-speed scanning in human memory. *Science, 153,* 652–654.

Strayer, D. L., & Johnston, W. A. (2001). Driven to distraction: Dual-task studies of simulated driving and conversing on a cellular telephone. *Psychological Science, 12,* 462–466.

Stroop, J. R. (1935). Studies of interference in serial verbal reactions. *Journal of Experimental Psychology, 18,* 643–662. (Reprinted in 1992 in the *Journal of Experimental Psychology: General, 121,* 15–23.)

Styles, E. A. (1997). *The psychology of attention*. Hove, England: Psychology Press.

Treisman, A. M. (1964). Selective attention in man. *British Medical Bulletin, 20,* 12–16.

Treisman, A. M., & Gelade, G. (1980). A feature integration theory of attention. *Cognitive Psychology, 12,* 97–136.

Vogel, E. K., Luck, S. J., & Shapiro, K. L. (1998). Electrophysiological evidence for a postperceptual locus of suppression during the attentional blink. *Journal of Experimental Psychology: Human Perception and Performance, 24,* 1656–1674.

Waters, W. F., McDonald, D. G., & Koresko, R. L. (1977). Habituation of the orienting response: A gating mechanism subserving selective attention. *Psychophysiology, 14,* 228–236.

Weichselgartner, E., & Sperling, G. (1987). Dynamics of automatic and controlled visual attention. *Science, 238,* 778–780.

Wood, N., & Cowan, N. (1995a). The cocktail party phenomenon revisited: Attention and memory in the classic selective listening procedure of Cherry (1953). *Journal of Experimental Psychology: General, 124,* 243–262.

Wood, N., & Cowan, N. (1995b). The cocktail party phenomenon revisited: How frequent are attention shifts to one's name in an irrelevant auditory channel? *Journal of Experimental Psychology: Learning, Memory, and Cognition, 21,* 255–260.

6

SELECTIVE ATTENTION TASKS IN CLINICAL RESEARCH

JENNY YIEND AND ANDREW MATHEWS

There has been more than a decade of research into biased attentional processing in both emotionally disordered and analogue nonclinical populations. In this chapter, we review some of the more common methods that have been used to establish these biases, as well as discuss what can be inferred from them. We deal only with visual attention tasks because these have been used most frequently in clinically related studies. Early clinical work did investigate the auditory modality with dichotic listening tasks (see chap. 4, this volume) to probe selective attention (Mathews & MacLeod, 1986; Trandell & McNally, 1987), but this method fell out of favor when it was argued that there was no way to rule out transient shifts of attention between channels. Neither do we consider the so-called *flanker* tasks (Eriksen, 1995; Eriksen & Eriksen, 1974), in which targets appear closely surrounded by to-be-ignored distractors (see also Shafer and Laberge [1979] for a relevant extension of the task to semantic categories). Though this task has been applied to clinical populations (Fox, 1996; Mathews, May, Mogg, & Eysenck, 1990), it suffers from similar interpretational problems, as does the emotional Stroop task (see chap. 3, this volume). The interference observed could arise from sources other than the deployment of attention to an emotional attribute. Alternatives include emotional arousal itself or voluntary efforts to *prevent* attentional capture by the distracting aspect (de Ruiter & Brosschot, 1994). Even if attentional capture does underlie the interference effect, it is impossible to distinguish with this method whether the mechanism involves shifts in spatial localization of attention or preemption of central processing resources, or both.

For convenience, we refer to a tendency to favor attention to emotional (or specifically threatening) information in emotionally disordered groups, relative to controls, as *attentional bias*. In practice most of the literature in this area focuses on anxiety disorders because these groups show the most pronounced selective attentional effects. We do not mean to imply that "normal" groups are unbiased; indeed, there is a case for arguing that healthy individuals have a persistent positive bias, a tendency to selectively process positive information.

METHODS FOR ASSESSING ATTENTION

Visual Attention and Eye Movements

Posner (1980) and others have distinguished between overt shifts of visual attention, accompanied by eye movements, and covert attention, in which processing is focused on specific locations or objects in the absence of eye movements. In both cases, attention can be indexed with faster or more accurate detection of targets in the attended location. The advantage of measuring eye gaze is that it provides a continuous measure of attentional deployment in space.

A large number of devices for tracking eye movements are now commercially available. Of these, the best use remote motorized infrared sensors to track the motion of the eyeball, automatically adjusting for minor head movements. Such equipment is usually supplied with its own data reduction and analysis software, which allows easy extraction of the main dependent variables of interest (described below). This technology represents a significant advance on older systems, which typically employ fixed sensors, either mounted on glasses worn by the participant or attached to a stand at which participants sit. In both cases, considerable care is required to keep head movement to a minimum, which can be done with either a headrest (chin, nose, and forehead rests are usually used) or a bite bar. Although less effective at controlling head movements, the headrest is often preferred for clinical populations because it is considerably less intrusive but still provides acceptable data.

All eye monitoring equipment requires careful calibration for each participant prior to use. This calibration involves the participant fixating centrally and then sequentially at known locations around the screen (usually at the farthest points above, below, left of, and right of fixation) while the experimenter adjusts the range of the equipment. This process also provides a useful opportunity to ensure that the strength of the signal is adequate. Many sensors work by detecting the boundary between the colored iris and white cornea; it follows that participants with brown eyes elicit a stronger signal than those with blue or green. As with any continuous biological measure, the size of the data files produced by an eye tracker is considerable, and data storage and processing capacity is an important practical consideration.

As regards data acquisition and processing, there are no generally accepted standards, and even experts in the field acknowledge that many methodological issues remain unaddressed (Rayner, 1998). The concerned reader should refer to Inhoff and Radach (1998). Common practices include smoothing of the raw data with a moving average filter and the exclusion of trials containing eye blinks that can disrupt the pattern of fixations (e.g. Bradley, Mogg, & Millar, 2000). Dependent measures vary, but usually include one or more of the following, depending on the particular hypotheses of the study: location of first fixation, duration of first fixation, speed of first fixation, number of fixations to a given area, and total duration of fixations on an area. Rayner and Pollatsek (1987) provide an overview of the methodological and theoretical issues involved in eye movement research.

A limited range of clinically relevant studies use eye movements as an index of attention. Matthews and Antes (1992) measured eye movements during picture viewing and found that happy regions were fixated more frequently, for longer and sooner than were sad regions. In addition, dysphoric participants fixated sad regions more often than did nondysphoric participants. Hermans, Vansteenwegen, and Eelen (1999) examined eye fixations to threat (spiders) and nonthreat (flowers) pictures, presented together for three seconds, in students fearful of spiders. Both groups looked more at spiders early on, but fearful individuals were more likely than others to shift fixation away from spiders later on. Using a similar paradigm, but with displays of faces having different expressions that were presented together for 500 ms, Bradley et al. (2000) reported that many participants made few or no eye movements away from the initial fixation point. In those who did make eye movements, however, participants high in negative emotionality were more likely to fixate on faces with negative expressions than faces with positive expressions. Patients with generalized anxiety disorder showed similar effects: Eye movements were more frequent in this group and favored shifts toward threatening faces rather than other expressions (Mogg, Millar, & Bradley, 2000).

The use of eye movements to index attention certainly offers scope for further work, as long as the more complex practical requirements of the technique can be overcome. However, it is important to remember that covert attention shifts can occur without eye movements, particularly to briefly presented distractors. Under these circumstances, a target detection task may be preferable.

Target Detection Tasks

One of the best known methods of investigating selective attention within the clinical literature is the attentional probe task first described by MacLeod, Mathews, and Tata (1986). The task is akin to the cued attention task developed by Posner (1980) and involves displaying two words simultaneously for 500 ms, above and below a fixation point. The words disappear from view, and a target then follows unpredictably in the location of one or the other word. MacLeod et al. found that when one of the words was threatening (e.g., death) and the other was not (e.g., table), anxious patients were relatively faster to detect the target when it replaced a threatening word than when the target replaced the nonthreat word. This result was taken as evidence that attention of anxious individuals was captured by the threatening word, and so a target in the same place benefited from the fact that attention was engaged at that location.

Since then there have been many replications with the same or similar methods, with a variety of clinical populations. Results appear to be unaffected by minor variations in procedure. For example, subsequent researchers have used target identification tasks (using for example dots, arrows, or letters) and target localization tasks (Mogg & Bradley, 1999) rather than simple detection tasks, allowing catch trials (when no probe appears) to be dispensed with and avoiding the need to report false alarm rates. Indeed, Mogg and Bradley (1999) recommend a probe position task (where is the probe?) as being better than the more common probe classification task (what is the type of probe?) because it produces faster reaction times, fewer errors, and a similar effect size.

With the identification or localization tasks, errors can now occur on any trial, and these need to be scored and excluded from later analysis. As regards outliers, reaction times below 100 ms are usually classed as being anticipatory responses and excluded. Long reaction time outliers can be defined in a variety of ways including the following: values falling more than two or three standard deviations from the mean, either by participants separately or for the dataset as a whole; values beyond that at which the histogram of the data becomes asymmetrical; and values beyond which the histogram falls to single observations. Typically, errors and reaction time outliers together constitute less than 4% of the total dataset.

A striking departure from the original MacLeod et al. study is that most subsequent work has dropped the requirement for participants to read aloud one of the two words before the probe display appears. MacLeod et al. found that this task caused a general speeding to probes replacing words that had been read. Although reading aloud did not obscure the critical speeding to threat probed words, subsequent data have shown that the additional read-aloud task is redundant. Thus, in most later studies either the word stimuli are not explicitly mentioned or participants are simply told to ignore them and fixate on the central cross. Another important factor is the proximity of the stimuli to the central fixation point. Proximity is usually described in terms of visual angle, which is a measure of the size of the object's projection on the retina. This angle depends on both viewing distance (d) and object height (h) and can be calculated with the formula $\tan \alpha = h/d$, where α is the visual angle. Most studies ensure that each stimulus of the pair subtends a visual angle of between 2 and 3 degrees with fixation. This angle ensures that stimuli are close enough to fixation to allow some preattentive processing of content, but not so close that the critical reaction time differences are lost.

One of the most significant methodological variations is the interval between word and target appearance (stimulus onset asynchrony, SOA). Several studies have looked at SOA and found evidence of continued attentional vigilance to threat throughout the first second or so. Derryberry and Reed (2002) found the expected anxiety-related effects at an SOA of 250 ms, although the effects were reduced at 500 ms, and other studies have reported similar biases up to 1,250 ms SOA (Bradley, Mogg, Falla, & Hamilton, 1998). Shifts of attention toward and then away from emotional stimuli are likely to vary according to both individual differences (e.g., in attentional control, see Derryberry & Reed, 2002; in depressed versus anxious mood, see McCabe & Toman, 2000) and the nature of the stimuli used. For example, more salient and complex location cues, such as faces or pictures, are likely to take longer to process and may thus delay the onset of any shift away. At a longer SOA (around a second or more), people are able to shift attention voluntarily, so they may elect to do so in order to minimize discomfort related to aversive information, consistent with the eye gaze data reported earlier. In general, SOAs of below 100 ms would be considered by many to limit processing effects to those that are largely automatic, whereas anything over 1,000 ms is likely to allow sufficient time for controlled processes to become active. The researcher should always remember that the degree of automaticity and control involved in any task duration varies according to the nature of the task itself.

Other variations on the original design include positioning stimuli pairs on either side of fixation rather than above and below. With this arrangement, care should be taken to ensure that any identification task does not add unwanted error variance by interfering with left/right target position. For example, targets such as leftward and rightward pointing arrows or the letters L and R would speed reaction times when target type and target position were congruent and slow reactions times when incongruent. Although this interference should not confound the interpretation of between-group differences on the trial types of interest, it could add unnecessary variance to the data, thereby reducing the sensitivity of statistical tests, such as analysis of variance, to reveal those differences. A similar situation emerges when one considers the spatial correspondence between response keys and target locations. In the so-called Simon effect (Lu & Proctor, 1995; Simon & Rudell, 1967), reaction times are faster when the location of the target and the position of the correct response key are compatible (e.g., both on the left) than when the same factors are incompatible (e.g., one left and one right). It is again advisable to avoid such interference by aligning response keys along an axis orthogonal to target location, so that for targets appearing left and right, say, response keys should be upper and lower. In summary, the optimum selection of target type and response options should maximize the mapping between the two, making the task easy to learn, while minimizing the kind of unwanted interference effects described above. One such example would be to use left and right pointing arrows, corresponding to left and right response keys, but to display above and below fixation.

A related issue is the importance of full counterbalancing. Within each condition, the relative position of picture type, target location, and target type should be nested so that each possible combination occurs an equal number of times. Thus, if threat/neutral stimuli pairs are used, equal numbers of threat (and neutral) should appear on the left side of the pair as appear on the right (or up as down). For each threat (and neutral) location, half the trials should probe the threat itself, and the other half should probe the neutral (threat), and so on for each type of target within these categories. This practice reduces Type I errors (incorrect rejection of the null hypothesis) by ensuring that the contrasts of interest are not confounded with irrelevant features of the design such as target type, position, or probe type. Were such confounds to occur, then the experimenter would be unable to distinguish whether speeded reaction times to threat probes were due to attentional vigilance for threat or were merely a result of, say, a right hemisphere processing advantage for emotion (Davidson, 1993; Tomarken, Davidson, Wheeler, & Doss, 1992) because threat was more often probed on the left. Similarly, consider the consequences of poor counterbalancing combined with the presence of unwanted interference effects, discussed earlier. Under these conditions, it would be quite possible to produce misleading speeding to threat probed stimuli simply because these items were disproportionately followed by response-compatible targets. For instance, the left (or right) key response choice might coincide more often (compared with neutral probed stimuli) with the left (or right) position of the probed threat.

Mean reaction times are usually calculated across participants for each combination of threat position and probe position. These times can be reported separately for each probed location or, to simplify interpretation, averaged across locations into *threat position probed* versus *nonthreat position probed*. Effect sizes for the threat/neutral difference are usually 10 to 20 ms. Another common procedure is to move one step further and calculate an index of *attentional bias* simply by subtracting the threat probed average from the nonthreat probed average. If positive, the resulting values indicate attentional vigilance for threat and, if negative, they show attentional avoidance. Both averaging across probed location and using the attentional bias index have the advantage of simplicity and clarity for the reader and are particularly useful for illustrative purposes. However, it is advisable to also perform analyses on, and report means for, the data broken down by threat and probe location. Although more complex for the reader, these analyses allow comparison with the previous literature, which mostly uses indexed scores only for summary purposes. They also allow a check on whether any effects are due to latency differences when threats are probed, rather than baseline differences when nonthreat stimuli are probed.

A novel variation of the target detection task was recently described by Fox, Russo, Bowles, and Dutton (2001) and Yiend and Mathews (2001). The technique is based on the cued attention method described by Posner (1980), in which participants are required to fixate a central point while responding to targets (e.g., an asterisk or letter) that appear on either side. In so-called *valid* trials, attention has been attracted by a cue (e.g., a brief flash) on one side, before the target appears. The classic finding is that targets on the cued side are detected more rapidly. When targets appear on the other side, however, detection is slower than if no cue is provided. This finding has been taken as evidence that attention focused in a spatial location speeds detection of events in the same place, but slows detection elsewhere, presumably because attention has to be shifted to the new location. Yiend and Mathews and Fox et al. used emotional material (pictures and faces respectively) rather than light flashes as cues, to assess the spatial attentional effects of valenced material. Results obtained in these studies generally confirm those found with word pairs, with high anxious groups showing more evidence of attentional capture by threatening pictures than do low anxious controls. Note that use of single cues in this way allows dissection of the processes involved into attentional engagement versus disengagement of attention away from emotional stimuli, an issue we return to later.

The attentional blink is another target detection task, described in detail by Cowan (see chap. 5, this volume) and which has recently been used to investigate attention in subclinically anxious populations (P. Barnard & C. Ramponi, personal communication, September, 2002; B. Mackintosh, M. Munafo, & P. Barnard, personal communication, September, 2002). Preliminary experiments have used streams of words presented at a rate of about one every 170 ms and have required participants to report a target word preceded at varying intervals by a threat distractor. Results so far suggest that anxious individuals show a larger blink (higher percentage errors on target report) than do nonanxious individuals for threatening distractors. The clinical application of this technique therefore looks set to be exploited further in the future.

The Deployment of Attention Task

A related but distinct method developed by Gotlib and colleagues has been termed the *deployment of attention task* (DOAT; Gotlib, McLachlan, & Katz, 1988; McCabe & Gotlib, 1995). Again, two words are briefly presented (in the original study for 730 ms) above and below a fixation point and then both are replaced with rectangular patches of color, one red and one green. Similar to the attentional probe task, the visual angle between each word and fixation is 2.5 degrees. Participants' task is to report which color appears first. In fact, both colors occur at the same time, but the stimulus at the location being attended to at the time tends to be perceived as appearing first, in line with Titchener's (1908) Law of Prior Entry. The dependent measure is therefore the percentage of trials in which a given word type is attended to, as indicated by the color chosen. Gotlib et al. used three word type variations: manic and neutral word pairs, depressed and neutral pairs, and manic and depressed pairs.

In several applications of this method to depressed patients, including the original study, it has been shown that this clinical group does not appear to selectively attend to either positive or negative words; there are no systematic differences in which color is reported to occur first. Nondepressed controls, however, typically report seeing the color that replaced the neutral word before they see the color that replaced the depression-relevant word, which suggests that they attend to positive and ignore negative words. This finding has been interpreted as a maladaptive absence in the depressed of a positive or *protective* bias usually shown by nondepressed individuals.

Subsequent attempts to use this task with groups varying in anxiety have revealed apparent replication difficulties. Mogg et al. (1991) used the DOAT with both non-clinically anxious individuals and anxious patients, but initially failed to find the group differences in attention that one might expect given results (see above) from the attentional probe task. As well as using different samples, they used a method different from that of Gotlib et al.; they used two categories of threat relevant words—general threat and achievement threat—and reduced the duration of the word pair display to 500 ms. In a final experiment that precisely replicated the Gotlib et al. method, albeit still using an analogue anxious population, they succeeded in finding a group difference and showed that it was more highly correlated with state anxiety measures than with depression measures. Mogg et al. suggested that there was an inherent unreliability in the DOAT and that the previous differences between depressed and nondepressed groups might be due to the co-occurrence of anxiety.

In the ensuing debate, Gotlib and colleagues (McCabe & Gotlib, 1995; McCabe, Gotlib, & Martin, 2000; McCabe & Toman, 2000) replicated their original finding and showed that a depression-related absence of positive bias, as shown by the DOAT, remains significant even after anxiety is partialled out. They also argued that duration of word pair presentation is a critical factor in determining whether or not group differences are found. Furthermore, McCabe and Toman (2000) have shown that the effect persists at longer durations (up to 1,500 ms) and so cannot be explained by generally slower processing speeds (i.e., psychomotor retardation) on the part of the depressed. Thus, the results and interpretation of the DOAT remain a topic of active interest and debate.

The DOAT appears to be a reliable task, provided that durations over 730 ms are used. Indeed, one question for further research concerns the reasons for the absence of the effect at short durations. A second involves the relative contributions of anxiety and depression to the effect, and a third is whether this attentional paradigm differs from others in revealing biases in controls as opposed to comparison groups. However, for those whose prime concern is the use of a selective attention task to reveal anxiety-related differences, the probe detection task should remain the paradigm of first choice.

Face-in-the-Crowd Task

One critical feature common to the above methods is that the target to be detected is in itself emotionally neutral. This fact may be important because, if participants are to report on an emotional target, they may show a response bias favoring reporting (or not reporting) targets having emotional significance. Nonetheless, methods involving emotional targets, such as the *face-in-the-crowd* task (Hansen & Hansen, 1994), could contribute potentially important information about the type of attentional processes involved.

In the typical procedure, an array of faces is presented, and the participant is required to pick out the face (if any) with a discrepant expression as quickly as possible. In addition to requiring this "yes/no" buttonpress response, some versions of the task also require the location of any discrepant face to be reported subsequently. There are many possible combinations of target and distractor expressions, including detecting an angry face among an array of neutral ones (allowing conclusions about threat detection speed); happy among neutral (detection speed for positive stimuli); neutral among angry (distraction effects of anger); and neutral among happy (distraction effects of happiness). If only neutral distractors are used then target absent trials can be dispensed with and the task becomes a choice reaction time (e.g., positive or negative target; Eastwood, Smilek, & Merikle, 2001). The typical finding is that angry facial expressions are both detected faster and more distracting than neutral or happy ones.

The literature that uses the face-in-the-crowd method has largely been conducted on unselected participants, who nevertheless seem to show robust speeded detection of anger or threat (Eastwood et al., 2001; Fox et al., 2000; Juth, Karlsson, Lundqvist, & Öhman, 2000; Öhman, Flykt, & Esteves, 2001; Öhman, Lundqvist, & Esteves, 2001). However, the few studies that have looked at individual differences with this method have reported clear between-subjects differences in subclinical anxiety (Byrne & Eysenck, 1995), specific phobias (Öhman, Flykt, et al., 2001), and social anxiety (Gilboa-Schechtman, Foa, & Amir, 1999), and these findings qualify the results from unselected populations. It appears that scope remains to exploit this paradigm further within the clinical sphere.

The array itself is usually a rectangle of rows and columns of anywhere between 4 and 20 photographs of faces. However, without an apparent loss of sensitivity, Fox et al. (2000) used an eight-position circular arrangement, around a central fixation, with a radius of 5.1 degrees of visual angle. For any one array, the same facial identity (i.e., the same person) appears in every location of the array, including the discrepant expression. This fact means that all elements of the array are matched for perceptual features, so differential detection speed for the discrepant expression must be due to that expression itself. Within any one experiment, several facial identities (different models) are used, including male and female, always with the same identity in any one array. This methodology typically produces a core set of around 6 to 10 unique array identities per condition, which are then repeatedly presented. For *target present* trials, the location of the discrepant expression is randomly distributed across the array such that each possible location is sampled an equal number of times.

Whereas earlier studies used photographic images, later work has favored schematic faces (simple line drawings) because of the greater ease with which they can be matched for perceptual features. Indeed, the original report of Hansen and Hansen (1988) was criticized precisely because the speeded detection effect was found to be attributable to a confound, namely a small dark patch on the chin of the discrepant face (Purcell, Stewart, & Skov, 1996). This case illustrates the importance of matching for perceptual features, as far as possible, to avoid such confounded results. Most studies have used schematic faces consisting simply of a circle, mouth, eyes, and sometimes eyebrows. The five main facial expressions (anger, fear, sadness, happiness, disgust) can then easily be conveyed simply by altering the mouth and brow shape, and these stimuli seem to be just as effective in producing effects as are photographic images. In fact, the use of schematics allowed Fox et al. (2000) to explore the contribution of purely perceptual differences (as opposed to affective valence) to the phenomenon. They found that both presenting the mouth in isolation and inverting the faces eliminated the speeded detection of angry faces (although see Experiment 4 in Öhman, Lundquist, et al., 2001, for contradictory results). This result led them to conclude that the effect could not be carried by some enhanced perceptual salience of a downturned mouth, or other features of the angry face, but must instead relate to the affective meaning conveyed by the discrepant face.

Another stimulus variation implemented by Öhman and colleagues (Öhman, Flykt, et al., 2001) is to use threatening and neutral pictures, specifically snakes, spiders, mushrooms, and flowers. These were presented in arrays of either 2×2 or 3×3, and participants had to search for the discrepant picture, which was either neutral in an array of threat pictures or threat in an array of neutral pictures. They compared detection times for threat and neutral targets and found, as predicted, that threatening pictures were located more quickly than were nonthreatening ones. Furthermore, they claimed that search for these threat stimuli occurred in parallel because no slowing was found on the 3×3 array compared with the 2×2 array, although in the absence of proper search slopes (see below), this result should be treated with caution. Nevertheless, it does suggest that more ecologically valid stimuli can also be used to reveal face-in-the-crowd effects, provided the researcher is confident that perceptual confounds can be ruled out. For the researcher interested in comparing clinical groups with controls, one could tolerate a main effect caused by differences in the stimuli, not related to the disorder of interest. However, it is equally likely that the critical group differences might also be caused by poorly controlled perceptual elements, such as the color and form of blood or teeth, rather than by emotional valence per se. We consider these and other aspects of stimulus selection in a later section.

Array size has also been used as a critical manipulation to investigate the extent to which visual search for angry faces occurs in parallel. In the classic pop-out experiments (Treisman & Gelade, 1980), participants are just as fast to detect a target distinguished by a unique feature (e.g., color), no matter how many distractor items are present, whereas for more complex targets larger arrays slow down search. Typically detection times are plotted against increasing set size (number of distractors) and the search slope of the resulting graph is characteristically flat, or inclined. These slopes are taken to represent parallel and serial search processes, respectively. Several studies that used the face-in-the-crowd method have investigated the effect of array size, the most comprehensive being that of Eastwood et al. (2001). They used arrays of 7, 11, 15, and 19 schematic faces and either positive or negative targets among neutral distractors. The search slopes were not flat, but the slopes for negative targets were shallower than those for positive, which suggests a serial search that was faster for negative targets. Fox et al. (2000) obtained similar results for angry compared with happy targets and concluded that although pop-out did not occur, search for anger was particularly fast and efficient. Although necessary to estimate search time in a serial search, varying the array size is not essential to establish the basic effect. Thus, for the researcher simply interested in applying the basic technique, a single array size of between 2×3 and 3×4 is typical. Usually arrays are presented until response, although Fox et al. (2000) experimented with fixed display durations. They found that 300 ms was too short—it produced an unacceptably high level of errors (> 20% in most participants)—whereas 800 ms produced an acceptable error rate (< 11% errors) and effect size.

Analysis usually proceeds by consideration of nontarget and target trials separately. In the case of nontarget trials, participants are typically slower and more error prone when reporting target absence in angry arrays than in neutral or positive arrays. Beyond this finding, nontarget trials are unlikely to reveal anything of much interest. For target trials, it is important to take a hypothesis-driven approach in order for comparisons to be meaningful, particularly if many facial expressions have been used as both distractors and targets. The most obvious comparison to consider is differently valenced targets within neutral distractor arrays, which allows clean conclusions about the speed of detection of the expression concerned. Care should be taken when considering valenced arrays combined with valenced targets, as the effects will be a combination of distraction and detection. A neutral target embedded in a valenced array provides a good way of considering distraction effects alone. Finally, most authors wisely elect to perform a signal detection analysis, in addition to comparisons of mean reaction times, in order to establish sensitivity differences aside from any response biases that are likely to be produced by the emotional nature of the targets.

SELECTION OF STIMULI

The Role of Competition

One feature that appears common to all methods sensitive to attentional bias effects is that of competition for processing between two or more input stimuli. Thus, in both attentional search and interference tasks, participants are required to respond to a target while simultaneously ignoring a competing distractor. In contrast, there are typically no differences between high and low anxiety groups when a lexical or affective decision is made about a single word (Mathews & Milroy, 1994). Such differences do emerge, however, when two-letter strings, one of which is a threatening word, are simultaneously present, (MacLeod & Mathews, 1991). This pattern of results implies that the anxiety-related differences underlying attentional bias depend on variations in processing priority, in which anxiety-prone people give priority to threat, rather than being more efficient in processing threat information.

It is also possible to demonstrate anxiety-related differences when only one stimulus is present, provided that more than one attribute could be selectively processed. For example, if participants are required to make either affective or other semantic decisions about single words, no group differences are seen under conditions when participants have advance knowledge as to which decision will be required. When the decision required is varied unpredictably from trial to trial, however, anxiety-prone individuals make affective decisions relatively more quickly (Pury & Mineka, 2001). How is this difference to be understood? The most plausible explanation, in our view, is that when a simple decision of this sort is specified in advance, both high and low anxiety groups can perform it with equal efficiency. Processing priorities are revealed only when no advance knowledge is available, and the data suggest that anxiety-prone individuals are more likely to give priority to preparing for an affective than for a semantic decision.

Content of Stimuli Used

It is generally accepted practice to balance sets of threat/neutral/positive word stimuli used in attentional tasks for features such as word length, usage frequency, and emotionality or hedonic tone. Dimensions such as imageability, pronunceability, and concreteness may also be important to consider, depending on the particular study and hypotheses concerned. Norms frequently used include those given in Anderson (1968), John (1988), and Rubin and Friendly (1986) and a useful index of norms is given in Proctor and Vu (1999). Matching on such measures as frequency and word length appears to be a reasonable precaution, on the grounds that anything that makes reading words easier may influence the probability that the words are incidentally encoded. It may well be, however, that normative frequency of usage is less important than frequency with which the participants being studied use the selected words. Attempts to look at this issue, by comparing sets of words relevant to special interest groups (e.g., bird watchers), have not—in our estimation—been conclusive, but frequency alone is probably less important than the personal significance of words. Some support for this view derives from the consequences of treatment and recovery from emotional disorders. Attentional bias to threat invariably declines following recovery, yet it is arguable that treatment (at least cognitive behavioral therapy) usually involves more rather than less usage of the relevant words. We therefore suggest that frequency per se is less important than current significance of that word to the individual involved. For consideration of other content issues, including category coherence and the relevance of stimuli to the individual's current concerns, refer to MacLeod (see chap. 3, this volume).

Finally, as the reader will have noticed above, more recent studies in the clinical field have taken to using pictures and faces as stimuli in preference to words. This departure allows researchers to enhance the ecological validity of the attentional bias literature, and so far many effects previously found with words have held up with the use of more complex stimuli. Another advantage of the use of pictures is that the degree of threat portrayed can be varied on an almost-continuous scale. This possibility has led several researchers to examine the extent to which anxiety-related differences depend on the perceived degree of threat involved, as we discuss below. However, some obvious disadvantages are inherent in the use of such stimuli, such as the greatly increased difficulty of matching perceptual characteristics of different stimulus sets, and the lack of available normative data, such as frequency of prior exposure. Though the exploration of attentional biases among new, more realistic stimulus types is to be encouraged, researchers should be cautious that their hypotheses really warrant sacrificing the methodological rigor provided by well-balanced word sets.

Severity of Threat

Most theoretical accounts of attentional bias to threat suggest that the severity (or urgency) of the threat content must play a role in determining whether or not a particular stimulus or event captures attention (MacLeod et al., 1986; Mathews & Mackintosh, 1998; Mogg & Bradley, 1998). It is generally supposed that a severe and urgent threat should always capture attention, regardless of individual differences. Failure of such a basic adaptive mechanism would clearly have resulted in poor survival rates, and evolutionary processes will thus have favored its development and maintenance.

At the same time, attentional capture by all emotional or threat-related cues, no matter how mild and currently irrelevant, would result in constant interruptions to other ongoing tasks. Indeed, very mildly emotional drawings produce apparent attentional avoidance, whereas more severely threatening pictures capture attention in the same participants (Mackintosh & Mathews, 2003). Similarly, Wilson and MacLeod (2003) compared attention to paired pictures of faces with neutral expressions and with differing levels of threat. All participants detected targets in the location of mildly threatening faces more slowly, consistent with attentional avoidance. Attention tended to switch as threat level increased, but this switching occurred at a lower threat level in anxiety-prone individuals.

We therefore suppose that the information indicating the presence of threat must reach a certain threshold or criterion before it can effectively capture attention, and that such capture can be opposed by a top-down inhibitory process (see Mathews & Mackintosh, 1998). If so, then attentional bias in anxiety presumably reflects a lowered threshold for either allocation of attention to possible threats or deficient control processes, or both. These hypotheses remain to be explored, however, as does the nature of the threshold or criterion used to determine whether or not attention is to be allocated to a potential threat cue. For now, we conclude only that there may be an intermediate level of threat that is high enough to capture attention in some individuals, but not so severe as to do so in everyone.

MECHANISMS AND INTERPRETATION OF ATTENTIONAL BIAS DATA

Automatic or Controlled?

A persistent question debated by researchers concerns the extent to which attentional biases are automatic or controlled (McNally, 1995). The strongest evidence put forward to support the automatic argument is that effects sometimes persist when the relevant stimuli are masked and so cannot be reported (e.g. Mathews & MacLeod, 1996). Although this evidence certainly suggests that attentional bias effects can arise in the absence of full awareness of the provoking stimuli, it cannot be assumed that attentional bias effects meet other properties of automatic processing. For example, it may well be the case that biases depend on general strategic intentions, such as preparing to encounter possible dangers, as has been argued by Wells and Matthews (1994). Many other examples of such processing mixtures exist, such as the strategic intention to drive home, which sets various automated subroutines in motion, not all of which can be reported. Thus, we may respond to familiar landmarks by turning in a certain direction without being able to report on or recall either perceiving the cue or making the appropriate response. Furthermore, as will be discussed later, there is evidence that biases may be induced experimentally by practice, including attentional responses to masked stimuli whose presence cannot be reported. We therefore conclude that attentional bias could arise from habitually controlled strategies, although these strategies may then be implemented with cognitive processes operating outside of awareness.

There is in fact virtually no direct evidence about how attentional biases develop in real life, so the above suggestion must remain speculative. Attentional biases similar to those seen in adults are seen in anxious children aged 11 years and up (Vasey, El-Hag, & Daleiden, 1996) and can be extended to encompass new (previously neutral) stimuli by processes such as evaluative conditioning (Fulcher, Mathews, Mackintosh, & Law, 2001). Further research on the earliest stages of attention to emotional stimuli is clearly needed.

Engagement or Disengagement?

A number of recent studies have attempted to explore the nature of the attentional processes underlying bias in anxiety by investigating whether effects arise via differential engagement of attention or difficulties in disengagement. A typical engagement account would imply that a preattentive process, operating outside awareness, detects potential threats and directs attentional resources to that location. Alternatively, threat-related information may be encountered accidentally, but then hold the attention of anxious individuals more effectively. Fox et al. (2001) and Yiend and Mathews (2001) found support for the disengagement view. Single cues (faces or pictures) were presented briefly followed by a target in the same or different locations. Anxiety-related differences existed not when targets followed in the same location as the cues, but only when threatening cues were followed by targets in a different location. This implies that there were no differences in engagement, but that anxious individuals were slower to disengage attention from the threatening stimuli in order to find the target elsewhere.

These attentional biases cannot be attributed to disengagement effects alone. The cues appeared on the screen suddenly, and consequently can be assumed to have attracted attention equally in all participants, perhaps reducing sensitivity to any individual differences in engagement. However, when the target appeared elsewhere, differences in ease of disengagement might be more apparent. To provide a more sensitive test for engagement differences, face cues varying in both emotional expression and right/left direction of eye gaze were followed by letter targets on the left or right (Mathews, Fox, Yiend, & Calder, 2003). Anxious participants were faster to detect a target if it followed a fearful face, but only if gaze direction had indicated that location. As the target always appeared in a different location from the threat cue (the fearful face), this finding clearly implies differential engagement at the location of a potential (but not actual) threat. In summary, it seems likely that both engagement and disengagement differences in attention to potential threats may characterize high versus low anxious individuals.

CAUSAL IMPLICATIONS OF ATTENTIONAL BIAS

Attentional bias effects are interesting to the extent that they are consistent with a causal hypothesis, such as the hypothesis that biased processing causes both increased subjective risk and vulnerability to anxiety. Needless to say, virtually all the relevant evidence is correlational in nature and compatible with a reverse hypothesis (anxious mood causes bias) and/or noncausal relationships, in which both bias and anxious mood result from another unknown factor.

Progress toward establishing the true causal significance of attentional bias can be made by directly manipulating the putative causal factor (in this case, attentional bias) and testing for any effects on the supposed consequences (in this case, vulnerability to anxiety). The first obstacle to overcome is to discover a practical method of manipulating attention to threat, assuming that such control is indeed possible (as discussed earlier). A recent paper by MacLeod, Rutherford, Campbell, Ebsworthy, and Holker (2002) has provided the first indication of how this manipulation can be done. Volunteers were trained with the standard threat/neutral dual-cue method, with the modification that for some the target always replaced the threat word, while for others it always replaced the neutral word. After several hundred such training trials, participants were faster to respond in new-word test trials if the target replaced the same valence of word as in training. This finding provides evidence that attentional bias can indeed be induced experimentally. More important, anxiety rose more during a laboratory stress task in those who had been trained to attend to threatening rather than neutral words.

Although such a demonstration does not, of course, prove that naturally occurring biases operate in the same way, it does provide the first evidence that an induced attentional bias can cause changes in anxiety. It is important to note, however, that the training procedure itself was not sufficient to produce anxiety differences; there were no differences in mood between groups after training. Instead, training an attentional bias appears to have prepared participants to attend to features of a stressful event that, depending on how they are processed, have the capacity to evoke more or less anxiety. Thus, induced attentional bias can influence how new and potentially threatening information is processed, rather than producing anxiety in and of itself.

CLINICAL IMPLICATIONS AND FUTURE DIRECTIONS

Investigations of attention to emotional cues can clearly provide new insights into cognitive differences between clinical groups and suggest new hypotheses about etiology. Researchers should be more cautious about concluding that such measures can be directly useful in assessing individual clinical clients. For example, although within group studies, attention to particular classes of stimuli is associated with diagnosis, there is probably too much variation among members of each group to allow these measures to be used as diagnostic tools. The most that could be claimed at present is that attention to particular classes of word may provide some information about individual areas of emotional concern if this information is not more easily obtained by self-report.

Similarly, although attention to emotional cues appears to change as expected after recovery, there seems no obvious advantage to using such measures to assess treatment outcome. Attentional measures might prove to be helpful in predicting relapse or response to future stress (cf. MacLeod & Hagan, 1992), but more evidence is needed. Another possibility that could usefully be explored is whether changes in attention are related to specific processes of cognitive change in therapy. Perhaps the most promising possibility for understanding mechanisms and for clinical applications is that of experimental modification. Future research will undoubtedly be directed at developing bias modification as an analogue to cognitive treatments, both to improve our understanding of the causal status of bias and to use as a tool for understanding processes of change.

REFERENCES

Anderson, N. H. (1968). Likableness rating of 555 personality-trait words. *Journal of Personality and Social Psychology, 9,* 272–279.

Bradley, B. P., Mogg, K., Falla, S. J., & Hamilton, L. R. (1998). Attentional bias for threatening facial expressions in anxiety: Manipulation of stimulus duration. *Cognition & Emotion, 12,* 737–753.

Bradley, B. P., Mogg, K., & Millar, N. H. (2000). Covert and overt orienting of attention to emotional faces in anxiety. *Cognition & Emotion, 14,* 789–808.

Byrne, A., & Eysenck, M. W. (1995). Trait anxiety, anxious mood and threat detection. *Cognition & Emotion, 9,* 549–562.

Davidson, R. J. (1993). Cerebral asymmetry and emotion: Conceptual and methodological conundrums. *Cognition & Emotion, 7,* 115–138.

de Ruiter, C., & Brosschot, J. F. (1994). The emotional Stroop interference effect in anxiety: Attentional bias or cognitive avoidance? *Behaviour Research and Therapy, 32,* 315–319.

Derryberry, D., & Reed, M. A. (2002). Anxiety-related attentional biases and their regulation by attentional control. *Journal of Abnormal Psychology, 111,* 225–236.

Eastwood, J. D., Smilek, D., & Merikle, P. M. (2001). Differential attentional guidance by unattended faces expressing positive and negative emotion. *Perception & Psychophysics, 63,* 1004–1013.

Eriksen, C. W. (1995). The Flankers task and response competition: A useful tool for investigating a variety of cognitive problems. *Visual Cognition, 2,* 101–118.

Eriksen, B. A., & Eriksen, C. W. (1974). Effects of noise letters on the identification of a target in a non search task. *Perception & Psychophysics, 16,* 143–149.

Fox, E. (1996). Selective processing of threatening words in anxiety: The role of awareness. *Cognition & Emotion, 10,* 449–480.

Fox, E., Lester, V., Russo, R., Bowles, R. J., Pichler, A., & Dutton, K. (2000). Facial expressions of emotion: Are angry faces detected more efficiently? *Cognition & Emotion, 14,* 61–92.

Fox, E., Russo, R., Bowles, R., & Dutton, K. (2001). Do threatening stimuli draw or hold visual attention in subclinical anxiety? *Journal of Experimental Psychology: General, 130,* 681–700.

Fulcher, E. P., Mathews, A., Mackintosh, B., & Law, S. (2001). Evaluative learning and the allocation of attention to emotional stimuli. *Cognitive Therapy and Research, 25,* 261–280.

Gilboa-Schechtman, E., Foa, E. B., & Amir, N. (1999). Attentional biases for facial expressions in social phobia: The face-in-the-crowd paradigm. *Cognition & Emotion, 13,* 305–318.

Gotlib, I. H., McLachlan, A. L., & Katz, A. N. (1988). Biases in visual attention in depressed and non-depressed individuals. *Cognition & Emotion, 2,* 185–200.

Hansen, C. H., & Hansen, R. D. (1988). Finding the face in the crowd: An anger superiority effect. *Journal of Personality and Social Psychology, 54,* 917–924.

Hansen, C. H., & Hansen, R. D. (1994). Automatic emotion: Attention and facial efference. In P. M. Niedenthal & S. Kitayama (Eds.), *The heart's eye: Emotional influences in perception and attention* (pp. 217–243). San Diego: Academic Press.

Hermans, D., Vansteenwegen, D., & Eelen, P. (1999). Eye movement registration as a continuous index of attention deployment: Data from a group of spider anxious students. *Cognition & Emotion, 13*, 419–434.

Inhoff, A. W., & Radach, R. (1998). Definition and computation of oculomotor measures in the study of cognitive processes. In G. Underwood (Ed.), *Eye guidance in reading and scene perception* (pp. 29–54). Oxford, England: Elsevier.

John, C. H. (1988). Emotionality ratings and free-association norms of 240 emotional and non-emotional words. *Cognition & Emotion, 2*, 49–70.

Juth, P., Karlsson, A., Lundqvist, D., & Öhman, A. (2000). Finding a face in the crowd: Effects of emotional expression, direction and social anxiety [meeting abstract]. *International Journal of Psychology, 35*, 434.

Lu, C. H., & Proctor, R. W. (1995). The influence of irrelevant location information on performance: A review of the Simon and Spatial Stroop Effects. *Psychonomic Bulletin & Review, 2*, 174–207.

Mackintosh, B., & Mathews, A. (2003). Don't look now: Attentional avoidance of emotionally valenced cues. *Cognition & Emotion, 17*, 623–646.

MacLeod, C., & Hagan, R. (1992). Individual differences in the selective processing of threatening information, and emotional responses to a stressful life event. *Behaviour Research and Therapy, 30*, 151–161.

MacLeod, C., & Mathews, A. (1991). Biased cognitive operations in anxiety: Accessibility of information or assignment of processing priorities? *Behaviour Research and Therapy, 6*, 599–610.

MacLeod, C., Mathews, A., & Tata, P. (1986). Attentional bias in emotional disorders. *Journal of Abnormal Psychology, 95*, 15–20.

MacLeod, C., Rutherford, E., Campbell, L., Ebsworthy, G., & Holker, L. (2002). Selective attention and emotional vulnerability: Assessing the causal basis of their association through the experimental induction of attentional bias. *Journal of Abnormal Psychology, 111*, 107–123.

Mathews, A., Fox, E., Yiend, J., & Calder, A. (2003). The face of fear: Effects of eye gaze and emotion on visual attention. *Visual Cognition, 10*, 823–835.

Mathews, A., & Mackintosh, B. (1998). A cognitive model of selective processing in anxiety. *Cognitive Therapy and Research, 22*, 539–560.

Mathews, A., & MacLeod, C. (1986). Discrimination of threat cues without awareness in anxiety states. *Journal of Abnormal Psychology, 95*, 131–138.

Mathews, A., May, J., Mogg, K., & Eysenck, M. (1990). Attentional bias in anxiety: Selective search or defective filtering. *Journal of Abnormal Psychology, 99*, 166–173.

Mathews, A., & Milroy, R. (1994). Processing of emotional meaning in anxiety. *Cognition & Emotion, 8*, 535–553.

Matthews, G. R., & Antes, J. R. (1992). Visual attention and depression: Cognitive biases in the eye fixations of the dysphoric and the nondepressed. *Cognitive Therapy and Research, 16*, 359–371.

McCabe, S. B., & Gotlib, I. H. (1995). Selective attention and clinical depression: Performance on a deployment-of-attention task. *Journal of Abnormal Psychology, 104,* 241–245.

McCabe, S. B., Gotlib, I. H., & Martin, R. A. (2000). Cognitive vulnerability for depression: Deployment of attention as a function of history of depression and current mood state. *Cognitive Therapy and Research, 24,* 427–444.

McCabe, S. B., & Toman, P. E. (2000). Stimulus exposure duration in a deployment-of-attention task: Effects on dysphoric, recently dysphoric, and nondysphoric individuals. *Cognition & Emotion, 14,* 125–142.

McNally, R. J. (1995). Automaticity and the anxiety disorders. *Behaviour Research and Therapy, 33,* 747–754.

Mogg, K., & Bradley, B. P. (1998). A cognitive-motivational analysis of anxiety. *Behaviour Research and Therapy, 36,* 809–848.

Mogg, K., & Bradley, B. P. (1999). Some methodological issues in assessing attentional biases for threatening faces in anxiety: A replication study using a modified version of the probe detection task. *Behaviour Research and Therapy, 37,* 595–604.

Mogg, K., Mathews, A. M., May, J., Grove, M., Eysenck, M., & Weinman, J. (1991). Assessment of cognitive bias in anxiety and depression using a colour perception task. *Cognition & Emotion, 5,* 221–238.

Mogg, K., Millar, N., & Bradley, B. P. (2000). Biases in eye movements to threatening facial expressions in generalized anxiety disorder and depressive disorder. *Journal of Abnormal Psychology, 109,* 695–704.

Öhman, A., Flykt, A., & Esteves, F. (2001). Emotion drives attention: Detecting the snake in the grass. *Journal of Experimental Psychology: General, 130,* 466–478.

Öhman, A., Lundqvist, D., & Esteves, F. (2001). The face in the crowd revisited: A threat advantage with schematic stimuli. *Journal of Personality and Social Psychology, 80,* 381–396.

Posner, M. I. (1980). Orienting of attention. *Quarterly Journal of Experimental Psychology, 32,* 3–25.

Proctor, R. W., & Vu, K.-P. L. (1999). Index of norms and ratings published in the psychonomic society journals. *Behaviour Research Methods, Instruments, & Computers, 31,* 659–667.

Purcell, D. G., Stewart, A. L., & Skov, R. B. (1996). It takes a confounded face to pop out of a crowd. *Perception, 25,* 1091–1108.

Pury, C. L. S., & Mineka, S. (2001). Differential encoding of affective and nonaffective content information in trait anxiety. *Cognition & Emotion, 15,* 659–693.

Rayner, K. (1998). Eye movements in reading and information processing: 20 years of research. *Psychological Bulletin, 124,* 372–422.

Rayner, K., & Pollatsek, A. (1987). Eye-movements in reading: A tutorial review. *Attention and Performance, 12,* 327–362.

Rubin, D. C., & Friendly, M. (1986). Predicting which words get recalled: Measures of free recall, availability, goodness, emotionality, and pronunciability for 925 nouns. *Memory & Cognition, 14,* 79–94.

Shafer, W. O., & Laberge, D. (1979). Automatic processing of unattended words. *Journal of Verbal Learning and Verbal Behaviour, 18,* 413–426.

Simon, J. R., & Rudell, A. P. (1967). Auditory S-R compatibility: The effect of an irrelevant cue on information processing. *Journal of Applied Psychology, 51,* 300–304.

Titchener, E. B. (1908). *Lectures on the elementary psychology of feeling and attention.* New York: Macmillan.

Tomarken, A. J., Davidson, R. J., Wheeler, R. E., & Doss, R. C. (1992). Individual-differences in anterior brain asymmetry and fundamental dimensions of emotion. *Journal of Personality and Social Psychology, 62,* 676–687.

Trandell, D. V., & McNally, R. J. (1987). Perception of threat cues in post-traumatic stress disorder: Semantic processing without awareness. *Behaviour Research and Therapy, 6,* 469–476.

Treisman, A. M., & Gelade, G. (1980). A feature-integration theory of attention. *Cognitive Psychology, 12,* 97–136.

Vasey, M. W., El-Hag, N., & Daleiden, E. L. (1996). Anxiety and the processing of emotionally threatening stimuli: Distinctive patterns of selective attention among high- and low-test-anxious children. *Child Development, 67,* 1173–1185.

Wells, A., & Matthews, G. (1994). *Attention and emotion: A clinical perspective.* Hove, England: Erlbaum.

Wilson, E., & MacLeod, C. (2003). Contrasting two accounts of anxiety-linked attentional bias: Selective attention to varying levels of stimulus threat intensity. *Journal of Abnormal Psychology, 112,* 212–218.

Yiend, J., & Mathews, A. (2001). Anxiety and attention to threatening pictures. *The Quarterly Journal of Experimental Psychology, 54A,* 665–681.

III

IMPLICIT MEMORY TASKS

7

IMPLICIT MEMORY TASKS: RETENTION WITHOUT CONSCIOUS RECOLLECTION

HENRY L. ROEDIGER III AND NADER AMIR

Implicit memory refers to the influence of past events in current behavior when people are not trying to retrieve the past events and when they are usually not even aware of the events' influence. The contrast is with explicit memory, which refers to conscious attempts to retrieve memories of past events. On implicit memory tests there is no conscious effort to retrieve studied material, whereas on explicit memory tests instructions refer to a specific encoding event. Graf and Schacter (1985) first proposed the distinction between explicit and implicit memory, although the history of the idea of conscious and unconscious forms of memory is much older (see Schacter, 1987, for a historical review). Others have used the terms *direct memory tests* and *indirect memory tests* to refer to the same contrasts as between explicit and implicit memory (Richardson-Klavehn & Bjork, 1988; Segal, 1966).

The customary use of the terms *memory* or *remembering* refers to explicit, conscious recollection during which people attempt to travel back in time mentally to relive or reexperience past events. However, many behaviors people perform reflect past learning even when no conscious attempts at retrieval occur; therefore, these behaviors reflect the manifestation of implicit memory. Some of these behaviors involve motor skills. When you tie your shoes or ride a bicycle or walk, you need not consciously retrieve your first attempts to learn these skills. The same is true of other types of learning. You may have noticed that it is much easier to read a passage of text if you have read it before, even if you are not consciously trying to remember the original time you read the passage (Kolers, 1976). Therefore, repetition of procedures is important in expression of both mental and physical skills. Similar phenomena occur in various clinical states. For example, individuals with clinical depression often report that negative thoughts about past failures come to them without them wanting to have the thought. In anxiety disorders, previous experiences with threat-relevant situations may lead to more salient threat cues for the afflicted individual.

As these examples indicate, implicit expressions of knowledge are sometimes referred to as occurring rather automatically, or at least as having an automatic component (Jacoby & Dallas, 1981). Explicit recollection is often proposed to be primarily consciously controlled, whereas implicit retention is more automatic; however, without special precautions and procedures, it is difficult to provide tests that reflect pure manifestations of explicit or implicit processes (Jacoby, 1991). Although the term *automatic* is often used in the clinical literature (e.g., negative automatic thoughts), few researchers have specifically examined the contribution of automatic processes to implicit memory (see Kazes et al., 1999, for an example of this approach).

Explicit and implicit memory tests can often be relatively similar in laboratory situations. For example, after study of a target word such as *elephant* in a long list, participants may be given a cue such as ele-; on an explicit test they would be asked to recall a word from the list that began with these letters, whereas on an implicit memory test they would be told to respond with the first word that comes to mind and they could say *element*, *elegant*, *electricity*, and so on, in addition to *elephant*. Any of these words is correct on the implicit test from the participant's viewpoint. On the explicit test, the measure of interest is probability of recall of the target word, and usually the guessing rate (that is, the probability of producing *elephant* to the cue if the word *elephant* had not been in the list) is quite low. On the implicit test, in which the participant is told to produce the first word to come to mind, the baseline probability of producing *elephant* when the word had not been presented in the prior list may be higher because it is an acceptable response. The measure of interest in implicit memory tests is the difference between the probability of producing the response when the target item had been presented in the list relative to the case when it had not been presented; this measure is referred to as priming, because the presentation of the word in the list usually primes its production on the later test (relative to the baseline condition).

The tests described above are called word stem completion (the implicit form of the test) and word stem cued recall (the explicit form). In many research projects, investigators compare performance on an implicit and an explicit test, as these tests are affected by either subject variables (different types of people) or independent variables (those under the experimenter's control). Word stem completion and word stem cued recall are often compared because they differ only in the instructions participants are given just before the test (Schacter, Bowers, & Booker, 1989). Everything else (materials, encoding instructions, test cues, etc.) is held constant. However, many other explicit and implicit memory tests are widely used. The most popular explicit memory tests are free recall (recalling a list in any order), recognition memory (either a forced or multiple choice test, or free choice or yes/no test), and cued recall with various types of cues besides word stems (e.g., *tusk* might be used as a cue for *elephant*). In all these cases, participants are instructed to try to recall or recognize recently studied material.

Likewise, many implicit memory tests have been developed. In practically all cases of implicit tests, the comparison of interest is between a nonprimed condition and a primed condition, with some cue serving as a prompt to produce a response. Participants are instructed to say the first item or items that come to mind. The cues can be word stems (ele-), word fragments (try to fill in letters to make e_e_h_n_ a word), or brief flashes of words in which participants try to guess their identities (a test called perceptual or word identification). Verbal materials are not always used, as people can study pictures and then be tested with a fragmented form of the picture or be given a brief flash of a picture and be asked to guess what it is. These tests are but a few examples of the many varieties of implicit memory measures that have been developed by cognitive psychologists. Clinical investigators have modified these tests to suit the clinical needs of studying specific populations or because of the theoretical viewpoint being investigated. For example, when studying social anxiety, researchers have presented their participants with simulated social interaction videos. Implicit memory is revealed if previously seen videos are rated as clearer than are novel videos.

The forms of implicit test described above are called perceptual (or data-driven) implicit memory tests (Blaxton, 1989; Roediger & Blaxton 1987). The participant's task in these tests is always to guess the identity of an object from an impoverished perceptual clue. Manipulation of perceptual factors during study (such as presenting words visually or auditorily) greatly affects performance on perceptual implicit tests. Another primary class of implicit memory tests is conceptual tests. For example, after studying *elephant*, participants might be asked to generate the names of all the animals that they could think of in 30 seconds (a category association test); or they might be asked to generate associations to the word *tusk* (a free association test); or they might be asked to answer the question "What animal aided Hannibal on his attack on Rome?" In each case the measure of interest is again priming: the difference between producing *elephant* if the item had been recently presented and producing *elephant* if the word had not been recently presented.

These tasks are called conceptual or meaning-based tests, because the cue for producing the answer is related to the target on the basis of meaning rather than perceptual resemblance. More important, the variables that affect these conceptual implicit memory tasks are quite different from the ones that affect perceptual tasks. For example, modality of presentation has no effect on the amount of priming, but manipulations of meaning have a great effect (e.g., Blaxton, 1989; Srinivas & Roediger, 1990). Conceptual implicit memory tests are of particular relevance to clinical conditions where psychopathologists have postulated the role of implicit memory for material relevant to the clinical conditions (e.g., depression; Watkins, 2002). Perceptual implicit memory tests are more relevant to clinical conditions that involve a pervasive deterioration of memory functioning in explicit memory tests but spared functioning in implicit memory tests, although both perceptual and conceptual tests can be used in these cases.

The study of implicit memory tests grew out of clinical situations, in particular those involving neuropsychologists studying the abilities of memory-impaired (amnesic) patients. In the late 1960s, Warrington and Weiskrantz (1968, 1970) reported the first research that used what are today called implicit memory paradigms. One of their studies can serve as a good starting point (1970, Experiment 2). They presented four amnesic patients (three with Korsakoff's syndrome and one with a temporal lobectomy) with words to remember and then assessed their retention on four different tests (for different lists of words). A total of 16 patients without brain damage were similarly tested. Two of the four tests would today be classified as involving explicit memory (free recall and recognition) and the other two as assessing implicit retention (naming of fragmented words in which each letter was degraded and word stem completion, described above, of three-letter cues such as ele-). In free recall, people recalled words in any order on a blank sheet of paper. In recognition, the studied words were intermixed with new words and people had to judge which ones had been previously studied. The other two tasks—word fragment and word-stem completion—seem to have been presented to the participants as word guessing games (although the instructions given were not provided in the original report of the experiment). The measure of performance was priming or completion of the fragment or stem above the baseline.

Warrington and Weiskrantz's (1970) results are presented in Figure 7.1, with explicit test performance at the top and priming on the implicit tests at the bottom. In the top two panels, it is apparent that amnesic patients performed much worse in both free recall and recognition than did control patients. This is, in some sense, not surprising. After all, the way one becomes classified as a memory-impaired or amnesic patient is by performing poorly on memory tests (as well as not being able to remember normally in situations outside the lab).

The remarkable results reported by Warrington and Weiskrantz (1970) are shown in the bottom two panels. Priming on the implicit memory tests

Explicit Tests

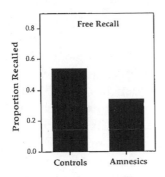

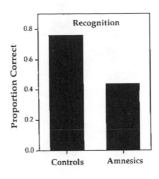

Implicit Tests

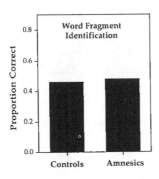

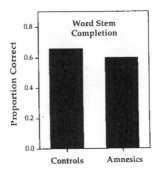

Figure 7.1. Performance of amnesic and control patients on four memory tasks: two explicit (free recall and recognition) and two implicit (word fragment and word stem completion). Amnesic patients showed much worse performance than did controls on the two explicit memory tests, but showed equal priming on the two implicit memory tests. Data from "Amnesic Syndrome: Consolidation or Retrieval?" by E. K. Warrington and L. Weiskrantz, 1970, *Nature,* p. 630.

was of equal magnitude for both groups. Because the items used had been normed to have a very low completion rate if the words had not been studied, these priming effects definitely reflect a form of memory. However, the form seems quite different from that measured on standard, explicit memory tests. The fact that the patients show normal priming indicates that experiences of these patients are somehow being encoded and retained; the difficulty seems to be in expressing retention on tests that require effortful, deliberate, conscious recollection. On implicit tests, which seem more automatic in nature and on which people do not deliberately try to remember the past, the patients and the controls show equal priming. These striking dissociations between memory-impaired and control patients on implicit memory tests were replicated by other groups (e.g., Graf, Squire, & Mandler, 1984).

Many other types of patients have been studied and compared using explicit and implicit memory tests, as we explore in chapters 8 and 9

Experimental psychologists took up these implicit or indirect tests of memory and were quick to show dissociations similar to those found with patient groups by the manipulation of independent variables. Overall, the data show a strong dissociation between explicit and implicit tests of memory. Just as memory-impaired patients display large deficits on explicit tests relative to control participants, experimental conditions (e.g., questions about physical appearance of words) that lead to large deficits on explicit tests (Craik & Tulving, 1975) can produce normal levels of priming (Jacoby & Dallas, 1981). These strong dissociations both in patient populations and with variables under experimental control are why so many researchers have investigated implicit memory tests and their comparison with explicit tests. Attempting to understand what these differences reveal about human memory and its vicissitudes has been in the forefront of psychology for the past 20 years or more.

Clinical psychologists have attempted to use the methods developed by cognitive psychologists to elucidate the nature of various clinical conditions. Although this research must be informed by the findings from cognitive psychology, a number of unique challenges and unique rewards are evident in studies of implicit memory in clinical populations. For example, the materials used for tests of implicit memory in clinical populations need to be relevant to the clinical condition. This requirement, however, provides a considerable challenge to clinical scientists who also need to consider basic cognitive issues (e.g., the need to match materials on lexical features such as word frequency). These challenges are well worth the effort, because implicit tests offer the possibility of unique insights into the nature of different clinical conditions. These insights include a better description of the clinical phenomenon and prediction of future symptoms, as well as the possibility of developing better treatments for clinical populations.

Chapters 8 and 9 discuss the conduct of research with implicit memory tests. Roediger and Geraci (see chap. 8, this volume) discuss research on healthy adult populations and address, among other topics, the rather tricky issue of ensuring that implicit memory tests are really measuring memory indirectly and that participants are not aiding performance by attempting to consciously recollect information. Amir and Selvig (see chap. 9, this volume) are concerned with the important issue of adapting implicit memory tests to ask interesting questions of various clinical populations.

REFERENCES

Blaxton, T. A. (1989). Investigating dissociations among memory measures: Support for a transfer appropriate processing framework. *Journal of Experimental Psychology: Learning, Memory, and Cognition, 15,* 657–668.

Craik, F. I. M., & Tulving, E. (1975). Depth of processing and the retention of words in episodic memory. *Journal of Experimental Psychology: General, 104,* 268–294.

Graf, P. & Schacter, D. A. (1985). Implicit and explicit memory for new associations in normal and amnesic subjects. *Journal of Experimental Psychology: Learning, Memory, and Cognition, 11,* 501–518.

Graf, P., Squire, L. R., & Mandler, G. (1984). The information that amnesic patients do not forget. *Journal of Experimental Psychology: Learning, Memory, and Cognition, 10,* 164–178.

Jacoby, L. L. (1991). A process dissociation framework: Separating automatic from intentional uses of memory. *Journal of Memory & Language, 30,* 513–541.

Jacoby, L. L., & Dallas, M. (1981). On the relationship between autobiographical memory and perceptual learning. *Journal of Experimental Psychology: General, 110,* 306–340.

Kazes, M., Berthet, L., Danion, J.-M., Amado, I, Willard, D., Robert, P., & Poirier, M.-F. (1999). *Neuropsychology, 13,* 54–61.

Kolers, P. A. (1976). Reading a year later. *Journal of Experimental Psychology: Human Learning and Memory, 2,* 554–565.

Richardson-Klavehn, A., & Bjork, R. A. (1988). Measures of memory. *Annual Review of Psychology, 39,* 475–543.

Roediger, H. L., & Blaxton, T. A. (1987). Retrieval modes produce dissociations in memory for surface information. In D. Gorfein & R. R. Hoffman (Eds.), *Memory and cognitive processes: The Ebbinghaus Centennial Conference* (pp. 349–379). Hillsdale, NJ: Erlbaum.

Schacter, D. L. (1987). Implicit memory: History and current status. *Journal of Experimental Psychology: Learning, Memory, and Cognition, 13,* 501–518.

Schacter, D. L., Bowers, J., & Booker, J. (1989). Intention, awareness, and implicit memory: The retrieval intentionality criterion. In S. Lewandowsky, J. C. Dunn, & K. Kirsner (Eds.), *Implicit memory: Theoretical issues* (pp. 47–65). Hillsdale, NJ: Erlbaum.

Segal, S. J. (1966). Priming compared to recall: Following multiple exposures and delay. *Psychological Reports, 18,* 615–620.

Srinivas, K., & Roediger, H. L. (1990). Testing the nature of two implicit tests: Dissociations between conceptually-driven and data-driven processes. *Journal of Memory and Language, 29,* 389–412.

Warrington, E. K., & Weiskrantz, L. (1968). New method of testing long-term retention with special reference to amnesic patients. *Nature, 217,* 972–974.

Warrington, E. K., & Weiskrantz, L. (1970). Amnesic syndrome: Consolidation or retrieval? *Nature, 228,* 629–630.

Watkins, P. C. (2002). Implicit memory bias in depression. *Cognition and Emotion, 16,* 381–402.

8

IMPLICIT MEMORY TASKS IN COGNITIVE RESEARCH

HENRY L. ROEDIGER III AND LISA GERACI

Our aim in this chapter is to describe some important issues to consider when designing and conducting implicit memory experiments. These are both conceptual questions (how can one determine if a task is implicit?) and methodological and practical issues (the nitty-gritty issues of research). Many different methods have been used under the loose banner of *implicit memory research* and various traditions have developed. We cannot cover all approaches in one chapter, but we provide an overview of some relevant methods and techniques.

As discussed in chapter 7, explicit memory tests—those assessing conscious recollection—have typically been used in memory research. These tests assess memory directly, by asking people what they can recollect (with a whole variety of procedures). For example, participants may see a set of pictures and words and be asked to recall or recognize them at a later point. Many experiments assessing implicit memory are formally rather similar to explicit memory experiments in that participants may study pictures or words, and their memories are assessed in a later test. The difference is that implicit tests measure retention indirectly, usually by having participants perform some ostensibly unrelated tasks, such as trying to name fragmented words or pictures or generating as many items as possible that belong to a certain category. Thus, implicit retention is measured by the benefit from recent study of the word or picture on the task of interest. This benefit in performance is called priming (Schacter, 1987).

The first part of our chapter describes the two main types of implicit tests that have been used and that were introduced in the preliminary chapter: perceptual and conceptual tests. In the previous paragraph, the word fragment and picture fragment naming tests represent examples of perceptual implicit tests, in that performance relies on processing at the level of the percept, whereas the category generation test is a conceptual test because performance on it relies on processing at the meaning level. In the remainder of the chapter we discuss critical issues faced when employing these tests and experimental techniques that can be used to address these issues. We end the chapter with some general advice for procedures to employ when conducting implicit memory research.

TYPES OF IMPLICIT TESTS

The perceptual and conceptual test distinction was proposed by Roediger and Blaxton (1987), following a suggestion by Jacoby (1983b). Criteria for classifying a test as predominantly of one or the other type were proposed by Roediger, Weldon, and Challis (1989; see also Blaxton, 1989; Tulving & Schacter, 1990). We consider these types of tests below. In all tests, the measure of interest is either the probability of producing a response or the speed with which the response can be produced (see Toth, 2000, for a comprehensive list of implicit memory tests).

Perceptual Implicit Memory Tests

Perceptual tests are those in which participants are typically presented with a degraded or rapid presentation of a stimulus that must be identified. Priming on such tests is highly sensitive to the perceptual format used in presentation, such as stimulus modality (auditory or visual) or type of representation (e.g., picture or word). For example, degraded words (word fragments) show more priming for items that were presented as words than as pictures at study, but degraded pictures (picture fragments) show more priming for items that were presented as pictures than words at study (Weldon & Roediger, 1987). These tests are relatively insensitive to meaningful manipulations that greatly affect explicit tests, such as variations of orienting tasks in what are usually called levels-of-processing experiments (e.g., Jacoby & Dallas, 1981). Roediger (2003) estimated that 80% of all published implicit memory research has used perceptual implicit tests. We consider some of the most popular variations here. For the discussion below, we assume that participants have recently studied a long list of pictures and/or words. In such experiments, the items used refer to concrete objects that can be presented as either words or pictures. During the test, fragmented forms of words or pictures are presented along with some fragments representing nonstudied items, to serve as a baseline measure against which to assess priming. We turn now to some popular perceptual implicit memory tests.

Word and Picture Identification

In this type of test, the words or pictures are presented very briefly and are usually followed by a backward mask, with pretesting determining a good level of baseline performance (somewhere between 25% and 40%). The stimulus display and testing must be done by computer (or, in older research, a tachistoscope). Priming in this task is measured by the percentage of stimuli identified that had been previously presented relative to the nonstudied completion rate. Jacoby and Dallas (1981) used this technique with words in a seminal paper. Interestingly, participants report that primed items on identification tests appear to stay on the screen longer than the new words, even though they are presented for the same amount of time. In turn, subsequent studies have used these subjective reports as a measure of priming (Witherspoon & Allan, 1985). We describe this type of implicit test below.

A variant on this identification technique is to present test stimuli in increasingly complete fragments; for example, the participant gets a much degraded fragment of a picture or word, a less degraded version, and so on until the picture or word is identified. In this case, the level of degradation needed to identify the picture is the measure of interest. Snodgrass's work (Snodgrass & Corwin, 1988; Snodgrass, Smith, Feenan, & Corwin, 1987) provides a good reference for such experiments. Similarly, words can also be slowly revealed on the screen, with each successive screen presenting a clearer and more complete view of the word, with the degree of clarification needed for identification serving as the dependent measure of priming (see Hashtroudi, Ferguson, Rappold, & Chronsniak, 1988; and Johnston, Hawley, & Elliot, 1991, for examples).

Word and Picture Fragment Completion

The word fragment completion test also involves giving people degraded forms of words. Here, people see words with missing letters, such as e_e_h_n_ or a_ _a_ _in, and are asked to guess the items (*elephant* and *assassin* in these cases). Tulving, Schacter, and Stark (1982) first developed this test, which has been used frequently. Typically, participants are given about 15 seconds to complete the fragment, and often only one word in the English language will complete it. If participants cannot complete the fragment, they leave it blank and advance to the next test fragment. The picture fragment naming test is similar, except that a fragmented picture (one with missing line and corner segments) is given, and the participant's task is to name the picture from a single long exposure. Priming in both tests is measured by subtracting the proportion of fragments completed in the baseline (nonstudied) condition from the proportion completed after items had been in the study list. Weldon, Roediger, Beitel, and Johnston (1995) provide experimental examples of both word fragment and picture fragment priming.

Word Stem Completion

This is perhaps the most popular task for studying perceptual implicit memory and was used in much of the early research with brain-damaged patients (e.g., Squire, Shimamura, & Graf, 1987; Warrington & Weiskrantz, 1970). The word stem completion test is similar to the word fragment completion test, in that participants are given a perceptually degraded version of a word and are asked to complete it with the first word that comes to mind. In this task, however, they are presented with the first three letters of the word (e.g., str-) after participants had studied *strawberry*. Again, priming is measured by subtracting the proportion of word stems completed with nonstudied words from the proportion of stems completed with studied words. Unlike the case of word fragment completion, word stem completion experiments are usually designed such that 10 or more completions are possible for any word stem. This means participants can always complete the stem, and so they find the task easier than word fragment completion in which many items are skipped. One problem is that base rates are often low (10% or so) in this task and the amount of priming obtained is sometimes small (relative to priming on word fragment completion tests). Still, in direct comparisons of word fragment and word stem completion, the tests behave rather similarly (Rajaram & Roediger, 1993; Roediger, Weldon, Stadler, & Riegler, 1992). Nelson and his colleagues have developed variants of stem completion tests in which participants get the last few letters of words rather than the first few letters (e.g., Nelson, Schreiber, & Holley, 1992).

Other Perceptual Tests

Several other perceptual implicit tasks have been used, although much less frequently than ones described in the previous sections. As in the previous tests, participants study stimuli (typically, pictures or words) and are given a task to examine the influence of the studied stimuli on performance. First, there are auditory counterparts to most of the tests already described, such that one can have an auditory identification task that involves identifying words presented in noise, or auditory equivalents of word stem and word fragment completion (see Pilotti, Bergman, Gallo, Sommers, & Roediger, 2000; Pilotti, Gallo, & Roediger, 2000; Schacter & Church, 1992). Other tests include duration judgments as discussed earlier (how long was the stimulus presented?), the lexical decision task (deciding whether or not a letter string is a word; see Duchek & Neely, 1989), the anagram solution task (solving anagrams for studied and nonstudied words, see Srinivas & Roediger,

1990), and the homophone spelling task (showing priming in spelling an auditorily presented word such as *reed* when this sound/meaning of the word had been primed; see Jacoby & Witherspoon, 1982).

Two nonverbal tasks are picture naming (Mitchell & Brown, 1988), in which participants quickly name pictures, and object decision, in which participants see drawn forms and have to decide whether each could represent a real object (Schacter, Cooper, & Delaney, 1990). As in the lexical decision task, the participant must make a decision by pressing one of two keys to indicate whether the presented object is possible or impossible (rather like deciding that a letter string is or is not a word). Although all of these tests are usually considered perceptual implicit memory tests, it is difficult in some cases to apply the operations specified by Roediger et al. (1989) to determine if they meet the proposed criteria. Still, there is reason to believe that these tests are perceptual in nature.

Performance on the implicit memory tests just described depends on perceptual analysis of items, and priming depends primarily on the match in perceptual processing between study and test presentations (Roediger, 1990). A reasonable question is whether these tests are more or less equivalent to one another, or whether they differ in important ways. It is surprising that relatively few attempts have been made to compare perceptual implicit tests directly, although it is known that the verbal and pictorial types of test differ markedly in the types of prior experience that produce priming (Weldon & Roediger, 1987; Weldon et al., 1995). As mentioned earlier, this sort of inquiry does show distinctions among these types of perceptual tests (studying words leads to an advantage on verbal tests, whereas studying pictures leads to an advantage on picture tests).

Rajaram and Roediger (1993) directly compared priming on four verbal implicit memory tests that involved visual test presentations of words: word identification, word fragment completion, word stem completion, and anagram solution. Groups of participants were exposed to items during study by reading words, hearing words, seeing pictures representing the names of the item, or (for the baseline condition) not being presented with the items at all. After study, participants received one of four types of test. The amount of priming from the three study conditions relative to the baseline is shown in Figure 8.1. As can be seen, despite some differences in priming across the four tests, visual presentations of words always produced greater priming than did auditory presentations, whereas both created more priming than did pictorial presentations. (In many experiments, little or no priming occurs from studying pictures on verbal tests and, similarly, little priming occurs from studying words on pictorial tests; see McDermott & Roediger, 1994; Srinivas, 1993). Of course, other tests such as homophone spelling may reveal a quite different pattern, but at least with regard to the four tests they used, Rajaram and Roediger concluded that these verbal implicit memory tests were broadly similar across these variables.

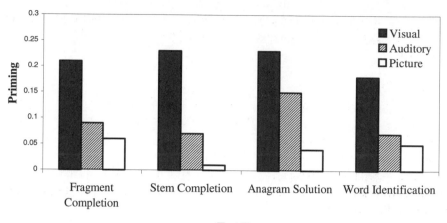

Figure 8.1. Relative priming on four implicit memory tests as a function of study condition. From "Direct Comparison of Four Implicit Memory Tests," by S. Rajaram and H. L. Roediger III, 1993, *Journal of Experimental Psychology: Learning, Memory, and Cognition, 19,* pp. 765–776. Copyright 1993 by the American Psychological Association. Reprinted with permission.

Conceptual Implicit Memory Tests

Conceptual tests represent the other class of implicit memory tests. These tests are relatively insensitive to perceptual factors manipulated at encoding (e.g., reading rather than hearing words does not affect priming). Instead, priming on these tests relies on the similarity of conceptual analysis of the items between study and test. The greater the overlap in conceptual processing, the greater the priming on these tests. As with perceptual implicit test items, performance on the nonstudied (baseline) conditions should be assessed to ensure that it is neither too high nor too low to observe priming. A general problem on some conceptual implicit tests is that the levels of priming can be fairly low, which makes them hard to study as a function of independent variables. In addition, these tests are much less frequently used and studied relative to perceptual tests. Perhaps 10% of all implicit memory tests have used conceptual implicit tests, and relatively few studies have employed both perceptual and conceptual implicit tests (a tradition begun by Blaxton, 1989).

Word Association

Perhaps the most commonly used conceptual implicit test is the word association test (see Shimamura & Squire, 1984). Participants study a list of words (e.g., including *bread*) and during the test they are given a set of weakly associated words (e.g., *wheat*) and are asked to produce associated words for 15 or 30 seconds. The interest is in how much prior study of *bread* will prime people to produce it as an associate to *wheat*, relative to the nonprimed condition (producing *bread* as an associate to *wheat* when *bread* was not studied in the list).

Category Production

The category exemplar production test is similar to the word association test, except that people are given category names on the test and are asked to produce as many examples from the category as they can in 30 seconds. So, participants study a list of words that are all from different categories (e.g., *trout, shoes, bureau*) and are later given a list of categories corresponding to studied items (e.g., *fish, clothing, furniture*) and some corresponding to nonstudied items (e.g., *professions*). At test, participants read the category labels and are told to write down category members within a specified period of time. Priming is obtained when people are more likely to produce a category exemplar when they have studied it than when they have not. Srinivas and Roediger (1990) provide an example of this test.

General Knowledge

Another way to measure conceptual implicit memory is to have people study a list of words (e.g., *strawberry*) that are answers to general knowledge questions (e.g., "What fruit wears its seed on the outside of its skin?"). Blaxton (1989) used this test. Included in the test, of course, are several general knowledge questions for which answers have not been presented in the study phase, to assess priming. The increase in general knowledge answers for studied items over nonstudied items is attributable to priming.

Other Conceptual Tests

There are several other conceptual implicit memory tests that can be used. These tests differ from the tests just described in two ways. First, they do not require production of the studied word, which is sometime preferable with certain populations that may differ in production ability (such as younger and older adults). Second, these tests also differ slightly from the others in that they contain the percept of the studied word. As such, these tests may demonstrate some perceptual priming, in addition to conceptual priming.

One example is the category verification test. As with the category production test, participants study lists of items from different categories (e.g., *strawberry*). At test, however, they are given a category name and a possible exemplar and are asked to indicate whether or not the item is a member of the category (*A type of fruit: strawberry*). Because people rarely make errors on this test, priming is typically measured in reaction time to either verify or disconfirm category membership. Priming is measured by examining the decrease in reaction time to respond to studied exemplars as compared with nonstudied exemplars. Tenpenny and Shoben (1992) provide a good example of use of this test.

Other tests include subjective judgments of fame and truth. In the case of fame, people read nonfamous names (Sebastian Weisdorf). On a later test people judge whether a name is of a famous person. Familiarity with the names (as a result of study) is misattributed to the belief that the name is famous, so Sebastian Weisdorf may be mistakenly judged to be a famous name (Jacoby & Kelley, 1987). One can also ask people whether certain statements are true or false (e.g., Hasher, Goldstein, & Toppino, 1977). In this test, as in the previous one, people are more likely to say that a statement is true when they have seen the statement previously than when they have not, the mere-truth effect. Thus, implicit memory is measured by a change in one's subjective judgments. Changes in subjective judgments have also been demonstrated for judgments of difficulty: people judge that anagrams are easier when they have studied their solutions than when they have not (Kelley & Jacoby, 1996), and they judge that reading passages is easier when they have read them before than when they have not (Kelley, 1999).

The study of conceptual implicit memory tests is still in its infancy. Many variants of these tests can be created from numerous conceptual tasks. The study of conceptual implicit tests may, in the long run, be seen as more important than perceptual tests. After all, the knowledge distilled from educational experiences and from other forms of past learning is typically expressed in making judgments and decisions in life with more of an implicit than an explicit retrieval orientation. That is, in making a decision in business we rarely consciously think back to what we have learned but rather seem to bring the totality of our past experience to bear in making a current judgment. Our past experience with the relevant concepts then is expressed in our judgments, decisions, and behavior.

CRITICAL ISSUES IN IMPLICIT MEMORY RESEARCH

In this section of the chapter we consider some central issues in implicit memory research that all researchers face, along with tips on how to handle these issues. In many cases, there are no absolute right or wrong answers to tricky issues raised during such research, but rather more and less effective ways to address them.

Equating Processing Demands

In a typical study exploring implicit memory, the experimental contrast is between performance on one explicit memory test and one implicit memory test with some independent or participant variable manipulated. For example, Roediger and Blaxton (1987) contrasted free recall with word fragment completion as a function of modality of presentation; Jacoby and Dallas (1981) contrasted performance on perceptual identification with recognition memory. The attempt in these cases is to compare a conscious, aware (recollective, explicit) form of memory with one that is unconscious or unaware or nonrecollective or implicit. Operationally, explicit and implicit tests differ by instructions, with the former tests using intentional recollection instructions ("recall or recognize recent events") and the latter using incidental retrieval instructions in which participants are simply told to perform the task as well as possible (Jacoby, 1984; Roediger & McDermott, 1993). Although this intentional/incidental contrast is the variable of interest, one confounding issue is that explicit and implicit tasks differ in processing demands that the tasks place on the cognitive system. For example, free recall and word fragment completion, two tasks studied by Roediger and Blaxton (1987) among others, differ not only in their intentionality of retrieval, but also in their processing demands. Most implicit memory tests require perceptual reanalysis of the studied item in completing the task, whereas typical explicit tests draw more on conceptual processing (Roediger, 1990). Recognition and perceptual identification, the tests used by Jacoby and Dallas (1981), seem better because in both tasks participants receive the whole stimulus. However, even these two tasks may differ somewhat in their processing demands because in one test the item is presented slowly (recognition) and in the other it is presented for very brief periods (30 ms). The simultaneous mismatch in processing demands and intention to retrieve between explicit and implicit tasks can hamper the conclusion drawn in comparisons between test types.

One solution that can be employed to blunt this problem has been called the *retrieval intentionality criterion* by Schacter, Bowers, and Booker (1989). Experiments that use the retrieval intentionality criterion hold constant all conditions of testing except for the instructions, which should either tell the participant to refer to the study list to do the task (explicit instructions) or make no mention of the study session (implicit instructions). (Study conditions in explicit and implicit test comparisons are held constant as a matter of course.)

Consider an experiment by Roediger et al. (1992). In one condition, participants studied a long list of words under two encoding conditions, one that directed participants' attention to the physical features of words and the other of which directed attention to meaning. At test, four different groups of participants were given either word stems or word fragments as cues with either intentional (explicit) or incidental (implicit) instructions. Note that the processing demands of the test are now equated; two groups of participants are tested with word stems under either explicit or implicit instructions, and two other groups receive word fragments with the same instructions.

The results of Roediger et al.'s (1992) experiment are shown in Figure 8.2 (for word stem tests) and Figure 8.3 (for word fragment tests). In each case, the type of orienting task (physical or semantic) had a large effect on

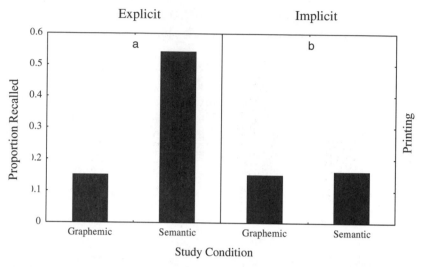

Figure 8.2. Performance on the stem completion task as a function of the type of instructions (explicit or implicit) and study condition. From "Direct Comparison of Two Implicit Memory Tests: Word Fragment and Word Stem Completion," by H. L. Roediger, M. S. Weldon, M. L. Stadler, and G. L. Riegler, 1992, *Journal of Experimental Psychology: Learning, Memory, and Cognition, 18,* pp. 1251–1269. Copyright 1992 by the American Psychological Association. Reprinted with permission.

performance on the explicit test but little or no effect on the amount of priming on the implicit test, even with processing requirements (producing an item to a stem or fragment) held constant. The important point is that strong differences between explicit and implicit tests can still be found even with the overt processing demands of the task equated.

The retrieval intentionality criterion is used on some perceptual implicit tests, but it is difficult to extend the logic to all implicit tests. For example, in word identification, where items are presented extremely briefly, it would be difficult to have an explicit counterpart of the test that equated processing requirements (although see Richardson-Klavehn, Lee, Joubran, & Bjork, 1994, Experiment 3). Similarly, the logic can be used on conceptual implicit memory tests, but because these tests and explicit tests are both conceptual in nature, it might be harder to find dissociations between tests.

Another criterion that has been generally used to define tests as implicit is whether the test shows preserved priming in amnesic patients. The assumption is that amnesics are at least impaired in explicit, conscious recollection and in the most severe cases, such as H. M. (Milner, 1966), K. C. (Tulving, 1989), or E. P. (Hamann & Squire, 1997; Stark & Squire, 2000), such a form of memory may be lacking altogether. The important point is that strong differences between explicit and implicit tests can still be found even with the overt processing demands of the task equated. If such patients show perfectly intact priming on a task, then the task would seem to be rea-

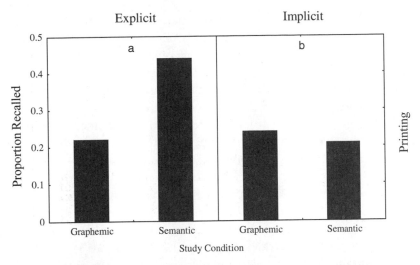

Explicit   Implicit

Figure 8.3. Performance on the fragment completion task as a function of the type of instructions (explicit or implicit) and study condition. From "Direct Comparison of Two Implicit Memory Tests: Word Fragment and Word Stem Completion," by H. L. Roediger, M. S. Weldon, M. L. Stadler, and G. L. Riegler, 1992, *Journal of Experimental Psychology: Learning, Memory, and Cognition, 18,* pp. 1251–1269. Copyright 1992 by the American Psychological Association. Reprinted with permission.

sonably classified as implicit. This logic is true as far as it goes, but the fact that amnesic patients show intact priming on the task in one experiment does not necessarily mean that the task has the same status when used under somewhat different conditions, with different participant groups, in other experiments. Nonetheless, some tasks are generally classified as implicit because of having met the criterion of being intact in amnesic patients. We turn next to the general problem of minimizing aware uses of memory in healthy populations of participants.

Limiting Conscious Recollection on Implicit Tests

Implicit tests are designed to measure unintentional uses of memory, but many researchers have worried that performance on these tests can become contaminated by consciously controlled uses of memory. Such contamination is not a great danger when patients with severe memory impairments are tested, but much implicit memory research uses healthy participants such as college students. These participants are told to perform a task (such as completing word fragments or word stems) to the best of their ability, with no mention made of the possibility of using conscious recollection. Still, participants may realize during the course of the test that some items they are producing correspond to those to which they were exposed earlier in the experiment, and they may then begin to engage in conscious recollection.

Consider the test of word fragment completion. As discussed previously, in this test participants study a list of words (e.g., *booklet*) and are later given fragments of those words (e.g., b_o_ _et), as well as other fragments of nonstudied words. Participants are told to complete the fragment with the first word that comes to mind. The danger is that the participant will notice that the solution to the word fragment appeared in the previous study list and then begin to treat the rest of the test as an explicit memory test, intentionally trying to complete each fragment with a studied word (Schacter et al., 1989). In the light of this concern, care should be taken to create conditions that limit participants' awareness of the relation between study and test to minimize the probability that participants will turn the implicit test into an explicit test.

Several strategies might be used to try to ensure that an implicit test will measure incidental retrieval (Roediger & McDermott, 1993). One strategy is to use incidental learning instructions before encoding. That is, the fact that participants are in an experiment about memory at all is disguised. Participants may be told that they are in a psycholinguistics experiment in which they will have several tasks involving characteristics of words, or in a perception task involving the rating of pictures. Words or pictures could then be presented, and participants could be asked to rate them on various characteristics. After this first phase, participants may be given various filler tasks before they are then given the implicit memory test (e.g., completing fragmented pictures or words). They are told that the task is a psycholinguistic (or perceptual) task that will measure how various types of word or picture fragments cue perception of words and pictures. With these cover stories (and mild deception) participants are less likely to use intentional recollection during the test.

Often the experimenter wants to use intentional learning instructions during study, so the strategy described earlier cannot be used. (Actually, evidence from several experiments shows that the intentional/incidental manipulation during study does not influence priming on implicit tests, anyway; see Roediger & McDermott, 1993, for a review). In this situation researchers customarily present the implicit memory test as one in a series of distractor tasks (part of some other research project) before the (explicit) memory test that participants expect (e.g., Weldon & Roediger, 1987). For example, after studying a list of words under intentional encoding conditions, participants may solve arithmetic problems, then may try to complete fragmented forms of famous names (B_n_ am_n F_a_kl_n) and then a series of fragmented words (the implicit test). At the beginning of the word fragment completion test, the first 30 items might be filler fragments that are not part of the experimental conditions to ensure that participants have an incidental retrieval orientation with respect to the study list (that is, they just see their task as one of completing fragments, not remembering). Even after list items are introduced, keeping the proportion of studied items on the test list low may help to ensure an implicit retrieval orientation, too (although see Challis & Roediger, 1993). For example, if the participants studied 50 words, a researcher might use a test list that contains a total of 150 test word fragments, so that only one out of three studied words appears in the test. (As noted earlier, these studied items should not appear early in the test list, either.) After completing the word fragment test, participants may be given the recall or recognition test that they expect. Also, when the test fragments or stems are presented at a relatively rapid rate, the test seems to be more purely incidental (Weldon, 1993).

The previous example considered word fragment completion, but the same considerations apply to other implicit tests. As in the example with 50 studied words and 150 test fragments, it is critical to use rather large stimulus sets in implicit memory tests, for at least two reasons. First, if the researcher has participants study a list of only 10 items and then gives the test of 30 items 20 minutes later, it is quite likely that participants may recognize the 10 studied items as having been from the previous phase of the experiment, and so they may be encouraged to engage in explicit retrieval strategies to recall the items. Second, with at least 40 or more study items, it becomes inefficient for participants to engage in explicit strategies even if they do recognize some items as being from the study list. That is, it is easier for them to solve the task at hand with an implicit retrieval orientation than to try to consciously retrieve items from the list, and one might assume participants will use an easy strategy relative to a hard one.

Some researchers have argued that the great worry about contamination of implicit tests by intentional strategies is overblown (Roediger & McDermott, 1993). However, it can be argued that some implicit tests may be more susceptible to explicit contamination than others. In particular, implicit tests that require speeded responses may not provide adequate time to think back and explicitly recall items from the study list. For example, in word or picture identification tests, items are displayed on the computer screen, and participants are required to name them as quickly as possible. Because the stimulus presentation is fast and the test is speeded, there is little time, and little advantage, for participants to try to recall whether the words appeared in the previous list. How can a researcher gauge if an implicit test is compromised by intentional recollection?

DETECTING AWARENESS AND EXPLICIT CONTAMINATION ON IMPLICIT TESTS

Even with all of these precautions in place, it is still possible for participants to become aware that some of the items on the test were from the study phase of the experiment. How can one assess if this is a problem? Several techniques are available.

Posttest Questionnaires

A posttest questionnaire can be included after any implicit memory test to assess retrospective awareness of the study–test relationship and the possible use of explicit memory strategies. For example, Bowers and Schacter (1990) developed a set of questions to determine whether participants were aware of the fact that the task involved production of list items and whether participants changed their retrieval strategy if they did become aware. Their technique has been adopted by many other researchers. The typical strategy is to begin probing with open-ended questions (e.g., "Did you notice any relation between the word fragment test we gave you and other parts of the experiment?") and move on to more specific questions. However, the meaning of such questionnaire data is open to interpretation, depending on how leading the question is and what participants may have done if they did become aware. For example, many participants may realize that some items on the test appeared in the study list, but they might realize this only after they have completed the fragment or named the stem. That is, retrieval may have been completely incidental, with recognition occurring after the implicit retrieval has occurred. This problem—dubbed *involuntary conscious recollection* by Richardson-Klavehn, Gardiner, and Java (1994)—may not compromise the measurement of priming on implicit memory tests unless participants report changing their strategy to use conscious recollection in the retrieval attempt itself (answering "yes" to the question, "Did you try to remember items from the list when you were given the fragments?"). Still, posttest questionnaire data can be useful because they can permit the researcher to analyze participants' performance separately on the basis of their type of awareness of the relation between the study and test (completely unaware; aware that study items appeared on the test but no change in reported strategy; aware with a change reported in strategy, etc.). This practice is increasingly used in the literature and has demonstrated some interesting dissociations (e.g., Geraci & Rajaram, 2002).

Retrieval Intentionality Criterion

A second strategy to assess whether implicit memory tests are compromised by intentional recollection is the retrieval intentionality criterion discussed earlier. Consider work with word-stem completion and word-fragment completion tests. In both cases the stems or fragments are displayed for several seconds (rather than for fractions of a second, as in word identification tests). Participants tend to respond relatively quickly to word stems and provide a response for almost all stems on the test. On the word fragment test, however, the responses are often slow, and many fragments are not completed even after 10 or 15 seconds. Squire et al. (1987) proposed that word stem tests were more likely to measure incidental retrieval relative to word fragment tests because of these differences and others.

Roediger et al. (1992), in an experiment described earlier, tested Squire et al.'s hypothesis by using the retrieval intentionality criterion. They manipulated the type of orienting task participants performed on words during study (a perceptual or a semantic task) and then gave word fragment and word stem tests with both implicit and explicit instructions. The results have already been shown earlier, but let's examine them again with this issue in mind. For the word-stem test, the manipulation of orienting task had a large effect on the explicit form of the test (see the righthand panel of Figure 8.2) but no effect on the implicit test. This outcome replicates the finding of Graf and Mandler (1984), among others, showing that a manipulation of orienting task affects intentional but not incidental retrieval. Now look at the results of the word fragment completion test in Figure 8.3. The basic pattern of results is the same as in word-stem completion. The explicit form of the test shows a large effect of orienting task, but the implicit form of the test shows no effect. If participants were using intentional recollection in the word fragment completion test, performance should resemble (at least to some degree) the results in Figure 8.3b, which shows performance under intentional retrieval conditions. However, the same amount of priming occurred under semantic encoding conditions and under perceptual encoding conditions, which means that word stem and word fragment completion tests seem equally free of contamination by explicit retrieval strategies.

The retrieval intentionality criterion is difficult to apply in all types of implicit memory tests. For example, the strategy of varying orienting task during study and showing a lack of effect on an implicit test does not work for conceptual implicit tests, because these tests (even when measuring incidental retrieval) show positive effects of semantic relative to perceptual processing (e.g., Srinivas & Roediger, 1990). Therefore, other types of dissociations must be used for conceptual implicit tests. That is, the retrieval intentionality criterion can still be used, but other variables must be manipulated to show dissociations between explicit and implicit forms of the test (e.g., see work by Hashtroudi et al., 1988).

Process Dissociation Procedure

A third strategy of separating intentional from incidental retrieval has been proposed by Jacoby (1991). He argued that attempts to isolate pure types of processing (incidental or automatic processing on the one hand, and intentional or consciously controlled processing on the other) are unlikely to be completely successful even when questionnaires or the retrieval intentionality criterion are used. So, although implicit tests are designed and assumed oftentimes to rely on unconscious automatic processes, they are not immune to more consciously controlled processes. Similarly, and just as seriously, explicit memory tests may be affected by incidental or automatic retrieval. To address these issues Jacoby and his colleagues developed the process dissociation procedure (PDP) that incorporates a technique called the opposition method (see Jacoby, 1991, 1998; Jacoby, Toth, & Yonelinas, 1993). Here we sketch in the logic of the procedure, but the method can be a bit tricky to use; perhaps the best general user's guide to the PDP is in Jacoby (1998).

In the PDP technique as applied to implicit memory tests, participants study a set of material such as words in a list (often under several encoding conditions) and then take one of two types of tests with different retrieval instructions called inclusion and exclusion instructions. The test cues are held constant (e.g., the same word stems might be presented on both the inclusion and exclusion test). Consider again a word-stem completion test (see Jacoby et al., 1993 for an experiment that used this procedure). After studying a long list of words such as *mercy* under various encoding conditions, participants are given the stems of words, such as mer¬, that could be completed with either a studied word on the previous list (e.g., *mercy*) or a nonstudied word (e.g., *merit*). On a typical cued recall test, people would be given a cue and asked to use the cue to remember the studied word. Here, as in all explicit memory tests, correct recall of the item could be achieved through either intentional recollection of the study episode or a more automatic process in which the item pops to mind and is then recognized. The inclusion test instructions are similar to those in a typical explicit memory task in that participants are asked to respond to the cue with an item from the study list; however, if they cannot remember the item, they are instructed to guess, so the test includes the product of intentional recollection and, failing that, incidental or automatic priming resulting from familiarity. On an exclusion test, participants are told to respond to the word stem without using a word from the studied list. So, if *mercy* comes to mind and they recognize it from the list, they should not respond with *mercy* but they must respond with *merit* or *merchant* or some other word beginning with *mer*. Now participants' use of conscious recollection opposes their responding with a list word; if they respond with the list word (above the nonstudied base rate of producing the list word when it has not been recently studied) then this effect is due to incidental retrieval that is unopposed by recollection.

The logic of the PDP is that inclusion performance is driven by both intentional and incidental (or automatic) retrieval, whereas exclusion performance is produced only by incidental (automatic) retrieval. If we assume that these processes are independent, then an estimate of intentional recollection in a particular condition or a particular participant can be derived by subtracting performance under the exclusion instruction from performance under inclusion instruction. That is, if Inclusion performance = Probability of retrieval using intentional recollection + Probability of recollection using automatic retrieval, whereas Exclusion performance = Probability of recollection using automatic retrieval, then the difference between the two reflects the influence of intentional recollection.

Probability of recall in the exclusion condition represents a measure of performance that is driven by incidental or automatic processes. This automatic use of memory is analogous to implicit memory (in that it is the information that leaks into memory and affects behavior without intention or awareness). However, several researchers (Richardson-Klavehn & Gardiner, 1996; Richardson-Klavehn et al., 1994) have suggested that the automatic form of memory measured by the PDP may not be completely analogous to priming on implicit memory tests because the PDP assumes that forms of memory that are automatic are also unconscious. Indeed, there is some research suggesting that this may not be true and that, as discussed earlier, there may be involuntary conscious recollection such as when an item is retrieved automatically but then the person recognizes it as having been from the recent study experience. The point is that volition, or intention to retrieve, can be a separate and orthogonal construct from conscious awareness. Although this theoretical discussion is somewhat of an aside, the problem does cut to the core of measuring the construct of implicit memory, which is retrieval affected by recent experience occurring without intention or volition.

ADDITIONAL TIPS FOR CONDUCTING IMPLICIT MEMORY EXPERIMENTS

In this last section we return to a few issues that are relevant to designing and carrying out experiments on implicit memory. We have mentioned these earlier, in passing, but deal with them more fully in this section. These are the related issues of norming materials to determine appropriate base-rate levels of performance and pretesting experimental conditions to ensure the existence of priming in the procedures.

Preexperimental norming of material is critical to ensuring sensitive tests of priming. Ideally, it is best to arrange conditions so that performance in the baseline condition is in the range of 25% to 35%. In other words, for a word-fragment completion test, the baseline completion rate should be fairly low so that one can obtain priming of various magnitudes (if it is possible). If the base-rate completion level is too high, it is difficult to obtain priming because performance may be near the ceiling of the scale. Conversely, base-rate levels that are too low might mean that the tasks created are too difficult and that one could not show priming because of floor effects. Baseline issues must be considered in all implicit memory tests. For example, in a task such as category exemplar production, one must be careful to choose exemplars that are not the most common or uncommon items in the category (don't pick *robin* or *kiwi* in the *birds* category because of the danger of ceiling and floor effects, respectively). As these examples demonstrate, norming of test materials is a critical first step in conducting an implicit memory study. Unfortunately, no sets of norms exist for many different implicit memory tests, although authors of many articles do supply their materials for those studies (but rarely do they supply the baseline completion rates for each possible item).

Another helpful step is to try to discern the approximate amount of priming that can be expected from different tests before one conducts an experiment. Prior pilot testing can help answer this question and then researchers can tinker with materials or procedures if they believe that problems exist. In general, perceptual implicit memory tests such as word fragment completion show priming rates of about 20% to 40%. If you obtain priming levels much higher than that, you may want to check whether your findings may have been compromised by explicit memory performance. Priming on conceptual implicit tests is generally much lower—around 5% to 20%. For this reason, it can be much more difficult to (a) obtain priming and (b) obtain differences in priming across experimental conditions with conceptual implicit memory tests.

Another practical issue to keep in mind when designing a study is the average priming duration for the task you want to use. The average priming duration is important to know to help you decide on an appropriate test delay. The duration of priming for perceptual tests may be more robust than for conceptual tests. Priming on perceptual tasks can be very long-lasting, with some studies showing evidence of priming for days (Jacoby, 1983a; Tulving et al., 1982) or weeks (Komatsu & Ohta, 1984; Sloman, Hayman, Ohta, Law, & Tulving, 1988), and evidence for long-lasting perceptual priming is even found in amnesic patients (Cave & Squire, 1992). On the other hand, priming, as measured by conceptual tests, has been shown to decrease sharply within an hour and a half (Hamann, 1990; but see Goshen-Gottstein & Kempinsky, 2001, for evidence of some conceptual priming for up to three weeks). However, most typical experiments with college students have used relatively immediate tests, so this consideration has not played too much of a role.

CONCLUSION

Conducting implicit memory research can be quite tricky, although the recommendations provided in this chapter can help researchers begin. Our other advice is to obtain some of the major articles that address the technique(s) you wish to use and carefully read the methods sections of those papers. However, watch for the fact that the field can change in its research practices as techniques improve on the basis of past work. For example, Jacoby and Dallas (1981) provided a classic demonstration using the implicit test of word identification, Tulving et al. (1982) first used the word fragment completion test, and Jacoby (1991) launched the process dissociation procedure. However, any of these researchers would probably make somewhat different choices in designing these experiments today, as the field has progressed. Therefore, it is good to model your new efforts with excellent recent examples from the literature on these techniques, which might show you how experimental procedures have changed and improved over time.

REFERENCES

Blaxton, T. A. (1989). Investigating dissociations among memory measures: Support for a transfer-appropriate processing framework. *Journal of Experimental Psychology: Learning, Memory, and Cognition, 15,* 657–668.

Bowers, J. S., & Schacter, D. L. (1990). Implicit memory and test awareness. *Journal of Experimental Psychology: Learning, Memory, and Cognition, 16,* 404–416.

Cave, C. B., & Squire, L. R. (1992). Intact and long-lasting repetition priming in amnesia. *Journal of Experimental Psychology: Learning, Memory, and Cognition, 18,* 509–520.

Challis, B. H., & Roediger, H. L. (1993). The effect of proportion overlap and repeated testing on primed word fragment completion. *Canadian Journal of Experimental Psychology, 47,* 113–123.

Duchek, J. M., & Neely, J. H. (1989). A dissociative word-frequency levels-of-processing interaction in episodic recognition and lexical decision tasks. *Memory & Cognition, 17,* 148–166.

Geraci, L., & Rajaram, S. (2002). The orthographic distinctiveness effect on direct and indirect tests of memory: Delineating the awareness and processing requirements. *Journal of Memory and Language, 47,* 273–291.

Goshen-Gottstein, Y., & Kempinsky, H. (2001). Probing memory with conceptual cues at multiple retention intervals: A comparison of forgetting rates on implicit and explicit tests. *Psychonomic Bulletin & Review, 8,* 139–146.

Graf, P., & Mandler, G. (1984). Activation makes words more accessible, but not necessarily more retrievable. *Journal of Verbal Learning and Verbal Behavior, 23,* 553–568.

Hamann, S. B. (1990). Level-of-processing effects in conceptually driven implicit tasks. *Journal of Experimental Psychology: Learning, Memory, and Cognition, 16,* 970–977.

Hamann, S. B., & Squire, L. R. (1997). Intact perceptual memory in the absence of conscious memory. *Behavioral Neuroscience, 111,* 850–854.

Hasher, L., Goldstein, D., & Toppino, T. (1977). Frequency and the conference of retrieval validity. *Journal of Verbal Learning and Verbal Behavior, 16,* 107–112.

Hashtroudi, S., Ferguson, S. A., Rappold, V. A., & Chrosniak, L. D. (1988). Data-driven and conceptually driven processes in partial-word identification and recognition. *Journal of Experimental Psychology: Learning, Memory, and Cognition, 14*, 749–757.

Jacoby, L. L. (1983a). Perceptual enhancement: Persistent effects of an experience. *Journal of Experimental Psychology: Learning, Memory, and Cognition, 9*, 21–38.

Jacoby, L. L. (1983b). Remembering the data: Analyzing interactive processes of reading. *Journal of Verbal Learning and Verbal Behavior, 22*, 485–508.

Jacoby, L. L. (1984). Incidental versus intentional retrieval: Remembering and awareness as separate issues. In L. R. Squire & N. Butters (Eds.), *Neuropsychology of memory* (pp. 145–156). New York: Guilford Press.

Jacoby, L. L. (1991). A process dissociation framework: Separating automatic from intentional uses of memory. *Journal of Memory and Language, 30*, 513–541.

Jacoby, L. L. (1998). Invariance in automatic influences of memory: Toward a user's guide for the process-dissociation procedure. *Journal of Experimental Psychology: Learning, Memory, and Cognition, 24*, 3–26.

Jacoby, L. L., & Dallas, M. (1981). On the relationship between autobiographical memory and perceptual learning. *Journal of Experimental Psychology: General, 110*, 306–340.

Jacoby, L. L., & Kelley, C. M. (1987). Unconscious influences of memory for a prior event. *Personality and Social Psychology Bulletin, 13*, 314–336.

Jacoby, L. L., Toth, J. P., & Yonelinas, A. P. (1993). Separating conscious and unconscious influences of memory: Measuring recollection. *Journal of Experimental Psychology: General, 122*, 139–154.

Jacoby, L. L., & Witherspoon, D. (1982). Remembering without awareness. *Canadian Journal of Psychology, 36*, 300–324.

Johnston, W. A., Hawley, K. J., & Elliot, J. M. (1991). Contribution of perceptual fluency to recognition judgments. *Journal of Experimental Psychology: Learning, Memory, and Cognition, 17*, 210–223.

Kelley, C. M. (1999). Subjective experience as basis of "objective" judgments: Effects of past experience on judgments of difficulty. In D. Gopher & A. Koriat (Eds.), *Attention and performance XVII* (pp. 515–536). Cambridge, MA: MIT Press.

Kelley, C. M., & Jacoby, L. L. (1996). Adult egocentrism: Subjective experience versus analytic bases for judgment. *Journal of Memory and Language, 35*, 157–175.

Komatsu, S., & Ohta, N. (1984). Priming effects in word-fragments completion for short- and long-term retention intervals. *Japanese Psychological Research, 26*, 194–200.

McDermott, K. B., & Roediger, H. L. (1994). Effects of imagery on perceptual implicit memory tests. *Journal of Experimental Psychology: Learning, Memory, and Cognition, 20*, 1379–1390.

Milner, B. (1966). Amnesia following operation on the temporal lobes. In C. Whitty & O. Zangwill (Eds.), *Amnesia* (pp. 109–133). London: Butterworth.

Mitchell, D. B., & Brown, A. S. (1988). Persistent repetition priming in picture naming and its dissociation from recognition memory. *Journal of Experimental Psychology: Learning, Memory, and Cognition, 14,* 213–222.

Nelson, D. L., Schreiber, T. A., & Holley, P. E. (1992). The retrieval of controlled and automatic aspects of meaning on direct and indirect tests. *Memory & Cognition, 20,* 671–684.

Pilotti, M., Bergman, E. T., Gallo, D. A., Sommers, M., & Roediger, H. L. (2000). Direct comparison of auditory implicit memory tests. *Psychonomic Bulletin & Review, 7,* 347–353.

Pilotti, M., Gallo, D. A., & Roediger, H. L. (2000). Effects of hearing words, imaging hearing words and reading on auditory implicit and explicit memory tests. *Memory & Cognition, 28,* 1406–1418.

Rajaram, S., & Roediger, H. L., III. (1993). Direct comparison of four implicit memory tests. *Journal of Experimental Psychology: Learning, Memory, and Cognition, 19,* 765–776.

Richardson-Klavehn, A., & Gardiner, J. M. (1996). Cross-modality priming in stem completion reflects conscious memory, but not voluntary memory. *Psychonomic Bulletin & Review, 3,* 238–249.

Richardson-Klavehn, A., Gardiner, J. M., & Java, R. I. (1994). Involuntary conscious memory and the method of opposition. *Memory, 2,* 1–29.

Richardson-Klavehn, A., Lee, M. G., Joubran, R., & Bjork, R. A. (1994). Intention and awareness in perceptual identification priming. *Memory & Cognition, 22,* 293–312.

Roediger, H. L. (1990). Implicit memory: retention without remembering. *American Psychologist, 45,* 1043–1056.

Roediger, H. L. (2003). Reconsidering implicit memory. In J. S. Bowers & C. Marsolek (Eds.), *Rethinking implicit memory* (pp. 3–18). Oxford, England: Oxford University Press.

Roediger, H. L., & Blaxton, T. A. (1987). Effects of varying modality, surface features, and retention interval on priming in word-fragment completion. *Memory & Cognition, 15,* 379–388.

Roediger, H. L., III, & McDermott, K. B. (1993). Implicit memory in normal human subjects. In F. Boller & J. Grafman (Series Eds.) & H. Spinnler & F. Boller (Vol. Eds.), *Handbook of neuropsychology: Vol. 8. Memory, dementia, perception of time, music and faces* (pp. 63–131). Amsterdam: Elsevier.

Roediger, H. L., Weldon, M. S., & Challis, B. H. (1989). Explaining dissociations between implicit and explicit measures of retention: A processing account. In H. L. Roediger & F. I. M. Craik (Eds.), *Varieties of memory and consciousness: Essays in honor of Endel Tulving* (pp. 3–41). Hillsdale, NJ: Erlbaum.

Roediger, H. L., Weldon, M. S., Stadler, M. L., & Riegler, G. L. (1992). Direct comparison of two implicit memory tests: Word fragment and word stem completion. *Journal of Experimental Psychology: Learning, Memory, and Cognition, 18,* 1251–1269.

Schacter, D. L. (1987). Implicit memory: History and current status. *Journal of Experimental Psychology: Learning, Memory, and Cognition, 13*, 501–518.

Schacter, D. L., Bowers, J., & Booker, J. (1989). Intention, awareness, and implicit memory: The retrieval intentionality criterion. In S. Lewandowsky, J. C. Dunn, & K. Kirsner (Eds.), *Implicit memory: Theoretical Issues* (pp. 47–65). Hillsdale, NJ: Erlbaum.

Schacter, D. L., & Church, B. A. (1992). Auditory priming: Implicit and explicit memory for words and voices. *Journal of Experimental Psychology: Learning, Memory, and Cognition, 18*, 915–930.

Schacter, D. L., Cooper, L. A., & Delaney, S. M. (1990). Implicit memory for unfamiliar objects depends on access to structural descriptions. *Journal of Experimental Psychology: General, 119*, 5–24.

Shimamura, A. P., & Squire, L. R. (1984). Paired-associate learning and priming effects in amnesia: A neuropsychological study. *Journal of Experimental Psychology: General, 113*, 556–570

Sloman, S. A., Hayman, C. G., Ohta, N., Law, J., & Tulving, E. (1988). Forgetting in primed fragment completion. *Journal of Experimental Psychology: Learning, Memory, and Cognition, 14*, 223–239.

Snodgrass, J. G., & Corwin, J. (1988). Perceptual identification thresholds for 150 fragmented pictures from the Snodgrass and Vanderwart picture set. *Perceptual & Motor Skills, 67*, 3–36.

Snodgrass, J. G., Smith, B., Feenan, K., & Corwin, J. (1987). Fragmenting pictures on the Apple Macintosh computer for experimental and clinical applications. *Behavior Research Methods, Instruments, & Computers, 19*, 270–274.

Squire, L. R., Shimamura, A. P., & Graf, P. (1987). Strength and duration of priming effects in normal subjects and amnesic patients. *Neuropsychology, 25*, 195–210.

Srinivas, K. (1993). Perceptual specificity in nonverbal priming. *Journal of Experimental Psychology: Learning, Memory, and Cognition, 19*, 582–602.

Srinivas, K., & Roediger, H. L., III. (1990). Classifying implicit memory tests: Category association and anagram solution. *Journal of Memory and Language, 29*, 389–412.

Stark, C. E. L., & Squire, L. R. (2000). Recognition memory and familiarity judgments in severe amnesia: No evidence for a contribution of repetition priming. *Behavioral Neuroscience, 114*, 459–467.

Tenpenny, P. L., & Shoben, E. J. (1992). Component processes and the utility of the conceptually-driven/data-driven distinction. *Journal of Experimental Psychology: Learning, Memory, and Cognition, 18*, 25–42.

Toth, J. P. (2000). Nonconscious forms of human memory. In E. Tulving & F. I. M. Craik (Eds.), *The Oxford handbook of memory* (pp. 245–266). New York: Oxford University Press.

Tulving, E. (1989). Memory: Performance, knowledge, and experience. *European Journal of Cognitive Psychology, 1*, 3–26.

Tulving, E., & Schacter, D. L. (1990). Priming and human memory systems. *Science, 247*, 301–306.

Tulving, E., Schacter, D. L., & Stark, H. A. (1982). Priming effects in word-fragment completion are independent of recognition memory. *Journal of Experimental Psychology: Human Learning and Memory, 8*, 336–342.

Warrington, E. K., & Weiskrantz, L. (1970). Amnesic syndrome: Consolidation or retrieval? *Nature, 228*, 628–630.

Weldon, M. S. (1993). The time course of perceptual and conceptual contributions to word fragment completion priming. *Journal of Experimental Psychology: Learning, Memory, and Cognition, 19*, 1010–1023.

Weldon, M. S., & Roediger, H. L., III. (1987). Altering retrieval demands reverses the picture superiority effect. *Memory & Cognition, 15*, 269–280.

Weldon, M. S., & Roediger, H. L., Beitel, D. A., & Johnston, T. R. (1995). Perceptual and conceptual processes in implicit and explicit tests with picture fragment and word fragment cues. *Journal of Memory and Language, 34*, 268–285.

Witherspoon, D., & Allan, L. G. (1985). The effect of a prior presentation on temporal judgments in a perceptual identification task. *Memory & Cognition, 13*, 101–111.

9

IMPLICIT MEMORY TASKS IN CLINICAL RESEARCH

NADER AMIR AND AMY SELVIG

Roediger and Geraci (see chap. 8, this volume) provided guidelines for conducting research involving implicit memory. In this chapter we focus on the utility of implicit memory research in understanding various clinical populations. Such investigations may help identify the etiology of various clinical conditions as well as influence the development of appropriate treatments for such conditions. For example, the observation that implicit memory is intact in patients with Korsakoff's syndrome stimulated interest in determining the extent to which memory processes may be spared in this population. This research suggests that Korsakoff's syndrome appears to affect not the memory in general but some aspects of memory process (i.e., explicit, effortful processes) instead. These observations prompted a better understanding of the disease and may result in better treatments for patients. For example, clinicians may take advantage of patients' intact implicit memory by repeatedly exposing them to important information and procedures (e.g., De Vreese, Neri, Fioravanti, Belloi, & Zanetti, 2001).

We would like to thank Courtney Beard for her help in the preparation of this chapter. The preparation of this chapter was supported by a faculty development grant from the Institute for Behavioral Research at University of Georgia awarded to Nader Amir.

CONCEPTUAL ISSUES

Intact Versus Enhanced Implicit Memory

The discovery of intact implicit memory in Korsakoff's patients was an important step in understanding the neuropsychology of this disorder. Thus, the crucial finding in this area was the presence of intact implicit memory in a population that should have shown impaired memory. However, researchers have also examined the hypothesis that some clinical conditions may be associated with enhanced implicit memory for certain types of material. Specifically, there is some indication that compared with nonpatients, individuals with depression and anxiety may have enhanced implicit memory for material relevant to their condition. These findings run counter to the traditional view of psychopathology that disorder means diminished abilities. In this chapter we discuss both types of implicit memory alterations: intact implicit memory when explicit memory is impaired, and enhanced implicit memory compared with normal functioning.

Conceptual Versus Perceptual Tasks

Some clinical conditions involve alterations in implicit memory when materials are related to the clinical condition (e.g., negative words in depression). Other clinical conditions involve implicit memory changes regardless of the content of the material. This distinction is captured by the dissociation between conceptual and perceptual implicit memory tasks (Roediger & McDermott, 1992). Perceptual implicit memory tasks are strongly influenced by orthographic, perceptual aspects of the material (i.e., are data driven) rather than by their conceptual, semantic aspects (e.g., Roediger, Buckner, & McDermott, 1999; Roediger & McDermott, 1992). For example, if individuals are first exposed to words written in uppercase letters during the study phase and later shown stems in lowercase letters during the test phase, priming effects diminish (Roediger & Blaxton, 1987). On the other hand, conceptual implicit memory tasks are strongly influenced by the meaning of the study and test material. For example, generating the to-be-studied materials rather simply reading them will lead to improved performance in conceptually driven tests (Roediger, Weldon, & Challis, 1989).

Clinical investigators have focused on various tasks to elucidate the role of these two implicit memory processes in clinical populations. Clinical conditions (e.g., epilepsy) in which memory impairment is likely to affect memory for all types of materials are best tested with both perceptual and conceptual tasks. On the other hand, if memory alterations are thought to occur only when material relevant to the clinical condition is presented (e.g., depression-related words in mood disorders), then it is important to use conceptual implicit memory tasks that are sensitive to the meaning of the material (Watkins, 2002). Indeed, because of their relative insensitivity to semantics, perceptual implicit memory tasks have limited relevance for the study of automatic access to meaningful emotional memories (McNally, 1994).

An example of the former approach is a study by Billingsley, McAndrews, and Smith (2002). These researchers examined implicit and explicit memory in temporal lobe epilepsy using a perceptual implicit memory task (i.e., word identification) and a conceptual implicit memory task (i.e., missing word generation). The performance of participants with temporal lobe epilepsy did not differ from controls on either conceptual or perceptual implicit memory tasks. However, participants with temporal lobe epilepsy showed deficits in their explicit memory for the material (i.e., recall). An example of the content-sensitive approach is summarized by Watkins (2002): Implicit memory for depression-related words seems to be confined to conceptual implicit memory tasks. In summary, when clinical states are examined, it is important to choose tasks that are a sensitive measure of the mechanism thought to play a role in that particular clinical condition.

Automatic Versus Strategic Cognitive Processes

Cognitive psychologists posit that information processing occurs at different stages (e.g., Bargh, 1989; Shiffrin & Schneider, 1977). One parsimonious conceptualization divides information processing into automatic and strategic processes (Shiffrin & Schneider, 1977). Automatic processes are thought to be (a) capacity-free with respect to resources, effort, and energy; (b) unconscious, not requiring awareness; and (c) unintentional, involuntary, or obligatory (McNally, 1995). Strategic processes, on the other hand, are thought to be (a) resource limited; (b) effortful, involving conscious attention; and (c) intentional or under voluntary control. Standard definitions of implicit memory suggest that this type of memory should be automatic in the sense that it is "revealed when previous experiences facilitate performance on a task that does not require *conscious* or *intentional* recollection of those experiences" (Schacter, 1992, p. 561, italics added). However, it has been difficult to conclude that implicit memory tasks involve unconscious and unintentional recollection in healthy participants (Schacter, Bowers, & Booker, 1989). Individuals with amnesia may perform without awareness or intention by virtue of their disorder, but clinical samples without severe memory impairment (e.g., anxiety, depression) are likely to have the same level of awareness and intention as do healthy participants.

This lack of specificity of the meaning of automaticity leaves researchers who study memory-intact clinical samples with an apparent dilemma: Of what value is the study of implicit memory if it does not tap into fully automatic processes? The solution rests in the definition of automaticity used in studies of these clinical states. The processes involved in some clinical states (e.g., anxiety, depression, eating disorders) may not be automatic in the sense of being outside of conscious awareness, but automatic in the sense of being involuntary (McNally, 1995). Therefore, researchers using implicit memory tasks should use paradigms that appear to reflect the particular aspects of automaticity associated with the target condition. Furthermore, most implicit memory tests involve both automatic and strategic processes (i.e., the tasks are not "process pure;" Jacoby, 1991). This realization has led some theorists to suggest that to understand the components involved in a task, one needs to adopt a process dissociation approach (Jacoby, 1991; Jacoby & Kelly, 1991; Jacoby, Toth, & Yonelinas, 1993). This approach was described by Roediger and Geraci (see chap. 8, this volume).

Definitional Difficulties in Studies of Implicit Memory

Another area where implicit memory paradigms have been questioned is in the role of intentionality and awareness in the clinical state because various investigators have used different definitions of implicit memory. In a recent review of the role of intentionality and awareness in implicit memory paradigms, Butler and Berry (2001) concluded that there is very little evidence that implicit memory paradigms involve nonconscious processes. Although conscious processes may be involved in conceptual implicit memory tasks, in clinical states these processes may be unintentional. Thus, the distinction between unintentional conscious and unintentional unconscious implicit memory may be of paramount importance to clinical psychologists. Furthermore, this distinction may be related to the clinical presentation. For example, in anxiety, implicit memory bias may be involved as an unintentional yet conscious memory for threat-relevant information. Indeed, individuals with anxiety often report that they do not try to recall information about threat relevant encounters, but that these thoughts come to mind without their intentional retrieval. Such an unintentional, yet conscious, retrieval of threat-relevant information may be the hallmark of anxiety.

Summary

The issues raised above should be taken into consideration when implicit memory is examined in clinical conditions. Below we provide a review of some of the studies that use implicit memory to examine clinical populations. To aid this review we propose a conceptual framework suggested by McNally (1996). That is, some conditions involve general implicit memory functioning whereas others involve implicit memory for certain content material. The former studies are examples of content-independent implicit memory. The latter studies are examples of content-sensitive implicit memory.

STUDIES OF CONTENT-INDEPENDENT IMPLICIT MEMORY

Alzheimer's Disease

Research on implicit memory in Alzheimer's disease (AD) has produced mixed results (for reviews, see Fleischman et al., 1995; Meiran & Jelicic, 1995). Several researchers have attempted to explain the mixed results by applying the distinction between conceptual and perceptual implicit memory processes. For example, most studies of perceptual implicit memory support the hypothesis that this implicit memory process is preserved in AD. Participants with AD have repeatedly shown preserved implicit memory in studies that use word identification (e.g., Koivisto, Portin, Rinne, 1996; Verfaellie, Keane, & Johnson, 2000), word pronunciation (e.g., Balota & Duchek, 1991; Ober, Shenaut, Jagust, & Stillman, 1991), picture identification (e.g., Gabrieli, Vaidya, & Stone, 1999; Park et al., 1998), and lexical decision (Balota & Ferraro, 1996; Ober et al., 1991).

Studies of conceptual implicit memory in AD have produced mixed results (for reviews see Fleischman et al., 1995; Lazzara, Yonelinas, & Ober, 2001; Maki, 1995; Meiran & Jelicic, 1995). For example, when using the free association task as a measure of implicit memory in AD, Carlesimo, Fadda, Marfia, and Caltagirone (1995) found that participants with AD were less likely to generate items that were presented in an earlier study phase than were participants in the control group. On the other hand, Vaidya, Gabrieli, and Monti (1999) failed to find this effect. Similar inconsistencies exist in studies that use the exemplar generation task (e.g., Maki & Knopman, 1996; Vaidya et al., 1999).

At least two theories have been proposed to account for the discrepant results. Maki and Knopman (1996) used the transfer appropriate processing (TAP) approach (Morris, Bransford, & Franks, 1977; Roediger & McDermott, 1993) to explain the discrepant results. According to the TAP, the similarity between processes used at study and at test determine performance on the test. Therefore, in AD, studies that have used similar processes at encoding and test have produced priming scores similar to those achieved by controls in the AD group. On the other hand, studies that have not matched processes at encoding and test have shown a priming deficit in AD. Maki and Knopman (1996) used this account to explain the results of both perceptual and conceptual implicit memory tests in AD. Fleischman et al. (1999) suggested that the mixed results of studies of implicit memory in AD may result from methodological differences across studies, as well as the composition of the control group used. These researchers stressed the importance of age-matched control groups and considerations of dementia ratings when implicit memory in this population is studied.

In summary, individuals with AD appear to have deficits in conceptual but not perceptual implicit memory when compared with non-AD individuals. However, difficulties remain in interpreting the results because the effects are greatly influenced by methodological differences, as well as the composition of the control group, across studies.

Amnesia

Amnesia is characterized by an inability to remember new episodes and facts accompanied by intact performance in other cognitive domains (Squire, 1992a). Implicit memory has generally been regarded as one domain that is intact in amnesia. However, it is not clear whether observed memory deficits in this disorder are associated with deficits in conscious recollection (for reviews, see Cohen & Eichenbaum, 1993; Squire, 1992a, 1992b) or deficits in encoding (e.g., Goshen-Gottstein, Moscovitch, & Melo, 2000). Studies of implicit memory in amnesia may provide a methodology for examining the above distinction. To this end, researchers have compared implicit memory for preamnesia information (previously encoded information) with implicit memory for novel information. A recent meta-analysis of studies of implicit memory in amnesia concluded that participants with amnesia perform similarly to those without amnesia on implicit memory tests for familiar information. However, comparison groups perform better than do amnesia groups on implicit memory tests for novel information (Gooding, Mayes, & van Eijk, 2000). Thus, amnesia may be associated with diminished ability to encode new information in implicit memory tests as well as explicit memory tests.

Schizophrenia

Although individuals with schizophrenia experience many symptoms congruent with cognitive impairment (e.g., disordered speech), evidence suggests that implicit memory may be intact in this population (for a review see Linscott & Knight, 2001). For example, individuals with schizophrenia perform at levels similar to those of controls in repetition priming (e.g., Gras-Vincendon et al., 1994), semantic priming (e.g., Stirling, Hellewell, & Hewitt, 1997), lexical priming (Schmand, Kop, Kuipers, & Bosveld, 1992), biased spelling of homophones (e.g., Clare, McKenna, Mortimer, & Baddeley, 1993), and word association (Bazin & Perruchet, 1996).

Researchers have also used Jacoby's (Jacoby, 1991; Jacoby & Kelley, 1991; Jacoby et al., 1993; Toth, Reingold, & Jacoby, 1994) process dissociation approach to examine the contributions of conscious and unconscious processes to intact priming in schizophrenia. For example, Kazes et al. (1999) found that participants with schizophrenia showed lower contribution of conscious processes in their priming performance than did controls. However, the contribution of nonconscious processes to priming was similar in the schizophrenia and the control groups. Linscott and Knight (2001) also

used a process dissociation approach to examine implicit memory in schizophrenia. These researchers found that compared with controls, individuals
with schizophrenia may show an enhanced contribution of nonconscious
processes to priming.

In summary, individuals with schizophrenia appear to have intact implicit memory and diminished explicit memory. There is also some evidence
that when the influences of nonconscious processes are taken into account,
individuals with schizophrenia may in fact have better implicit memory than
do individuals without schizophrenia.

Other Studies of Content-Independent Implicit Memory

Researchers have also used content-independent implicit memory to
examine other clinical conditions. For example, Maki, Bylsma, and Brandt
(2000) examined implicit memory (rhyme and category exemplar generation) and explicit memory (recognition of previously heard words) in individuals with Huntington's disease (HD). These researchers reported that HD
patients showed intact implicit memory and impaired explicit memory.
Scarrabelotti and Carroll (1998) examined implicit (stem completion) and
explicit (recall) memory in individuals with multiple sclerosis (MS). Similar
to the Maki et al. (2000) study, these researchers found intact implicit memory
in the MS patients and a marked impairment in explicit memory. These
researchers applied Jacoby's process dissociation approach and concluded that
both conscious and nonconscious processes contributed to the intact implicit memory performance in the MS group.

STUDIES OF CONTENT-DEPENDENT IMPLICIT MEMORY

Anxiety

The role of implicit memory bias for threat-relevant information in
anxiety has been the topic of much research (for a recent review see, Coles &
Heimberg, 2002). Individuals with different anxiety disorders share many
features including avoidance of feared consequence and physiological symptoms of anxiety. Despite these similarities, there are clear distinctions among
them (e.g., object of fear, severity, comorbidity pattern, age of onset). These
distinctions may contribute to differences in implicit memory among the
anxiety disordered populations.

*Investigation of Implicit Memory in Anxiety With the Word Stem
Completion Task*

In the word-stem completion task, participants study a list of words
(e.g., *apple*) during encoding. During the test phase participants see word

stems (app-) or word fragments (a_p_e) and are asked to complete the fragment with the first word that comes to mind. Implicit memory is revealed if a higher percentage of the word fragments are completed with studied words than with the nonstudied words.

Using this paradigm, Cloitre, Shear, Cancienne, and Zeitlin (1994) found that individuals with panic disorder (PD) completed more stems with studied threat words than did clinicians or nonanxious controls (NACs). However, three subsequent investigations failed to find an implicit memory bias for threat words in PD patients with the word stem completion task (Banos, Medina, & Pascual, 2001; Lundh, Czyzykow, & Öst, 1997; Rapee, 1994).

Two studies examined implicit memory bias for threat in individuals with social phobia (SP) with the stem completion task (Lundh & Öst, 1997; Rapee, McCallum, Melville, Ravenscroft, & Rodney, 1994). Both studies failed to find evidence for implicit memory bias for threat in social anxiety. However, in the Lundh and Öst study individuals with nongeneralized SP (i.e., having anxiety symptoms in a specific type of social situation such as public speaking) did show larger implicit memory for social threat words than did controls or individuals with generalized SP (i.e., having anxiety symptoms in a variety of social situations).

Two studies examined implicit memory bias for threat in individuals with generalized anxiety disorder (GAD) with the stem completion task (Mathews, Mogg, Kentish, & Eysenck, 1995; Mathews, Mogg, May, & Eysenck, 1989). In the first study (Mathews et al., 1989) individuals with GAD showed an implicit memory bias for threat-relevant information but controls did not. In the second study (Mathews et al., 1995) there was no evidence of an implicit memory bias for threat in the GAD groups. However, the target words in the latter study had only been studied orthographically (participants counted the number of *e*'s in each word). In summary, there is little consistent evidence for an implicit memory bias in anxiety with the stem completion task.

Investigation of Implicit Memory in Anxiety With the Perceptual Identification Task

In the perceptual identification task, participants are first presented with a study list. During the test phase they are presented with the studied words intermixed with novel words for a very brief duration (e.g., 50 ms). Participants are asked try to identify the word. Mathews et al. (1989) used the perceptual identification task to assess implicit memory in individuals with GAD. These researchers found that GAD participants identified more studied threat words than novel threat words compared with controls. MacLeod and McLaughlin (1995) replicated these findings. McNally and Amir (1996) used a perceptual identification task to compare traumatized Vietnam veterans with and without posttraumatic stress disorder (PTSD).

Although both groups exhibited implicit memory by accurately identifying more old words than new words, this priming effect was not enhanced for trauma words in the PTSD group. Finally, Lundh, Wikstrom, Westerlund, and Öst (1999) reported that PD patients identified more panic-related words than did controls on a perceptual identification task, but that groups did not differ with respect to interpersonal threat or neutral words. In summary, with the exception of PTSD, there is reliable evidence for an implicit memory bias for threat with the perceptual identification task.

Investigation of Implicit Memory in Anxiety With the Lexical Decision Task

In the lexical decision task, participants are asked to decide whether a series of briefly presented letters form a word. Studied words are identified more quickly and more accurately than are novel words, which reveals implicit memory for prior presentation of the words. Bradley, Mogg, and Williams (1995) examined implicit memory for emotion-congruent information in GAD participants, depressed participants, and controls with the lexical decision paradigm. During the encoding phase, participants saw a block of primes and rated each word for how often they would use the word. They then completed a lexical decision task. GAD patients did not show preferential priming for anxiety-related words. Individuals with depression, however, did show an implicit memory bias for negative words (see section on depression below).

Investigation of Implicit Memory in Anxiety With the Noise-Judgment Task

In the noise-judgment paradigm (Jacoby, Allan, Collins, & Larwill, 1988) participants first hear a set of sentences and repeat them aloud. Next, participants hear these old sentences intermixed with a new set of sentences, all presented against a background of noise. Participants are asked to repeat the sentences and to rate the volume of the background noise. Jacoby et al. (1988) found that noise accompanying old sentences was rated as less loud than noise accompanying new sentences. This differential noise rating for the old and new sentences was interpreted as reflecting implicit memory for the former. Foa, Amir, Gershuny, Molnar, and Kozak (1997) used Jacoby et al.'s (1988) noise-judgment paradigm to investigate implicit memory in individuals with obsessive–compulsive disorder (OCD). These authors did not find any evidence for an implicit memory bias for threat in OCD.

Using a hybrid version of Jacoby et al.'s (1988) noise-judgment paradigm with Schacter and Church's (1995) modification, Amir, McNally, Riemann, and Clements (1996) examined implicit memory bias for threat-relevant sentences in PD individuals and NACs. Results revealed that under the low volume of noise, individuals with PD demonstrated an implicit memory bias for threat information whereas NACs did not. In a follow-up and extension of the above study, Amir, McNally, and Wiegratz (1996) examined implicit memory bias for threat in Vietnam combat veterans with and without PTSD. Individuals with PTSD rated the noise accompanying old threat-relevant sentences as less loud than noise accompanying old non-threat-relevant sentences. In a third experiment using the same paradigm, Amir, Foa, and Coles (2000) employed the noise-judgment task to investigate implicit memory bias for threat in individuals with generalized social phobia (GSP) and NACs. Results revealed that the GSP group, but not the control group, demonstrated an implicit memory bias for social threat sentences.

Investigators have also used the clarity-rating task to examine implicit memory. The clarity-rating task is modeled after the noise-judgment paradigm introduced by Jacoby et al. (1988) and involves an encoding and a test phase. During the encoding phase, participants view brief video clips that involve an actor or actress approaching the camera and commenting on some aspect of the viewer's action, physical appearance, or belongings. Half of these videos are positive (e.g., "I really like your shoes") and half are negative (e.g., "That is a horrible haircut"). During the test phase participants view another set of videos, half of which they have viewed during encoding (*old*) and half of which they had not seen earlier (*new*). Implicit memory for old videos is revealed if these old videos are rated as more clear (i.e., focused, crisp) than new videos on a five-point Likert scale. Amir, Briks, Bower, and Freshman (2003) employed a video clarity judgment task to investigate implicit memory for threat in socially anxious individuals, dysphoric individuals, and nonanxious controls. Socially anxious individuals showed a larger implicit memory effect for negative videos than did nonanxious and dysphoric controls.

In summary, the results of studies that use the noise/clarity-rating task as a measure of implicit memory converge to suggest that anxious individuals may show a threat-related bias in this task. However, as with most other implicit memory measures, this measure of implicit memory has a number of significant advantages and disadvantages. For example, researchers have used sentences, videos, and pictures in variations of this task. As such, this task provides some degree of flexibility for use with different clinical populations (e.g., children with anxiety) who may have difficulty conducting other implicit memory tasks (e.g., stem completion). However, the degree of variation in clarity (or *fuzziness*) introduced into the materials seems to be crucial. Some studies have manipulated this variable by presenting sentences under low, medium, or high white noise. The variation in clarity was used to provide the participants with a varied range of background noise for the judgment task. However, in at least two of the studies implicit memory effects were observed only at certain noise levels. Other studies have used this task without varying the objective level of clarity during test. It is not clear whether either method is preferable, and extensive piloting may be necessary when new materials are used.

Summary

The results of studies examining implicit memory bias in anxiety are mixed. There are at least three reasons for these inconsistencies: (a) type of test used, (b) anxious population studied, and (c) the interaction of the two factors. Thus, it behooves researchers to pay attention to particular procedures used at encoding (e.g., orthographic vs. semantic), particular procedures used at test (e.g., word generation, word identification, or clarity rating), and the population under study. For example, most studies that used word stem completion did not find any priming effects. However, perceptual identification task and clarity-rating task have resulted in more consistent findings. Thus, when the role of implicit memory in anxious populations is examined, the latter tasks may be more appropriate.

Depression

A number of researchers have examined the role of implicit memory in depression (for a review see Watkins, 2002). Watkins (2002) suggested that the role of implicit memory bias in depression may be more important than that of explicit memory, noting that "it could be argued that the way this bias impacts the behavior and experience of depressed individuals is more through implicit or unintentional memory than through explicit processes" (p. 383). According to this perspective some of the hallmarks of depression, such as overgeneralization, could be seen as the result of tending to retrieve more unpleasant events, which results in inaccurate negative generalizations about life because of the implicit memory for these negative events.

Researchers have examined implicit memory in depression using the stem/fragment completion task (Watkins, Matthews, Williamson, & Fuller, 1992). However, these studies failed to find any evidence for implicit memory bias in depression. Other studies attempted to examine implicit memory with the free association task (Denny & Hunt, 1992; Watkins, Vache, Verney, & Mathews, 1996). In the free association task, participants are presented with cues and asked to generate related words. Implicit memory is revealed when a higher rate of studied words are generated compared with nonstudied words. For example, Watkins et al. (1996) presented their participants with a set of positive, negative, and neutral target words and asked them to imagine themselves in a scene involving each word. Participants were then asked some questions about the scene (e.g., whether they were the principal character in the scene). Following a filler task, participants were administered an association task that contained association cues that were related to the target words from both studied and unstudied targets. Priming was revealed by subtracting the number of unstudied targets from the number of studied targets produced. These researchers found that depressed individuals displayed more priming for negative words than did controls. Controls, on the other hand, showed more priming for positive words than did the depressed group.

Researchers have also examined implicit memory in depression using the lexical decision task (Bradley, Mogg, & Millar, 1996; Bradley et al., 1995). Both studies showed that individuals with depression are characterized by an implicit memory bias for negative words. For example, in the Bradley et al. (1995) study, depressed individuals were on average 48 ms faster in deciding if a primed depression-related target was a word or a nonword than in making the same decision for nonprimed depression-related words. No such effects were obtained for anxiety-related, positive, or neutral words. These results were replicated in nonclinical dysphoric participants (Bradley, Mogg, & Williams, 1994; Scott, Mogg, & Bradley, 2001).

In summary, a number of researchers have demonstrated an implicit memory bias for negative information in depression. There is some indication that when tasks are sensitive to the meaning of the material (i.e., are conceptually driven), individuals with depression show implicit memory bias for depression-related words. The results are mixed when researchers use perceptually driven tasks. Watkins, Martin, and Stern (2000) investigated the boundary conditions of implicit memory bias in depression by comparing conceptual and perceptual implicit memory tasks. These investigators administered four implicit tasks to their depressed participants: two perceptual and two conceptual. The perceptual implicit memory tasks were word stem completion and word identification. The conceptual implicit memory tasks were free association and semantic definition. In the semantic definition task, participants were provided with definitions and the first letter of a word and asked to generate the word. Implicit memory is revealed when studied words are generated at a higher rate than are nonstudied words. Results revealed that during the perceptual implicit memory tests there was no evidence for implicit memory bias for negative words in the depressed group. Findings for the conceptually driven tasks were mixed. Depressed individuals showed an implicit memory bias for negative words in the semantic definition task. No such results were obtained when the free association task was examined.

Other Studies of Content-Dependent Implicit Memory

Researchers have used content-dependent implicit memory to examine other clinical conditions. Some of these studies have failed to find implicit memory differences between clinical groups and control groups (e.g., Dirk, Guido, & Paul, 1998). Other investigators have found weak results (e.g., Heffelfinger, Calamari, & Zander, 2000). For example, Dirk et al. (1998) failed to find implicit memory (word-stem completion) differences between patients with anorexia nervosa and controls for anorexia-related words. Heffelfinger et al. (2000) used the noise-judgment task to compare implicit memory for cardiac-related words in a group of cardiac patients and a matched control group. The researchers found limited support for a cardiac-specific implicit memory bias in the cardiac patients. It is difficult to interpret the results of these studies because results of a single study in any clinical condition are open to multiple interpretations. Researchers should consider at least three explanations for null results from a single study: (a) implicit memory does not play a role in that clinical condition, (b) the particular implicit memory test is not sensitive to the implicit memory processes involved in that conditions, and (c) the particular sample was somehow unique.

CONCLUSION

The above review provides a summary of some of the studies of implicit memory in various clinical populations. On the basis of the extant studies of implicit memory in clinical states, a number of conclusions seem warranted. First, it is important to examine the reliability of any finding regarding implicit memory in any clinical state. Interested researchers would be well advised to use paradigms with both theoretical and empirical support in the particular condition. A second issue is construct validity of the implicit memory index for a clinical population. That is, are the findings specific to one clinical state? Only studies that include a clinical control group can address this issue (Garber & Hollon, 1991).

The above caveats notwithstanding, examination of implicit memory in clinical states can be a useful source of information in at least three domains. The first domain is the description of the clinical phenomenon. Clinical states are often demarcated in terms of self-report of symptoms. Some researchers have questioned the utility of self-report in clinical psychology. For example, MacLeod (1993, p. 171) has suggested that self-report will never meet the "standards of scientific acceptability." According to this perspective, although the cognitive revolution provided liberation in theory (i.e., researchers were freed to postulate latent constructs), it did not suggest a parallel liberation in method. That is, postulating a latent construct (e.g., information-processing mechanism) that may mediate between stimulus and response is in keeping with the cognitive revolution. However, using dependent variables that are subjective (e.g., appraisal of anxiety symptoms as dangerous) is not in keeping with the standard for scientific acceptability. Indeed, regardless of one's level of analysis, quantification of the dependent variables should remain intact in applications of cognitive psychology to clinical states. Examination of implicit memory in clinical conditions is one such dependent variable. As such it is an informative method of describing clinical conditions and may supplant information gained from self-report to help triangulate the clinical construct under study.

The second area where the examination of the role of implicit memory in clinical disorders can be informative is the delineation of etiological factors involved in any clinical condition. The value of such studies derives from the design of the experiment, not the use of a particular cognitive mechanism (e.g., implicit memory). Nevertheless, some promising data suggest that implicit memory may be a better predictor of future anxiety symptoms than are baseline anxiety symptoms (e.g., Amir, Selvig, & Elias, 2002). Finally, the third area where the examination of the role of implicit memory in a clinical disorders can be informative is the development of treatments for these conditions (e.g., De Vreese et al., 2001). As described in the introduction, patients with AD may be repeatedly exposed to important information to help prime such concepts in their memory in the absence of explicit recollection of the event.

In this chapter we have provided a broad perspective on one concept borrowed from cognitive psychology (i.e., implicit memory) that may help elucidate the mechanisms involved in various clinical conditions. We conclude that there is great potential for this domain of information to help explain the nature of various clinical states. Furthermore, the information gained from such studies can help with the description of the disorder, identification of etiological factors in the disorder, and potential treatment for the disorder. Specifically, interventions can be designed that capitalize on memory processes spared in clinical populations or help eliminate exaggerated memory in other clinical conditions.

REFERENCES

Amir, N., Briks, J., Bower, E., & Freshman, M. (2003). Implicit memory bias for negative social interactions in social anxiety. *Cognition & Emotion, 17,* 567–583.

Amir, N., Foa, E. B., & Coles, M. E. (2000). Implicit memory bias for threat-relevant information in individuals with generalized social phobia. *Journal of Abnormal Psychology, 109,* 713–720.

Amir, N., McNally, R. J., Riemann, B. C., & Clements, C. (1996). Implicit memory bias for threat in panic disorder: Application of the "white noise" paradigm. *Behaviour Research and Therapy, 34,* 157–162.

Amir, N., McNally, R. J., & Wiegratz, P. S. (1996). Implicit memory bias for threat in posttraumatic stress disorder. *Cognitive Therapy and Research, 20,* 625–635.

Amir, N., Selvig, A., & Elias, J. (2002, November). Implicit memory bias for trauma-related information in traumatized individuals with and without PTSD. In R. Bryant (Chair), *Information processing in PTSD.* Symposium conducted at the annual meeting of the Association for the Advancement of Behavior Therapy, Reno, NV.

Balota, D. A., & Duchek, J. M. (1991). Semantic priming effects, lexical repetition effects, and contextual disambiguation effects in healthy aged individuals with senile dementia of the Alzheimer's type. *Brain and Language, 40,* 18–20.

Balota, D. A., & Ferraro, F. R. (1996). Lexical, sublexical, and implicit memory processes in healthy young and healthy older adults and in individuals with dementia of the Alzheimer type. *Neuropsychology, 10,* 82–95.

Banos, R. M., Medina, P. M., & Pascual, J. (2001). Explicit and implicit memory biases in depression and panic disorder. *Behaviour Research and Therapy, 39,* 944–948.

Bargh, J. A. (1989). Conditional automaticity: Varieties of automatic influence in social perception and cognition. In T. S. Uleman & J. A. Bargh (Eds.), *Unintended thought* (pp. 3–51). New York: Guilford Press.

Bazin, N., & Perruchet, P. (1996). Implicit and explicit associative memory in patients with schizophrenia. *Schizophrenia Research, 22,* 241–248.

Billingsley, R. L., McAndrews, M. P., & Smith, M. L. (2002). Intact perceptual and conceptual priming in temporal lobe epilepsy: Neuroanatomical and methodological implications. *Neuropsychology, 16,* 92–101.

Bradley, B. P., Mogg, K., & Millar, N. (1996). Implicit memory bias in clinical and non-clinical depression. *Behaviour Research and Therapy, 34,* 865–879.

Bradley, B. P., Mogg, K., & Williams, R. (1994). Implicit and explicit memory for emotional information in non-clinical subjects. *Behaviour Research and Therapy, 32,* 65–78.

Bradley, B. P., Mogg, K., & Williams, R. (1995). Implicit and explicit memory for emotion-congruent information in clinical depression and anxiety. *Behaviour Research and Therapy, 33,* 755–770.

Butler, L. T., & Berry, D. C. (2001). Implicit memory: Intention and awareness revisited. *TRENDS in Cognitive Science, 5,* 192–197.

Carlesimo, G. A., Fadda, L., Martia, G., & Caltagirone, C. (1995). Explicit memory and repetition priming in dementia: Evidence for a common basic mechanism underlying conscious and unconscious retrieval deficits. *Journal of Clinical and Experimental Neuropsychology, 17,* 44–57.

Clare, L., McKenna, P. J., Mortimer, A. M., & Baddeley, A. D. (1993). Memory in schizophrenia: What is impaired and what is preserved? *Neuropsychologia, 31,* 1225–1241.

Cloitre, M., Shear, M. K., Cancienne, J., & Zeitlin, S. B. (1994). Implicit and explicit memory for catastrophic associations to bodily sensations words in panic. *Cognitive Therapy and Research, 18,* 225–240.

Cohen, N. J., & Eichenbaum, H. (1993). *Memory, amnesia, and the hippocampal system.* Cambridge, MA: MIT Press.

Coles, M. E., & Heimberg, R. G. (2002). Memory biases in the anxiety disorders: Current status. *Clinical Psychology Review, 22,* 587–627.

Denny, E. R., & Hunt, R. R. (1992). Affective valence and memory in depression: Dissociation of recall and fragment completion. *Journal of Abnormal Psychology, 101,* 575–580.

De Vreese, L. P., Neri, M., Fioravanti, M., Belloi, L., & Zanetti, O. (2001). Memory rehabilitation in Alzheimer's disease: A review of progress. *International Journal of Geriatric Psychiatry, 16,* 794–809.

Dirk, H., Guido, P., & Paul, E. (1998). Implicit and explicit memory for shape, body weight, and food-related words in patients with anorexia nervosa and nondieting controls. *Journal of Abnormal Psychology, 107,* 193–202.

Fleischman, D. A., Gabrieli, J. D. E., Gilley, D. W., Hauser, J. D., Lange, K. L., Dwornik, L. M., Bennett, D. A., & Wilson, R. S. (1999). Word-stem completion priming in healthy aging and Alzheimer's disease: The effects of age, cognitive status, and encoding. *Neuropsychology, 13,* 22–30.

Fleischman, D. A., Gabrieli, J. D. E., Reminger, S., Rinaldi, J., Morell, F., & Wilson, R. (1995). Conceptual priming in perceptual identification for patients with Alzheimer's disease and a patient with right occipital lobectomy. *Neuropsychology, 9,* 187–197.

Foa, E. B., Amir, N., Gershuny, B., Molnar, C., & Kozak, M. (1997). Implicit and explicit memory in obsessive-compulsive disorder. *Journal of Anxiety Disorders, 11,* 119–129.

Gabrieli, J. D. E., Vaidya, C. J., & Stone, M. (1999). Convergent behavioral and neuropsychological evidence for a distinction between identification and production forms of repetition priming. *Journal of Experimental Psychology: General, 128,* 479–498.

Garber, J., & Hollon, S. D. (1991) What can specificity designs say about causality in psychopathology research? *Psychological Bulletin, 110,* 129–136.

Gooding, P. A., Mayes, A. R., & van Eijk, R. (2000). A meta-analysis of indirect memory tests for novel material in organic amnesics. *Neuropsychologia, 38,* 666–676.

Goshen-Gottstein, Y., Moscovitch, M., & Melo, B. (2000). Intact implicit memory for newly formed verbal associations in amnesic patients following single study trials. *Neuropsychology, 14,* 570–578.

Gras-Vincendon, A., Danion, J.-M., Grange, D., Bilik, M., Willard-Schroeder, D., Sichel, J. P., & Singer, L. (1994). Explicit memory, repetition, priming and cognitive skill learning in schizophrenia. *Schizophrenia Research, 13,* 117–126.

Heffelfinger, S. K., Calamari, J. E., & Zander, J. R. (2000). Do patients with cardiac problems develop disease-specific schemas?: Evaluation of conceptual implicit memory. *International Journal of Rehabilitation and Health, 5,* 1–15.

Jacoby, L. L. (1991). A process dissociation framework: Separating automatic and intentional uses of memory. *Journal of Memory and Language, 30,* 513–541.

Jacoby, L. L., Allan, L. G., Collins, J. C., & Larwill, L. K. (1988). Memory influences subjective experience: Noise judgment. *Journal of Experimental Psychology: Learning, Memory, and Cognition, 14,* 240–247.

Jacoby, L. L., & Kelly, C. (1991). Unconscious influences of memory: Dissociations and automaticity. In A. D. Milner & M. D. Rugg (Eds.), *The neuropsychology of consciousness* (pp. 201–233). London: Academic Press.

Jacoby, L. L., Toth, J. P., & Yonelinas, A. P. (1993). Unconscious influences of memory: Dissociations and automaticity. *Journal of Experimental Psychology: General, 122,* 139–154.

Kazes, M., Berthet, L., Danion, J. M., Amado, I., Willard, D., Robert, P., & Poirier, M. F. (1999). Impairment of consciously controlled use of memory in schizophrenia. *Neuropsychology, 13,* 54–61.

Koivisto, M., Portin, R., & Rinne, J. O. (1996). Perceptual priming in Alzheimer's and Parkinson's diseases. *Neuropsychologia, 34,* 449–557.

Lazzara, M. M., Yonelinas, A. P., & Ober, B. A. (2001). Conceptual implicit memory performance in Alzheimer's disease. *Neuropsychology, 15,* 483–491.

Linscott, R. J., & Knight, R. G. (2001). Automatic hyperamnesia and impaired recollection in schizophrenia. *Neuropsychology, 15,* 576–585.

Lundh, L.-G., Czyzykow, S., & Öst, L. (1997). Explicit and implicit memory bias in panic disorder with agoraphobia. *Behaviour Research and Therapy, 35,* 1003–1014.

Lundh, L.-G., & Öst, L. (1997). Explicit and implicit memory bias in social phobia: The role of subdiagnostic type. *Behaviour Research and Therapy, 35,* 305–317.

Lundh, L.-G., Wikstrom, J., Westerlund, J., & Öst, L. (1999). Preattentive bias for emotional information in panic disorder with agoraphobia. *Journal of Abnormal Psychology, 108,* 222–232.

MacLeod, C. (1993). Cognition in clinical psychology: Measures, methods or models? *Behaviour Change, 10,* 169–195.

MacLeod, C., & McLaughlin, K. (1995). Implicit and explicit memory bias in anxiety: A conceptual replication. *Behaviour Research and Therapy, 33,* 1–14.

Maki, P. M. (1995). Is implicit memory preserved in Alzheimer's disease? Implications for theories of implicit memory. *Aging and Cognition, 2,* 192–205.

Maki, P. M., Bylsma, F. W., & Brandt, J. (2000). Conceptual and perceptual implicit memory in Huntington's disease. *Neuropsychology, 14,* 331–340.

Maki, P. M., & Knopman, D. S. (1996). Limitations of the distinctions between conceptual and perceptual implicit memory: A study of Alzheimer's disease. *Neuropsychology, 10,* 464–474.

Mathews, A., Mogg, K., Kentish, J., & Eysenck, M. (1995). Effect of psychological treatment on cognitive bias in generalized anxiety disorder. *Behaviour Research and Therapy, 33,* 293–303.

Mathews, A., Mogg, K., May, J., & Eysenck, M. (1989). Implicit and explicit memory bias in anxiety. *Journal of Abnormal Psychology, 98,* 236–240.

McNally, R. J. (1994). *Panic disorder: A critical analysis.* New York: Guilford Press.

McNally, R. J. (1995). Automaticity and the anxiety disorders. *Behaviour Research and Therapy, 33,* 747–757.

McNally, R. J. (1996). Cognitive bias in anxiety disorders. In D. Hope (Ed.), *Perspectives on anxiety, panic and fear* (pp. 211–250). Lincoln: University of Nebraska Press.

McNally, R. J., & Amir, N. (1996). Perceptual implicit memory for trauma-related information in posttraumatic stress disorder. *Cognition & Emotion, 10,* 551–556.

Meiran, N., & Jelicic, M. (1995). Implicit memory in Alzheimer's disease: A meta-analysis. *Neuropsychology, 9*, 291–303.

Morris, C. D., Bransford, J. D., & Franks, J. J. (1977). Levels of processing versus transfer appropriate processing. *Journal of Verbal Learning & Verbal Behavior, 16*, 519–533.

Ober, B. A., Shenaut, G. K., Jagust, W. J., & Stillman, R. C. (1991). Automatic semantic priming with various category relations in Alzheimer's disease and normal aging. *Psychology and Aging, 6*, 647–660.

Park, S. M., Gabrieli, J. D. E., Reminger, S. L., Monti, L. A., Fleischman, D. A., Wilson, R. S., Tinklenberg, J. R., & Yesavage, J. A. (1998). Preserved priming across study-test picture transformations in patients with Alzheimer's disease. *Neuropsychology, 12*, 340–352.

Rapee, R. M. (1994). Failure to replicate a memory bias in panic disorder. *Journal of Anxiety Disorders, 8*, 291–300.

Rapee, R. M., McCallum, S. L., Melville, L. F., Ravenscroft, H., & Rodney, J. M. (1994). Memory bias in social phobia. *Behaviour Research and Therapy, 32*, 89–99.

Roediger, H. L., & Blaxton, T. A. (1987). Effects of varying modality, surface features, and retention interval on priming in word-fragment completion. *Memory and Cognition, 15*, 379–388.

Roediger, H. L., Buckner, R. L., & McDermott, K. B. (1999). Components of processing. In J. K. Foster & M. Jelicic (Eds.), *Systems, process, or function?* (pp. 31–65). London: Oxford University Press.

Roediger, H. L., & McDermott, K. B. (1992). Depression and implicit memory: A commentary. *Journal of Abnormal Psychology, 101*, 587–591.

Roediger, H. L., & McDermott, K. B. (1993). Implicit memory in normal human subjects. In F. Boller & J. Grafman (Eds.), *Handbook of neuropsychology* (pp. 63–131). Amsterdam: Elsevier.

Roediger, H. L., Weldon, M. S., & Challis, B. H. (1989). Explaining dissociations between implicit and explicit measures of retention: A processing account. In H. L. Roediger & F. I. M. Craik (Eds.), *Varieties of memory and consciousness: Essays in honour of Endel Tulving* (pp. 3–14). Hillsdale, NJ: Erlbaum.

Scarrabelotti, M., & Carroll, M. (1998). Awareness of remembering achieved through automatic and conscious processes in multiple sclerosis. *Brain and Cognition, 38*, 577–588.

Schacter, D. L. (1992). Priming and multiple memory systems: Perceptual mechanisms of implicit memory. *Journal of Cognitive Neuroscience, 4*, 244–256.

Schachter, D. L., Bowers, J., & Booker, J. (1989). Intention, awareness, and implicit memory: The retrieval intentionality criterion. In S. Lewandowsky & J. C. Dunn (Eds.), *Implicit memory: Theoretical issues* (pp. 47–65). Hillsdale, NJ: Erlbaum.

Schacter, D. L., & Church, B. (1995). Implicit memory in amnestic patients: When is auditory priming spared? *Journal of the International Neuropsychological Society, 1*, 434–442.

Schmand, B., Kop, W. J., Kuipers, T., & Bosveld, J. (1992). Implicit learning in psychotic patients. *Schizophrenia Research, 7*, 55–64.

Scott, K. M., Mogg, K., & Bradley, B. (2001). Masked semantic priming of emotional information in subclinical depression. *Cognitive Therapy and Research, 25*, 505–524.

Shiffrin, R. M., & Schneider, W. (1977). Controlled and automatic information processing: II. Perceptual learning, automatic attending and a general theory. *Psychological Review, 84*, 127–190.

Squire, L. R. (1992a). Declarative and nondeclarative memory: Multiple brain systems supporting learning and memory. *Journal of Cognitive Neuroscience, 4*, 232–243.

Squire, L. R. (1992b). Memory and the hippocampus: A synthesis from findings with rats, monkeys, and humans. *Psychological Review, 99*, 195–231.

Stirling, J. D., Hellewell, J. S. E., & Hewitt, J. (1997). Verbal memory impairment in schizophrenia: No sparing of short-term recall. *Schizophrenia Research, 25*, 85–95.

Toth, J. P., Reingold, E. M., & Jacoby, L. L. (1994). Toward a redefinition of implicit memory: Process dissociations following elaborative processing and self-generation. *Journal of Experimental Psychology: Learning, Memory, and Cognition, 20*, 290–303.

Vaidya, C., Gabrieli, J. D. E., & Monti, L. A. (1999). Dissociation between two forms of conceptual priming in Alzheimer's disease. *Neuropsychology, 13*, 516–529.

Verfaellie, M., Keane, M. M., & Johnson, G. (2000). Preserved priming in auditory perceptual identification in Alzheimer's disease. *Neuropsychologia, 38*, 1581–1592.

Watkins, P. C. (2002). Implicit memory bias in depression. *Cognition & Emotion, 16*, 381–402.

Watkins, P. C., Martin, C. K., & Stern, L. D. (2000). Unconscious memory bias in depression: Perceptual and conceptual processes. *Journal of Abnormal Psychology, 109*, 282–289.

Watkins, P. C., Mathews, A., Williamson, D. A., & Fuller, R. D. (1992). Mood-congruent memory in depression: Emotional priming or elaboration? *Journal of Abnormal Psychology, 101*, 581–586.

Watkins, P. C., Vache, K., Verney, S. P., & Mathews, A. (1996). Unconscious mood-congruent memory bias in depression. *Journal of Abnormal Psychology, 105*, 34–41.

IV

DIRECTED FORGETTING TASKS

10

DIRECTED FORGETTING RESEARCH: FINDING COMMON GROUND

JONATHAN M. GOLDING AND RICHARD J. MCNALLY

Directed forgetting involves the use of explicit cues to designate specific information as irrelevant (i.e., to-be-forgotten information) or relevant (i.e., to-be-remembered information). The purpose of these cues is to diminish interference from to-be-forgotten information, thereby enhancing the effectiveness of memory. Accordingly, directed forgetting is a natural point of contact between cognitive and clinical psychologists.

Until recently, however, there has been limited cross talk between these two groups, despite their common interest in the mechanisms of forgetting. Some cognitive researchers may have been wary of venturing into the clinical domain, especially because it has been historically dominated by dubious concepts such as Freud's *repression*. Some clinical researchers may have been reluctant to venture into the cognitive domain, believing that studies on forgetting mere words in the laboratory must have questionable relevance for the forgetting of traumatic personal experiences. Finally, busy members of both groups may have been a bit parochial, reading only those journals already familiar to them.

Despite this shaky start, it now appears that common ground has finally been established between cognitive and clinical psychologists, and that each group can share in the excitement of their respective discoveries. Therefore, the chapters to follow present directed forgetting methodology, empirical results, and theory in a manner accessible to both groups of researchers. In chapter 11 (this volume), Golding presents a detailed review of directed forgetting research in cognitive psychology (see Golding & MacLeod, 1998). He describes the basic directed forgetting paradigm and how it has evolved over the years to include different ways of presenting information and explicit cues to individuals: word-by-word (the item method), list-by-list (the list method), and even cueing a single item as to be forgotten. Researchers now acknowledge that each presentation method likely produces forgetting through different memory mechanisms. For example, the item method leads to the differential encoding of information to be forgotten and to be remembered, and the list method leads to retrieval inhibition of the to-be-forgotten information.

In chapter 12 (this volume), McNally reviews directed forgetting of negative emotional material in a clinical context. After discussing problems with Freud's notions of repression and suppression, he considers practical issues arising from attempts to apply directed forgetting methods to test hypotheses about aberrant forgetting in patients with psychiatric disorders.

Both chapters examine the results of directed forgetting studies, making clear that although the phenomenon of directed forgetting is a robust finding, there are important cases in which an instruction to forget may become an *instruction to remember*. For example, sometimes the context in which a forget instruction is presented leads individuals to continue processing the to-be-forgotten information as relevant (e.g., a juror being told that certain evidence in court is inadmissible). Likewise, people with certain clinical disorders experience dysfunction in the ability to forget upsetting material (e.g., abuse survivors with posttraumatic stress disorder).

The directed forgetting paradigm offers researchers in cognitive and clinical psychology a chance to clarify how memory works by offering insight into when people forget and the mechanisms that lead to such forgetting. In this way, the paradigm brings together researchers who have often studied similar issues, but have been separated in their endeavors. Clearly, the time has come for cognitive psychologists to show applications of directed forgetting with clinical populations and for clinicians to use the paradigm to investigate cognitive correlates of psychopathology.

REFERENCES

Golding, J. M., & MacLeod, C. M. (Eds.). (1998). *Intentional forgetting: Interdisciplinary approaches*. Mahwah, NJ: Erlbaum.

11

DIRECTED FORGETTING TASKS
IN COGNITIVE RESEARCH

JONATHAN M. GOLDING

Is forgetting good or bad? If one asked people this forced-choice question, the majority of responses would likely be that forgetting is bad. People would think of all of the times they needed information and it was unavailable. Examples could include forgetting an item at a grocery store, a person's name, an answer to an exam question, or a telephone number. Compounding this viewpoint would be the increasing number of stories that describe the devastating effects of Alzheimer's disease on memory and the newest drugs that may combat forgetting. Despite the prevailing opinions about forgetting, it is important to understand that this aspect of memory is often misunderstood, and that forgetting really does have some positive virtues.

In fact, it has been argued that forgetting is critical to the efficient use of memory, because forgetting allows for memory updating (i.e., the adaptive nature of memory; e.g., Anderson & Milson, 1989; Kraemer & Golding, 1997). William James (1890, p. 488) noted that without such updating, humans are unable to deal with the "blooming, buzzing confusion" of information that impinges on them. Put another way, James (1890, p. 68) stated that "if we remembered everything, we should on most occasions be as ill off as if we remembered nothing." Thus, there are times when information *should* be forgotten, typically when such information is irrelevant to a particular task or has little future value. The issue of forgetting relevant information, perhaps because of its traumatic nature, is discussed in McNally (see chap. 12, this volume).

Given that forgetting can work to one's advantage, how does one know what to forget? Now things get a little tricky. Individuals sometimes must identify irrelevant information on the basis of implicit cues. For example, if I am talking to someone about the University of Kentucky–Duke basketball game last night and I comment on the weather, he may consider the latter to be irrelevant to the goal of our conversation and worthy of being forgotten. However, it is possible that even irrelevant comments will continue to be processed by a person. Luckily, we have another device for knowing what to forget (i.e., to-be-forgotten, or F information)—we can just tell a person. Sometimes, explicit cues are used to designate information as relevant or irrelevant. If one thinks something is irrelevant one simply directs or instructs the other person perhaps by using one of the following phrases: "forget that," "I didn't mean that," "disregard what I just said," or "oh, never mind." Typically, an instruction to forget specific information is followed by correct or relevant information (i.e., to-be-remembered, or R information).

An instruction to forget can be extremely effective in reducing interference (i.e., the potentially interfering effects of the F information). When this reduction in interference occurs it is typically referred to as *directed forgetting* (also termed *intentional forgetting*), and it has been studied in various experimental contexts for the past 40 years (for a recent edited volume see Golding & MacLeod, 1998; for recent reviews see R. A. Bjork, 1998; Golding & Long, 1998; Johnson, 1994; MacLeod, 1998, and for earlier reviews see R. A. Bjork, 1972; Epstein, 1972). It is important to keep in mind, however, that directed forgetting means different things to different researchers. In fact, the term *directed forgetting* was coined by cognitive psychologists investigating how memory interference can be reduced. There are now many researchers who investigate the effect of explicit cues on memory, although some of them rarely if ever use the term *directed forgetting* (e.g., Golding & Long, 1998). Moreover, some of these researchers are not interested in the actual retrieval of specific information, but in the impact of the to-be-forgotten information on other processes (e.g., impression formation, decision making). Nonetheless, as argued by Golding and Long (1998), these researchers are all using a similar paradigm and are all investigating how individuals use explicit cues to designate information as relevant and irrelevant.

THE BASIC PARADIGM

The basic directed forgetting paradigm involves presenting explicit cues to designate information F or R. Although participants do not expect to be tested on the F information, memory (or some other type of measure) for both types of information is usually assessed. The performance of participants presented with forget and remember cues (i.e., forget condition) can be compared with two other groups. One group does not receive the F information (control condition) and one group receives remember cues instead of forget cues for the same information (remember condition). A concrete example should help in thinking about the paradigm. Group 1 receives 10 F words and 10 R words, Group 2 receives only the 10 R words (no information is presented during the time experimental materials are presented to the other groups), and Group 3 receives the 10 R words, but instead of being instructed to forget the other 10 words, they are told to remember these words (i.e., 20 R words). The use of the above three groups in a directed forgetting study allows for the clearest interpretation of the results; however, many studies do not include all three conditions.

On the basis of the presentation of words described above, there are two primary ways to look at the data from a directed forgetting experiment. First, one can examine performance related to the same 10 R items in all three groups to see if there was a reduction in interference. (Although different performance measures can be used, I discuss memory-dependent variables because they are used most often.) If Group 1 (forget condition) was able to reduce interference because of the F words, memory performance for the 10 R words should be similar to that for Group 2 (control condition) who did not even have F words, and both of these participant groups' memory should be higher for the same 10 words in Group 3 (remember condition), whose participants had to remember twice as many words: Forget = Control > Remember. In effect, Group 1 was able to trim a list of 20 words to 10 words. MacLeod (1998) described analyzing the R items in this fashion as a cost–benefit analysis. Did the F words lead to a benefit or a cost in remembering the R items? A second way to examine the data is to analyze performance on the F items. MacLeod (1998) described this analysis as the *remember–forget (R-F) difference.* As he stated, "to the extent that the F words are successfully edited out, then the difference between the R and F items should be large" (p. 5; i.e., if the F words are forgotten, Forget < Remember). Ideally, the results of an experiment will include both higher recall of R items and lower recall of F items when compared with the appropriate control groups. This result, in fact, has been the case in many experiments with mostly undergraduates, but also with younger participants and elders (e.g., Golding & Long, 1998; MacLeod, 1998).

One may be wondering at this point whether a directed forgetting experiment really involves forgetting. Are participants losing access to the items, or are the results a nice example of demand characteristics (i.e., participants simply withhold F items during memory tasks)? Rest assured that researchers have examined this issue in several studies and have concluded that response withholding is not leading to the direct forgetting effect. Following the lead of earlier studies (R. A. Bjork & Woodward, 1973; Woodward & R. A. Bjork, 1971), MacLeod (1999) presented word lists to participants using the directed forgetting paradigm; he obtained the typical effect. He then offered 50 cents for each additional F word that was recalled. Alas, MacLeod (1999, p. 123) noted that "participants could recall almost no more items."

Item Method

Over time, two different methodologies have emerged to examine directed forgetting (e.g., Basden & Basden, 1998; Basden, Basden, & Gargano, 1993; MacLeod, 1998; e.g., also Marks & Dulaney, 2001). One of these methods is called the *item* (or *word*) method. The distinguishing aspect of the item method is that each item is presented with a random explicit cue (i.e., type of cue—forget or remember—is a within-participants factor). It is typically the case that each cue is presented soon after the item so that participants must initially encode the item to some degree (but see Paller, 1990, for an example of presenting each item–cue pair simultaneously). That is, until the cue appears, the participants do not know whether they can forget the word or not. The presentation time for both the items and the explicit cues is usually relatively short, a few seconds. The cue is often a single word (*forget*) or a series of letters (FFFFF), but it may even include changing the background color of the items being presented. There is usually a very short delay between item–cue pairs of about one second, but sometimes a cue is followed immediately by the next item. One or more lists of items may be presented to participants. If one list is presented to participants, memory performance of both the F and R items is tested, usually following some delay with an unrelated task to eliminate short-term memory effects. If multiple lists are presented, it is often the case that only memory of the R items is tested after each list, which thereby increases the validity of the explicit cues. However, this type of procedure is usually followed by a final memory test that includes both F and R items. An example of the item method with an abbreviated list is illustrated below.

        car
        "forget"
        bag
        "remember"
        plane
        "forget"
        arm
        "forget"
        bread
        "remember"
        floor
        "remember"

As for actual experiments with the item method, Basden et al. (1993, Experiment 3) is a nice illustration. In this experiment, 48 nouns (24 F and 24 R) were presented for two seconds apiece. The forget–remember cue for each word was presented for six seconds. The results for final recall showed that the remember–forget difference was quite large (R = .50, F = .05). As another example, Earles and Kersten (2002) presented 40 verb–noun actions (e.g., "break–toothpick") for eight seconds with each action followed by a forget or remember cue for six seconds. They found that for their undergraduate sample, recall of nonperformed actions that were to be remembered was .50 compared with recall of nonperformed actions recall that were to be forgotten, which was only .20. The results from item-method experiments for recall are quite impressive and robust (e.g., MacLeod, 1998). In addition, the item method reliably produces the directed forgetting effect with recognition as a dependent measure. For example, in Davis and Okada (1971) the remember–forget difference was significant with a yes/no recognition task (R = .70, F = .50; see also Basden et al., 1993; MacLeod, 1975, 1989). It should be noted that other measures besides recall and recognition have been used as dependent variables, including latency of response (e.g., Cruse & Jones, 1976), event-related brain potentials (Paller, 1990), and implicit measures of memory such as stem completion (e.g., MacLeod, 1989; Paller, 1990; see also MacLeod, 1998).

With regard to materials, experiments that use the item method typically use words, but other materials have been presented, such as syllables, consonants, and (as described previously) word pairs (e.g., MacLeod, 1998). It is also usually the case that the words are unrelated (but see Golding, MacLeod, & Long, 1994; Horton & Petruk, 1980) so that participants do not gain any advantage from semantic categories or relationships. The issue of relatedness or category membership, however, becomes a much more central issue with specific clinical populations (see chap. 12, this volume). It is typical that at least two lists of words are used in this type of experiment. These lists are counterbalanced so that each list can serve as both the F list and the R list. The words on each list are generally equated in terms of frequency of use of agreed-on norms (e.g., Kučera & Francis, 1967) and are sometimes equated with other norms, such as imageability or vividness. There is no set number of items that should be presented to participants, and the literature shows that various numbers have been used (e.g., MacLeod, 1998). However, if one is measuring recognition it is best to pilot test to be sure that there were enough items to avoid a ceiling effect with the R items. Finally, the number of F and R items is often equal.

List Method

The other method for investigating directed forgetting is called the *list* (or *blocked*) method; it involves having a particular list or set of items cued as

F or R. Most often, the forget cue is presented immediately after an initial list of items (List 1), with the R items (List 2) to follow. The reason for the forget cue varies (e.g., Golding & Long, 1998), but participants are usually instructed to forget the preceding set because it was practice or that a mistake was made in presenting these items. The forget cue is then followed by an instruction that the R set of items will then be presented (e.g., Geiselman, R. A. Bjork, & Fishman, 1983). Also, because the forget cue is much longer, it naturally follows that additional time is given for participants to read this cue. This type of method is illustrated below.

> car
> bag
> plane

"What you have done thus far has been practice; therefore, you should forget all of the to-be-learned words that you have been presented. The actual list will now be presented."

> arm
> bread
> floor

If a remember group is included (i.e., all of the items are to be remembered), the mid-list instruction will say something to the effect that "The first portion of the list has now been presented; continue to try to remember the items" (e.g., Geiselman et al., 1983). Following the presentation of the lists, there is typically a delay with some unrelated task to again eliminate short-term memory effects, and then performance is measured.

R. A. Bjork (1970, Experiment 1) performed a list method that experiment that serves as a good example. He presented participants with 64 lists. The lists were composed of one to eight syllable–word pairs presented on colored slides. Each pair was presented for three seconds. Participants were instructed that when the color of the slide changed, they were to forget all prior pairs in the lists. The number of prior pairs varied from one to three pairs. The results showed virtually no proactive interference from the forget pairs when recall of the R items was measured. Likewise, in Basden et al. (1993) the list method with only a forget condition (with 48 words presented for 8 seconds each, with 1 second between words) yielded a relatively large remember–forget difference for List 1 words on recall (R = .41, F = .20). Finally, Geiselman et al. (1983) included both a forget condition and a remember condition. They also showed a remember–forget difference for List 1 words (R = .75, F = .58). In addition, the cost–benefit analysis was significant. Recall of the List 2 R items was greater for the forget condition (.75) than the remember condition (.60).

In thinking about the list method, it should be noted that the forget–remember difference is typically smaller with the list method than the item method. It has been argued that the list method allows for a relatively greater opportunity to encode and relate F words together, and hence aid memory (Basden at al., 1993). This point will be discussed further in the next section.

Several additional points need to be made about the list method. First, the placement of the explicit cue can affect the results. That is, although the forget cue is usually placed right after List 1 and before List 2, it can be presented before List 1. However, this placement will likely decrease the probability that the List 1 words will be encoded. Also, the forget cue for List 1 can be placed after List 2, but this increases the likelihood that the List 1 words will not be forgotten as a result of extensive encoding. Some opposing viewpoints to this placement issue (Wyer & Budesheim, 1987; Wyer & Unverzagt, 1985) are discussed in the subsequent section. Second, the materials presented in the lists have varied a great deal (e.g., words, digits, sentences, and behaviors). In general, directed forgetting is found with different types of materials (see MacLeod, 1998, but see Golding & Long, 1998). Third, the number of items per list has varied. Related to the number of words per list, it has generally been the case that the lengths of List 1 and List 2 are identical. Fourth, participants are usually asked to either recall or recognize the items in each list. The importance of not having the same participants perform both memory tasks is to avoid contamination of the second task by the first task . If the same participants complete both tasks, one should examine recall and then look at what items were later recognized but not recalled. Also related to dependent measures, both explicit and implicit measures have been used with the list method. Fifth, it is important to control for output order. Thus, participants are often counterbalanced with regard to whether F and R items are remembered first or second. The problem with not counterbalancing is that if a participant recalls the R items first, recall of F items may suffer. The lower F performance may not be due to forgetting per se, but may simply reflect that waiting to remember these items may lead to an increase in proactive interference or forgetting as a result of decay. Geiselman et al. (1983; see also Sahakyan & Kelley, 2002) tested for this possibility and found no evidence output interference, but it is far from settled whether this is a significant problem.

A final point about the list method is that the reason given to the participants in the forget cue has been shown to be a very important factor in this type of study of directed forgetting. For example, I have investigated the effect of pragmatics on directed forgetting. Keenan, MacWhinney, and Mayhew (1977) define *pragmatics* as including information about the communicative situation, the temporal position of an utterance in the communication, knowledge about the speaker (e.g., intentions, beliefs, and knowledge of and attitude toward the listener), and information about the relationship between the speaker and listener. In my studies, I have varied the reason for the forget cue to determine whether explicit cues might be effective only to the extent that the pragmatic implication of the cue indicated that the designated information was indeed irrelevant.

In the first of several studies (Golding, Fowler, Long, & Latta, 1990), I presented behaviors to participants in an impression–formation context. The participants in the experimental condition were instructed to disregard some of the behaviors about another person because it was either confidential or incorrect (i.e., it was about someone else). The results showed that only those participants who were told that the F behaviors were incorrect did not use these behaviors when forming their impressions. The confidential information continued to be used by participants, as much as a group instruction to use the F information from the outset (i.e., the remember condition). These results have been supported in several studies that have (a) used role-playing (Golding et al., 1990; Golding, Sego, Hauselt, & Long, 1994); (b) used a more naturalistic context (Golding & Hauselt, 1994); (c) used a task involving person impression or object impression (Golding et al., 1990); and (d) had individual participants (e.g., Golding & Hauselt, 1994) or groups (Golding, Ellis, Hauselt, & Sego, 1998) make judgments about a target. It is interesting to note that in these studies the recall results have generally not supported the effect of pragmatics; F information has been recalled relatively well regardless of the type of forget instruction.

The studies involving pragmatics are important in showing that the use of explicit cues to segregate may be a function of the context in which the cue is presented. Just because information is cued as "to be forgotten" does not mean it will be treated that way (e.g., Fleming, Wegener, & Petty, 1999; Kassin & Sommers, 1997; Petty & Wegener, 1993; Wegener & Petty, 1995). Thus, if participants perceive the F information as relevant, it is likely that this information will continue to be processed (e.g., instructions to disregard inadmissible evidence in court). However, if participants really believe that the F information is of no value (as in a typical directed forgetting study with words) then the directed forgetting effect is likely to be found.

Single-Item Method

It is important to mention a third method with regard to directed forgetting. Some directed forgetting researchers include only a single piece of information to be forgotten. Included in these studies is research on instructions to disregard information in court (e.g., Kassin & Studebaker, 1998; Thompson & Fuqua, 1998), debriefing (e.g., Ross, Lepper, & Hubbard, 1975), hindsight bias (e.g., Fischhoff, 1975), corrective advertising (see Wilkie, McNeill, & Mazis, 1984, for a review), thought suppression (e.g., Wegner, 1989, 1994), and directions to a destination (Golding & Keenan, 1985). The results of most of these studies point to the idea that a single piece of information is extremely difficult to forget, especially if the to-be-forgotten information is seen as relevant to the task or context.

A few examples of the inability to forget a single item should suffice. First, in a classic psychology and law study, Sue, Smith, and Caldwell (1973) presented mock jurors with a robbery trial summary in one of three conditions: (a) no evidence that was critical to judging the defendant's guilt; (b) evidence critical to judging the defendant's guilt; and (c) evidence critical to judging the defendant's guilt, but with an additional instruction to disregard the evidence because it was inadmissible. It was shown that jurors continued to use the inadmissible evidence in determining guilt, but only in a weak version of the trial summary in which the other evidence did not clearly indicate guilt or innocence. The Sue et al. (1973) study examined instructions to disregard information that pertained to the crime, but such instructions have also been examined with regard to disregarding prior criminal records, pretrial publicity, police tactics, and how instructions to disregard are presented by a judge (e.g., Golding & Long, 1998; Kassin & Studebaker, 1998; Thompson & Fuqua, 1998).

Second, research on thought suppression has shown an inability to forget single items. In Wegner's classic study (Wegner, Schneider, Carter, & White, 1987, Experiment 1) participants reported into a tape recorder "everything that came to mind" for two five-minute periods. Participants were instructed to "try not to think of a white bear" (initial suppression group) or to "try to think of a white bear" (initial expression group) as they spoke. The instructions were reversed for the two groups in the second period. All groups were also asked to ring a bell if they said "white bear" or if "white bear" came to mind. The results showed that participants were not completely successful in suppressing the "white bear." Moreover, there was a rebound effect with regard to suppression—an increase in the frequency of thoughts about the white bear in the second period for the initial suppression group (see also Lavy & van den Hout, 1990).

Finally, research has investigated hindsight bias (see Hawkins & Hastie, 1990, for a review and Christensen-Szalanski & Willham, 1991, for a meta-analysis). Hindsight bias occurs when individuals who receive knowledge about the outcome of an event exhibit a change in their perceptions of the likelihood of that outcome, even when they are explicitly instructed to disregard that knowledge. In most of these studies, one group of participants (hindsight participants) is told the outcome of an event and another group is not told this outcome (foresight participants). A comparison is then made between these groups as to the likelihood of the event. In Fischhoff (1975) participants read descriptions of historical events (e.g., a near riot in Atlanta) and clinical cases; each description included four possible outcomes. Hindsight participants received information about what they were told was the "true" outcome, whereas foresight participants did not. Finally, the participants were asked to predict the likelihood of each of the four outcomes. It was found that hindsight participants assigned higher probabilities to the outcome they were told had actually occurred than did foresight participants, even when they had been instructed to disregard their outcome knowledge (i.e., to respond "as they would have had they not known the outcome"). These hindsight participants claimed that they "knew it all along."

One of the only successful attempts to achieve directed forgetting that has specifically used a single item was by Golding and Keenan (1985). They presented participants with a set of verbal directions to a destination. One group received a basic set of directions, one group received the basic set plus one additional direction to remember, and one group received the basic set and the additional direction, but they were instructed to forget the additional direction. On a verbal recall test of the directions there was no evidence of directed forgetting. However, when participants were asked to draw the directions (including the F directions) the group instructed to forget the additional direction did not recall this information.

THEORETICAL PERSPECTIVES

In discussing theoretical explanations for directed forgetting, one must be reminded of a point raised earlier: Directed forgetting means different things to different researchers. The importance of this is that (regrettably) a theoretical position (let alone empirical findings) in one area of psychology may not be mentioned or even known in another area of psychology (e.g., Golding & Long, 1998). Nonetheless, in trying to have readers understand directed forgetting it makes the most sense to begin a discussion of theoretical views of directed forgetting by reviewing mechanisms of directed forgetting that have been proposed within cognitive psychology before turning to theories from social psychology and ironic processing theory.

In discussing what I refer to as cognitive mechanisms of directed forgetting, one must step back and think a bit about the item method and list method described above. It is these two methodologies that consistently lead to directed forgetting. One might wonder about the utility of using these two methodologies for investigating directed forgetting. At first glance it may simply be two ways to show the same thing. In fact, the importance of using two different methodologies did not really fit into place until a clear theoretical explanation for the mechanisms leading to directed forgetting was clarified by Basden et al. (1993).

Initially, R. A. Bjork (1972) proposed two related encoding processes to account for directed forgetting: set differentiation and selective rehearsal. (He did not clearly distinguish between item and list methods.) Set differentiation involved the functional segregation of F and R items as a result of explicit cues. This segregation allowed for selective rehearsal of only the R information. Selective rehearsal led to an increase in R memory performance because fewer items needed to be rehearsed and fewer items needed to be searched during retrieval. Given that the F items were not processed to the same degree as the R items, they were relatively less accessible. This inaccessibility led to fewer F items recalled and recognized compared with R items.

Although R. A. Bjork's (1972) theoretical view gained strong support and is accepted today as an explanation for directed forgetting in certain contexts, during the initial 10 years of directed forgetting research a few investigators argued for another mechanism for this effect: retrieval inhibition. These researchers suggested that a forget cue may inhibit access routes to the F information during retrieval. Those who discussed this possibility (e.g., Reed, 1970; Weiner, 1968; Weiner & Reed, 1969; see also Roediger & Crowder, 1972) received either no mention or only a passing note as exceptions to the prevailing encoding position in other directed forgetting publications. It is likely that these studies received little attention because of the sheer amount of empirical evidence supporting R. A. Bjork combined with potential problems in methodology (e.g., Roediger & Crowder, 1972).

In recent years, there has been increasing empirical evidence to support retrieval inhibition as another mechanism leading to directed forgetting (e.g., Basden et al., 1993; R. A. Bjork, 1989; Geiselman & Bagheri, 1985; Geiselman et al., 1983; Harnishfeger & Pope, 1996; Kimball & Bjork, 2002; MacLeod, 1989; see also E. L. Bjork, R. A. Bjork, & Anderson, 1998). Among these studies, Geiselman et al. (1983) is typically cited as the first of the new wave of directed forgetting studies to offer evidence in support of retrieval inhibition. In Geiselman et al. (1983), participants were presented with two lists of concrete nouns, with an instruction to learn some words and to rate other words for pleasantness. The presentation of learn and rate instructions was interspersed, so that a participant would be given a *learn* word, then a *rate* word, then a *learn* word, and so on. All participants received two lists of words. In addition, some participants were told to forget the to-be-learned words from List 1 because List 1 had been a practice list.

Using the above methodology, Geiselman et al. (1983) found directed forgetting for the F words in the learn condition on a recall task. They also found directed forgetting for the F words in the rate condition on this memory task. Given that the rate words were assumed not to have been rehearsed (i.e., participants did not expect that they would be required to recall them), it was concluded that these words were inhibited during recall by a "process that blocks or inhibits access routes" (Geiselman et al., 1983, p. 70) to the F items. In addition, because participants were not told to forget the rate words, response withholding was unlikely (e.g., MacLeod, 1999). Additional support for retrieval inhibition was that it appeared that the retrieval routes to the F words were disrupted; participants had a difficult time classifying F words that they recalled as words that were to be forgotten. Finally, in another experiment Geiselman et al. (1983) used a recognition task with separate groups of participants and found no directed forgetting. The group instructed to forget was similar in their recognition performance as the remember group on both the F and R words. Because retrieval is minimized in a recognition task, the results for recognition were viewed as indicative of a release from the retrieval inhibition found in recall.

The results of Geiselman et al. (1983) and the emergence of retrieval inhibition as a mechanism of directed forgetting led researchers to examine the necessary conditions for retrieval inhibition. However, it was not until 10 years later that Basden et al. (1993) suggested what these conditions might be, and how these varied as a function of methodology. Specifically, Basden et al. (1993) emphasized that different mechanisms led to directed forgetting on the basis of how the materials and explicit cues were presented. For example, in Geiselman et al. (1983) the words were presented as a list prior to a forget cue. This type of presentation encourages participants to relate these words together as they encode them (i.e., relational processing; e.g., Hunt & Einstein, 1981). Even the rated words, although only incidentally learned, should be related to the learned words. When the forget cue is presented it should act on the list as a whole. Because it is assumed that all of the F words were encoded, any evidence of directed forgetting should be viewed as a result of a mechanism occurring at retrieval. Moreover, if this mechanism is that of retrieval inhibition (i.e., blocking) of the F words, there should be evidence of directed forgetting on recall but not on recognition.

Conversely, Basden et al. (1993) argued that the item method leads to distinctive processing, in which each word is processed as a function of its associated cue and not in relation to other words. In the case of words followed by a forget cue, participants should stop processing these words immediately upon presentation of the forget cue. This cessation of processing leads to the F words receiving relatively little processing at encoding. Because they are not encoded very well, the F words should show directed forgetting on all explicit memory tasks (i.e., recall and recognition). As an added point, because the F words were barely encoded in the item method, any evidence of directed forgetting (especially the forget–remember difference) should be greater with the item method than with the list method (e.g., Basden & Basden, 1998).

There is an interesting sidelight to the theoretical explanation described above. Although the Geiselman et al. (1983) study is most often cited as providing evidence for retrieval inhibition (e.g., Golding & MacLeod, 1998), no other published study has used the learn/rate paradigm to investigate retrieval inhibition during directed forgetting. However, a number of other studies show evidence of retrieval inhibition: Geiselman and Bagheri (1985) have used a test–retest paradigm with the item method. In this study, after an initial presentation and recall opportunity, unrecalled F and R items were presented a second time. A number of studies (Basden et al., 1993; Lehman, McKinley-Pace, Wilson, Slavsky, & Woodson, 1997; MacLeod, 1989; Paller, 1990) have investigated retrieval inhibition by using both implicit and explicit memory measures with the item method. Finally, E. L. Bjork and R. A. Bjork (1996); Harnishfeger and Pope (1996); and Zacks, Radvansky, and

Hasher (1996) have used variations of the list method paradigm without the learn/rate distinction.

An important theoretical point should be noted about discussions of retrieval inhibition and the list method. Research in social psychology that deals primarily with impression formation tasks does not always support the Basden et al. (1993) viewpoint. For example, there is a general formulation of social information processing called the bin model. The bin model is quite complex and is not described in detail here (see Isbell, Smith, & Wyer, 1998, for further discussion of the model). It views permanent memory as a set of content-addressable storage bins with each bin having unlimited capacity and identified by a header that specifies its referent and describes its content. The bin model states that the content of a bin depends on the presentation position of the F and R information. When F information is presented as a list before the R information, it is stored separately and thus should not influence or interfere with the R information: Each set of behaviors should be recalled well, and the F information should not influence impression formation. However, when the F behaviors are presented after the R behaviors, two bins are also constructed. In one of these bins is both the F and R information, whereas the other contains only the R information. This type of storage leads to interference, which thereby lowers recall of the F information and leads the F information to influence judgments related to the R information. The model has been empirically tested (Wyer & Unverzagt, 1985; see also Wyer & Budesheim, 1987), and the results generally support the predictions with regard to judgments and F recall. Thus far, there have been no published attempts to reconcile the findings of studies in cognitive psychology with those in social psychology, although Golding (2001) does offer some possibilities on why the results of social psychology studies contradict the findings of typical list method directed forgetting experiments.

In conclusion, a final point should be extended to those studies that present only a single item to participants to forget. Because these studies cross disparate domains, various theoretical positions have been presented for why individuals usually have difficulty forgetting the single item. In keeping with the examples I presented earlier (for other examples see Golding & Long, 1998), psychology and law explanations include the juror justice viewpoint. This view states that failure to heed a judge's instructions in the courtroom is due to different views of justice held by the court and by jurors (Thompson, Fong, & Rosenhan, 1981; see also Fleming et al., 1999). Because the court views justice with regard to due process and jurors view justice in terms of "right" outcomes, there is bound to be a clash over how to deal with information that is relevant to the court case, but should be disregarded. In fact, it would defy common justice or common sense for juries to ignore this information.

With regard to the inability of individuals to suppress thoughts, Wegner (1994) proposed the ironic process theory. He discussed the idea that mental control involves the interaction of two mental processes working together to promote a certain cognitive state. First, an intentional operating system searches for the mental contents that will yield a desired state—an effortful process. Second, an ironic monitoring system searches for mental contents that signal the failure to achieve the desired state—an automatic process. For example, when a person is trying to be happy, the intentional operating system searches for mental contents pertinent to happiness. However, the ironic monitoring system searches for mental contents that indicate happiness has not been achieved. Although typically mental control is achieved, if mental capacity is reduced for some reason (e.g., cognitive load, stress, or time pressure), the intentional operating system is undermined, and the contents of the ironic monitoring system will come into consciousness, thereby producing ironic effects such as intruding thoughts (e.g., Wegner & Erber, 1993).

A theoretical explanation of hindsight effects is Fischhoff's (1975, 1977; see also Hasher, Attig, & Alba, 1981) notion of *creeping determinism*. He stated that hindsight effects arise from processes that operate to create a coherent whole out of knowledge about an event. Thus, when a person hears the outcome of an event, he or she integrates the outcome with relevant prior knowledge. Moreover, because this assimilation occurs automatically, participants underestimate the influence of outcome knowledge on their perceptions, and thus overestimate how obvious the correct outcome appeared (e.g., Slovic & Fischhoff, 1977).

CONDUCTING DIRECTED FORGETTING RESEARCH

Hopefully, after reading this chapter one sees the value in using the directed forgetting paradigm to investigate specific issues related to clinical populations. If so, one needs to ask several questions (and subquestions) before moving ahead:

1. What is the goal in conducting an experiment with the directed forgetting paradigm? Does the investigation involve a particular ability to process information? For example, one may want to examine whether individuals can inhibit information. If they can, then one would likely choose the list method as part of the procedure.
2. What materials will be used? As stated earlier, many different materials have been used in directed forgetting research. This choice of materials may have important implications with regard to how participants process the information, especially if the items are not simply unrelated words.
3. How will one present the materials and cues? Currently, most directed forgetting research is conducted with computer pre-

sentation. However, one may decide that another type of presentation is useful (e.g., using a more naturalistic context).

4. How will one measure performance? One may simply want to use explicit memory measures such as recall or recognition. However, other explicit or implicit performance measures that can help one determine how individuals process the F information may be used. Also, will one examine whether order effects involving the F and R items have an impact on the results, and will one run separate groups of participants to examine each dependent measure?

5. What groups will be included in the study? Although there is general agreement that the most efficient way to examine directed forgetting is to include forget, remember, and control groups in the same experiment, few researchers do so. The problem in including all three conditions is the sheer number of participants required to complete the study.

It should be clear that directed forgetting is a useful paradigm to investigate a variety of phenomenon in many different contexts. McNally (see chap. 12, this volume) explains that directed forgetting has been of interest to clinicians for many years and that the directed forgetting paradigm can be used quite effectively with clinical populations to investigate various psychological issues. I hope that this chapter has given clinical researchers a starting point from which to conduct directed forgetting research and allows these investigators to share a common language of study with their colleagues in experimental psychology in their quest for important theoretical and applied advances.

REFERENCES

Anderson, J. R., & Milson, R. (1989). Human memory: An adaptive perspective. *Psychological Review, 96*, 703–719.

Basden, B. H., & Basden, D. R. (1998). Directed forgetting: A contrast of methods and interpretations. In J. M. Golding & C. M. MacLeod (Eds.), *Intentional forgetting: Interdisciplinary approaches* (pp. 139–172). Mahwah, NJ: Erlbaum.

Basden, B. H., Basden, D. R., & Gargano, G. J. (1993). Directed forgetting in implicit and explicit memory tests: A comparison of methods. *Journal of Experimental Psychology: Learning, Memory, and Cognition, 19*, 603–616.

Bjork, E. L., & Bjork, R. A. (1996). Continuing influences of to-be-forgotten information. *Consciousness and Cognition, 5*, 176–196.

Bjork, E. L., Bjork, R. A., & Anderson, M. C. (1998). Varieties of goal-directed forgetting. In J. M. Golding & C. M. MacLeod (Eds.), *Intentional forgetting: Interdisciplinary approaches* (pp. 103–137). Mahwah, NJ: Erlbaum.

Bjork, R. A. (1970). Positive forgetting: The noninterference of items intentionally forgotten. *Journal of Verbal Learning and Verbal Behavior, 9*, 255–268.

Bjork, R. A. (1972). Theoretical implications of directed forgetting. In A. W. Melton & E. Martin (Eds.), *Coding processes in human memory* (pp. 217–235). Washington, DC: Winston.

Bjork, R. A. (1989). Retrieval inhibition as an adaptive mechanism in human memory. In H. L. Roediger & F. I. M. Craik (Eds.), *Varieties of memory and consciousness: Essays in honour of Endel Tulving* (pp. 309–330). Hillsdale, NJ: Erlbaum.

Bjork, R. A. (1998). Intentional forgetting in perspective. In J. M. Golding & C. M. MacLeod (Eds.), *Intentional forgetting: Interdisciplinary approaches* (pp. 453–481). Mahwah, NJ: Erlbaum.

Bjork, R. A., & Woodward, A. E. (1973). Directed forgetting of individual words in free recall. *Journal of Experimental Psychology, 99*, 22–27.

Christensen-Szalanski, J. J., & Willham, C. F. (1991). The hindsight bias: A meta-analysis. *Organizational Behavior and Decision Processes, 48*, 147–168.

Cruse, D., & Jones, R. A. (1976). Intentional forgetting of tones in a choice recognition-time task. *Journal of Experimental Psychology: Human Learning and Memory, 2*, 577–585.

Davis, J. C., & Okada, R. (1971). Recognition and recall of previously forgotten items. *Journal of Experimental Psychology, 89*, 181–186.

Earles, J. L., & Kersten, A. W. (2002). Directed forgetting of actions by younger and older adults. *Psychonomic Bulletin and Review, 9*, 383–388.

Epstein, W. (1972). Mechanisms of directed forgetting. In G. H. Bower (Ed.), *The psychology of learning and motivation* (Vol. 6, pp. 147–191). New York: Academic Press.

Fischhoff, B. (1975). Hindsight-foresight: The effect of outcome knowledge on judgment under uncertainty. *Journal of Experimental Psychology: Human Perception and Performance, 1*, 288–299.

Fischhoff, B. (1977). Perceived informativeness of facts. *Journal of Experimental Psychology: Human Perception and Performance, 3*, 349–358.

Fleming, M. A., Wegener, D. T., & Petty, R. E. (1999). Procedural and legal motivations to correct for perceived judicial bias. *Journal of Experimental Social Psychology, 35*, 186–203.

Geiselman, R. E., & Bagheri, B. (1985). Repetition effects in directed forgetting: Evidence for retrieval inhibition. *Memory & Cognition, 13*, 57–62.

Geiselman, R. E., Bjork, R. A., & Fishman, D. L. (1983). Disrupted retrieval in directed forgetting: A link with posthypnotic amnesia. *Journal of Experimental Psychology: General, 112*, 58–72.

Golding, J. M. (2001, August). *Intentional forgetting in a social context*. Paper presented at the 109th Annual Convention of the American Psychological Association, San Francisco, CA.

Golding, J. M., Ellis, A. L., Hauselt, J., & Sego, S. A. (1998). Instructions to disregard potentially useful information in a group context. In J. M. Golding &

C. M. MacLeod (Eds.), *Intentional forgetting: Interdisciplinary approaches* (pp. 369–394). Mahwah, NJ: Erlbaum.

Golding, J. M., Fowler, S. B., Long, D. L., & Latta, H. (1990). Instructions to disregard potentially useful information: The effects of pragmatics on evaluative judgments and recall. *Journal of Memory and Language, 29,* 212–227.

Golding, J. M., & Hauselt, J. (1994). When instructions to forget become instructions to remember. *Personality and Social Psychology Bulletin, 20,* 178–183.

Golding, J. M., & Keenan, J. M. (1985). Directed forgetting and memory for directions to a destination. *American Journal of Psychology, 98,* 579–590.

Golding, J. M., & Long, D. L. (1998). There's more to intentional forgetting than directed forgetting: An integrative review. In J. M. Golding & C. M. MacLeod (Eds.), *Intentional forgetting: Interdisciplinary approaches* (pp. 59–102). Mahwah, NJ: Erlbaum.

Golding, J. M., & MacLeod, C. M. (1998). *Intentional forgetting: Interdisciplinary approaches.* Mahwah, NJ: Erlbaum.

Golding, J. M., MacLeod, C. M., & Long, D. L. (1994). You can't always forget what you want: Directed forgetting of related words. *Journal of Memory and Language, 33,* 493–510.

Golding, J. M., Sego, S. A., Hauselt, J., & Long, D. L. (1994). Pragmatics and the effect of instructions to forget information that varies in the magnitude of a trait. *The American Journal of Psychology, 107,* 223–243.

Harnishfeger, K. K., & Pope, R. S. (1996). Intending to forget: The development of cognitive retrieval inhibition in directed forgetting. *Journal of Experimental Child Psychology, 62,* 292–315.

Hasher, L., Attig, M. S., & Alba, J. A. (1981). I knew it all along: Or, did I? *Journal of Verbal Learning and Verbal Behavior, 20,* 86–96.

Hawkins, S. A., & Hastie, R. (1990). Hindsight: Biased judgments of past events after the outcomes are known. *Psychological Bulletin, 107,* 311–327.

Horton, K. D., & Petruk, R. (1980). Set differentiation and depth of processing in the directed forgetting paradigm. *Journal of Experimental Psychology: Human Learning and Memory, 2,* 566–576.

Hunt, R. R., & Einstein, G. O. (1981). Relational and item-specific information in memory. *Journal of Verbal Learning and Verbal Behavior, 20,* 497–514.

Isbell, L. M., Smith, H. L., & Wyer, R. S. (1998). Consequences of attempts to disregard social information. In J. M. Golding & C. M. MacLeod (Eds.), *Intentional forgetting: Interdisciplinary approaches* (pp. 289–320). Mahwah, NJ: Erlbaum.

James, W. (1890). *Principles of psychology: Vol. 1.* New York: Holt.

Johnson, H. M. (1994). Processes of successful intentional forgetting. *Psychological Bulletin, 116,* 274–292.

Kassin, S. M., & Sommers, S. R. (1997). Inadmissible testimony, instructions to disregard, and the jury: Substantive versus procedural considerations. *Personality and Social Psychology Bulletin, 23,* 1046–1054.

Kassin, S. M., & Studebaker, C. A. (1998). Instructions to disregard and the jury: Curative and paradoxical effects. In J. M. Golding & C. M. MacLeod (Eds.), *Intentional forgetting: Interdisciplinary approaches* (pp. 413–434). Mahwah, NJ: Erlbaum.

Keenan, J. M., MacWhinney, B., & Mayhew, D. (1977). Pragmatics in memory: A study of natural conversation. *Journal of Verbal Learning and Verbal Behavior, 16,* 549–560.

Kimball, D. R., & Bjork, R. A. (2002). Influences of intentional and unintentional forgetting on false memories. *Journal of Experimental Psychology: General, 131,* 116–130.

Kraemer, P. J., & Golding, J. M. (1997). Adaptive forgetting in animals. *Psychonomic Bulletin & Review, 4,* 480–491.

Kučera, H., & Francis, W. N. (1967). *Computational analysis of present-day American English.* Providence, RI: Brown University Press.

Lavy, E. H., & van den Hout, M. (1990). Thought suppression induces intrusions. *Behavioural Psychotherapy, 18,* 251–258.

Lehman, E. B., McKinley-Pace, M. J., Wilson, J., Slavsky, M. D., & Woodson, M. E. (1997). Direct and indirect measures of intentional forgetting in children and adults: Evidence for retrieval inhibition and reinstatement. *Journal of Experimental Child Psychology, 64,* 295–316.

MacLeod, C. M. (1975). Long-term recognition and recall following directed forgetting. *Journal of Experimental Psychology: Human Learning and Memory, 104,* 271–279.

MacLeod, C. M. (1989). Directed forgetting affects both direct and indirect tests of memory. *Journal of Experimental Psychology: Learning, Memory, and Cognition, 15,* 13–21.

MacLeod, C. M. (1998). Directed forgetting: The human memory literature. In J. M. Golding & C. M. MacLeod (Eds.), *Intentional forgetting: Interdisciplinary approaches* (pp. 1–57). Mahwah, NJ: Erlbaum.

MacLeod, C. M. (1999). The item and list methods of directed forgetting: Test differences and the role of demand characteristics. *Psychonomic Bulletin & Review, 6,* 123–129.

Marks, W., & Dulaney, C. L. (2001). Encoding processes and attentional inhibition in directed forgetting. *Journal of Experimental Psychology: Learning, Memory, and Cognition, 27,* 1464–1473.

Paller, K. A. (1990). Recall and stem-completion priming have different electrophysiological correlates and are modified differently by directed forgetting. *Journal of Experimental Psychology: Learning, Memory, and Cognition, 16,* 1021–1032.

Petty, R. E., & Wegener, D. T. (1993). Flexible correction processes in social judgment: Correcting for context-induced contrast. *Journal of Experimental Social Psychology, 40,* 137–165.

Reed, H. (1970). Studies of the interference process in short-term memory. *Journal of Experimental Psychology, 84,* 452–457.

Roediger, H. L., & Crowder, R. G. (1972). Instructed forgetting: Rehearsal control or retrieval inhibition (repression). *Cognitive Psychology, 3*, 244–254.

Ross, L., Lepper, M. R., & Hubbard, M. (1975). Perseverance in self-perception and social perception: Biased attributional processes in the debriefing paradigm. *Journal of Personality and Social Psychology, 32*, 880–892.

Sahakyan, L., & Kelley, C. M. (2002). A contextual change account of the directed forgetting effect. *Journal of Experimental Psychology: Learning, Memory, and Cognition, 28*, 1064–1072.

Slovic, P., & Fischhoff, B. (1977). On the psychology of experimental surprises. *Journal of Experimental Psychology: Human Perception and Performance, 3*, 544–551.

Sue, S., Smith, R. E., & Caldwell, C. (1973). Effects of inadmissible evidence on the decisions of simulated jurors: A moral dilemma. *Journal of Applied Social Psychology, 3*, 345–353.

Thompson, W. C., Fong, G. T., & Rosenhan, D. L. (1981). Inadmissible evidence and juror verdicts. *Journal of Personality and Social Psychology, 40*, 453–463.

Thompson, W. C., & Fuqua, J. (1998). "The jury will disregard . . ." : A brief guide to inadmissible evidence. In J. M. Golding & C. M. MacLeod (Eds.), *Intentional forgetting: Interdisciplinary approaches* (pp. 435–452). Mahwah, NJ: Erlbaum.

Wegener, D. T., & Petty, R. E. (1995). Flexible correction processes in social judgment: The role of naive theories in corrections for perceived bias. *Journal of Personality and Social Psychology, 68*, 36–51.

Wegner, D. M. (1989). *White bears and other unwanted thoughts*. New York: Viking Press.

Wegner, D. M. (1994). Ironic processes of mental control. *Psychological Review, 101*, 34–52.

Wegner, D. M., & Erber, R. (1993). Social foundations of mental control. In D. M. Wegner & J. W. Pennebaker (Eds.), *Handbook of mental control* (pp. 37–56). Englewood Cliffs, NJ: Prentice-Hall.

Wegner, D. M., Schneider, D. J., Carter, S., III, & White, L. (1987). Paradoxical effects of thought suppression. *Journal of Personality and Social Psychology, 53*, 5–13.

Weiner, B. (1968). Motivated forgetting and the study of repression. *Journal of Personality, 36*, 213–234.

Weiner, B., & Reed, H. (1969). Effects of the instructional sets to remember and forget on short-term retention: Studies of rehearsal control and retrieval inhibition (repression). *Journal of Experimental Psychology, 79*, 226–232.

Wilkie, W. L., McNeill, D. L., & Mazis, M. B. (1984). Marketing's "Scarlet Letter": The theory and practice of corrective advertising. *Journal of Marketing, 48*, 11–31.

Woodward, A. E., & Bjork, R. A. (1971). Forgetting and remembering in free recall: Intentional and unintentional. *Journal of Experimental Psychology, 89*, 109–116.

Wyer, R. S., & Budesheim, T. L. (1987). Person memory and judgments: The impact of information that one is told to disregard. *Journal of Personality and Social Psychology, 53,* 14–29.

Wyer, R. S., & Unverzagt, W. H. (1985). Effects of instructions to disregard information on its subsequent recall and use in making judgments. *Journal of Personality and Social Psychology, 48,* 533–549.

Zacks, R. T., Radvansky, G., & Hasher, L. (1996). Studies of directed forgetting in older adults. *Journal of Experimental Psychology: Learning, Memory, and Cognition, 32,* 143–156.

12

DIRECTED FORGETTING TASKS IN CLINICAL RESEARCH

RICHARD J. MCNALLY

Most people try to avoid thinking about unpleasant things. Few assertions in psychology could be more banal than this one. This bromidic claim conceals important issues concerning forgetting emotional material. For example, attempts to forget often fail. A desire to forget must not be confused with an ability to do so. As classic work by Wegner and his colleagues has shown, attempts to expel unwanted thoughts from awareness often backfire (Wegner, 1994; Wenzlaff & Wegner, 2000). Deliberate efforts not to think about a target thought often increase its frequency. This statement may be especially true when subjects try to forget personally upsetting topics (McNally & Ricciardi, 1996), including traumatic ones, such as memories of being raped (Shipherd & Beck, 1999).

If someone does manage to banish unwanted thoughts from awareness, what mechanism mediates this achievement? As every psychology undergraduate has been told, two psychodynamic candidates are repression and suppression. According to Chaplin's (1968, p. 423) dictionary of psychological terms, "repression should not be confused with suppression or inhibition.

Preparation of this article was supported in part by National Institute of Mental Health Grant MH61268 awarded to Richard J. McNally.

Both of the latter processes are voluntary. The essential mechanism of repression was held by Freud to be unconscious and involuntary." Contrary to this bit of folklore, Freud was strikingly cavalier about this issue, sometimes viewing repression as a conscious mechanism, sometimes viewing it as an unconscious one, and sometimes saying it could be either. Consider the following quotations, each exemplifying one of these three views. Seemingly discussing suppression, he once wrote that for hysteria to emerge, *"an idea must be intentionally repressed from consciousness* and excluded from associative modification" (Breuer & Freud, 1895/1955, p. 116, emphasis in original). Yet elsewhere he wrote that impulses, memories, and so forth are "stifled before they enter consciousness" (Freud, 1914/1957, p. 93)—a textbook description of repression. Yet he also wrote that "the essence of repression lies simply in turning something away, and keeping it at a distance, from the conscious" (1915/1962, p. 147).

Some scholars seem to regard Freud's vagueness about repression as a virtue. If repression means nothing more than trying not to think about something unpleasant, then perhaps Freud can be rescued from oblivion and his insights integrated into contemporary cognitive science (Erdelyi, 1990; Westen, 1998). For example, Erdelyi interprets research on directed forgetting as potentially vindicating Freud's views on repression.

But paring down the concept of repression to its bare-bones essence—trying not to think about something unpleasant—eliminates its distinctively Freudian character. What makes Freud's repression different from this everyday notion is its connection to other concepts in the psychoanalytic system. Once repression is stripped of its characteristic Freudian connotations, there will be little left to integrate with cognitive science.

In fact, experimental psychopathologists have been studying the remembering and forgetting of emotional material for more than a decade, and very little of this work has been inspired by psychoanalytic thinking (for reviews, see McNally, 1996; Williams, Watts, MacLeod, & Mathews, 1997). One need not be Freudian to investigate mechanisms of emotional forgetting.

The purposes of this chapter are twofold. First, I review several methodological issues that arise when researchers attempt to study forgetting of negative emotional material in clinical populations. Second, I summarize recent experiments on directed forgetting in these populations.

METHODOLOGICAL ISSUES

Golding (see chap. 11, this volume) describes the standard methods for studying forgetting in the cognitive psychology laboratory (e.g., item method, list method). Additional methodological issues arise when researchers attempt to adapt these procedures to investigate forgetting of affective material in clinical populations.

Pilot Research

Most universities have a seemingly unlimited supply of subjects for basic research. An abundance of subjects enables cognitive psychologists to fine-tune their methods in pilot studies prior to launching their experiments. Experimental psychopathologists seldom have the luxury of a functionally unlimited supply of psychiatric patients with the target diagnosis (e.g., panic disorder). But if one wishes to test hypotheses about forgetting emotional material, how is one to know whether the procedures are sufficiently sensitive and the material sufficiently evocative short of wasting precious patients in pilot studies? One possibility is to test undergraduates with a subclinical version of obsessive–compulsive disorder (OCD), social phobia, or other disorder. If stimuli are emotionally evocative for subclinical subjects, then they will likely work for real patients. One caveat is that students with subclinical versions of the disorder may be psychiatrically healthy precisely because the relevant cognitive mechanisms are intact for them, but not for the patients. For example, an inability to expel unwanted thoughts from awareness may be the derangement that distinguishes genuine OCD from its subclinical variant. Likewise, students with elevated scores on the Anxiety Sensitivity Index (Reiss, Peterson, Gursky, & McNally, 1986)—a questionnaire measure of the fear of fear, a notable feature of panic disorder (McNally, 1994)—exhibit few of the cognitive biases associated with the actual illness (McNally, Hornig, Hoffman, & Han, 1999).

To cope with this issue, psychopathologists have attempted to follow the methods of their cognitive colleagues as closely as possible, and have piloted either on a few patients or on subclinical subjects—and then have held their breath and hoped that all goes well.

Selecting Emotional Stimuli

Experimental cognitive research on emotional disorders can concern either content-independent or content-dependent biases. Some researchers have studied content-independent abnormalities, such as heightened distractibility in people with elevated anxiety levels (e.g., Eysenck, 1992). Others have investigated biases that become evident only when patients process certain kinds of material, often threatening and personally relevant. Just as cardiologists sometimes need to expose their patients to stress tests to unmask underlying heart problems, experimental psychopathologists often need to expose their patients to certain kinds of emotional material to uncover latent cognitive biases.

What considerations affect selection of stimuli? Most studies have involved lexical cues that afford flexibility and specificity to certain disorders. Some words are threatening to people with some disorders, whereas others are not. Use of lexical stimuli enables one to tailor cues to each disorder. For example, in an emotional Stroop experiment, Hope, Rapee, Heimberg, and Dombeck (1990) found that words threatening for panic disorder patients were not evocative for those with social phobia, whereas words threatening for social phobia patients were not evocative for those with panic disorder. All directed forgetting research on clinical populations has involved words that varied in emotional valence. We recently used pictorial threat cues in an emotional Stroop experiment for individuals with intense fear of snakes (Constantine, McNally, & Hornig, 2001). But it is difficult to identify pictorial cues to match the concerns of most people with anxiety and other emotional disorders. This can easily be done for fears of snakes and spiders, and using photographs of people expressing negative, evaluative facial expressions might work for people with social phobia. Pictorial threat cues might also work for certain groups of patients with posttraumatic stress disorder (PTSD). For example, one might test whether photographs of combat scenes, relative to other scenes, are more difficult to forget. After seeing a series of combat-related pictures, might veterans with PTSD subsequently recall more of those they were instructed to forget, relative to veterans without the disorder? As far as I know, no investigator has used directed forgetting methods to investigate forgetting of emotional pictures in people with psychiatric disorders.

If one plans to use lexical stimuli, how should one choose the words? For syndromes whose concerns are relatively homogeneous (e.g., social phobia, PTSD in Vietnam combat veterans), experimenters can draw up a list of words, have people with the diagnosis rate them on stress-relevance scales, and then select the words with the highest stress ratings (e.g., McNally et al., 1987). These words, in turn, can serve as the negative emotional stimuli in the experiment.

This method can be a bit risky when people with the same disorder vary in terms of their concerns. For example, some patients with panic disorder are preoccupied by fears of heart attack, but not impending insanity, whereas others worry about "going crazy" during their panics, but not about dying during them. Patients with OCD present an even greater problem; their concerns can be amazingly diverse. In one of our PTSD studies involving the emotional Stroop task, we included an additional control group of OCD patients with contamination obsessions (McNally, Kaspi, Riemann, & Zeitlin, 1990). As it turned out, our patients had such atypical obsessions (e.g., fears about contamination from cat dander, WD-40 lubricating oil, and LSD) that they failed to react to our standard set of words (e.g., feces, urine).

To get around this problem of phenomenologic heterogeneity within a diagnostic group, researchers sometimes have patients themselves select relevant stimuli from a long list of diagnostically relevant threat words (e.g., Kaspi, McNally, & Amir, 1995). Tolin, Hamlin, and Foa (2002) used this approach in a directed forgetting experiment with OCD patients. The advantage of this idiographic stimulus selection procedure is that it ensures that words in the negative category are, indeed, threatening for each patient. The potential disadvantage is that different subjects process different words. Accordingly, researchers may need to conduct additional analyses to ensure that idiographically selected words do not differ on other variables (e.g., mean frequency of usage), or if they do, that these variables are unrelated to performance on the task (Riemann & McNally, 1995). Another approach is to use a standard set of validated words, but have subjects rate the emotional relevance of each word on scales ranging from 0 (not at all threatening) to 7 (very threatening) after the experiment is concluded. One can then determine whether any failure to obtain predicted effects is attributable to the irrelevance of certain words for certain patients.

Assuming that one opts to use a standard set of negative emotional words, how many should be used? Unfortunately, for directed forgetting experiments, one needs a nontrivial number of words per emotional category. For example, we had to use 20 trauma-related words in our study of directed forgetting in adult survivors of childhood sexual abuse with PTSD (McNally, Metzger, Lasko, Clancy, & Pitman, 1998). Unfortunately, the more words one needs, the less relevant some of them might be. Words such as incest, molested, and assault are clearly tied to abuse, but words such as semen, tortured, and scream are less so.

Selecting Control Stimuli

In addition to the category of negative emotional words, how many other stimulus categories should one use? At a minimum, one needs emotionally neutral words, preferably members of a single category (e.g., household items, fruits). To ensure that any effects obtained with negative words are attributable to negativity, not to emotionality in general, one also needs a category of positive emotional words. In some cognitive studies (but none yet in the directed forgetting area), researchers have added a disorder-irrelevant category of negative words (e.g., negative words relevant for OCD, but not for PTSD) to test the specificity of the effect. One directed forgetting study included positive words (e.g., clean) relative to the concerns of OCD patients to discriminate disorder relevance from negativity (Tolin et al., 2002).

Most directed forgetting research has included negative, positive, and neutral stimulus categories, or negative and positive ones. Most researchers have also endeavored to match the stimulus categories in terms of word frequency (Francis & Kučera, 1982). That is, the mean frequency of occurrence of the negative words should not differ significantly from that of the neutral words or of the positive words. Frequency of occurrence can affect the likelihood of a word being recalled or recognized irrespective of whether the word had received instructions to be forgotten (an F word) or instructions to be remembered (an R word).

Selecting Control Groups

Because older people may not perform as well as younger ones in directed forgetting experiments, researchers need to select control subjects whose ages are similar to those of subjects in the clinical groups. Accordingly, selecting a group of undergraduates as control subjects is a questionable practice if one's clinical group comprises 55-year-old Vietnam combat veterans with PTSD.

Most studies on directed forgetting have involved at least an age- and sex-matched psychiatrically healthy control group. In one study on OCD, the researchers included a control group of patients with generalized social phobia (in addition to a healthy control group) to test whether deficits predicted for OCD do not, in fact, occur in another anxiety disorder group (Tolin et al., 2002). In studies on PTSD, researchers often include an equally traumatized group of individuals without the disorder in addition to a control group of nontraumatized healthy control subjects (McNally et al., 1998). Researchers can thus distinguish any effects attributable to PTSD per se from the effects of having been exposed to trauma.

DIRECTED FORGETTING EXPERIMENTS: THE ITEM METHOD

Experimental psychopathologists have used directed forgetting methods to test hypotheses arising from several perspectives. In this section, I briefly review this literature, organizing the findings around diagnostic group.

Trauma and PTSD

Few controversies in psychology have been as contentious as the one concerning the reality of repressed and recovered memories of childhood sexual abuse (McNally, 2003a, 2003c). Some theorists believe that children exposed to repeated trauma, such as incest, develop a dissociative or avoidant encoding style that enables them to disengage attention from threatening cues during inescapable episodes of molestation and direct it elsewhere (e.g., Herman & Schatzow, 1987; Terr, 1991). For example, a child may attend to wallpaper or a doorknob, or otherwise pretend that he or she is elsewhere during an episode of abuse. Unable to escape physically from the perpetrator, the abused child may escape mentally by dissociating attention. Although this avoidant encoding style may be adaptive in the short run by enabling the child to attenuate the impact of otherwise overwhelming emotional trauma, it may make it difficult for survivors to remember and process their abuse memories later in life, according to some theorists (Terr, 1991). Repressed or dissociated (and therefore unprocessed) memories of early abuse allegedly give rise to psychiatric symptoms later in life.

These theoretical considerations imply that psychiatrically impaired adult survivors of childhood sexual abuse should have acquired a superior ability to disengage attention from threat cues, thereby impairing subsequent memory for these cues. If these individuals have, indeed, acquired this cognitive style, then it ought to be evident in the laboratory.

Accordingly, we used an item-cuing directed forgetting task to test the ability to forget trauma words in three groups of women (McNally et al., 1998). One group comprised women with histories of serious sexual abuse (penetration) and who met criteria for PTSD. Another group comprised women with equally serious abuse histories, but who had no psychiatric disorder (including PTSD). The last group comprised women with neither an abuse history nor PTSD. Each subject viewed a series of words on a computer screen. Each word appeared for two seconds and was replaced by a cue directing the subject either to remember (RRRR) or to forget (FFFF) the previous word. The words were from three categories: trauma (e.g., abused, molested, incest, shame), positive (e.g., carefree, elation, sociable, affection), and neutral (e.g., household category: curtain, dishwasher, lamp, stairs). Immediately after this encoding phase, subjects were asked to write down as many words as they could remember, regardless of original instructions to remember or forget. The dissociative encoding hypothesis implies that abuse survivors with PTSD should recall few trauma R words relative to positive and neutral R words, and relative to healthy abuse survivors and nonabused control subjects who presumably lack the skill and motivation to expel trauma-related material from memory. Moreover, the avoidant tendencies of the PTSD group should reduce the number of trauma R words recalled relative to other R words and relative to the other groups.

The results were precisely the opposite of these predictions: Abuse survivors with PTSD exhibited memory deficits, but only for positive and neutral words they were supposed to remember. They did not exhibit an enhanced ability to forget trauma words. In fact, they remembered trauma words all too well, including those they were supposed to forget. Contrary to predictions of some trauma theorists (e.g., Terr, 1991), these data implied that psychiatrically impaired sexual abuse survivors are characterized by an inability to cease encoding trauma words and therefore a difficulty in forgetting them. Childhood sexual abuse survivors without PTSD resembled healthy control subjects in their directed forgetting performance. Both groups recalled R words more often than F words, irrespective of word type.

All the abuse survivors who exhibited a breakdown in the ability to forget suffered from current PTSD. By definition, they were plagued by intrusive recollections of their abuse, findings fully consistent with their directed forgetting performance. Accordingly, we next investigated directed forgetting of trauma cues in two other groups that might be expected to exhibit the superior ability to forget trauma cues (McNally, Clancy, & Schacter, 2001), as Terr, Herman, and other trauma theorists have predicted. One group comprised women who reported having recovered memories of childhood sexual abuse after not having thought about these experiences for long periods of time. We were unable to corroborate the accuracy of these reports. A second group comprised women who believed they harbored repressed memories of childhood sexual abuse. Subjects in this group inferred their abuse history from a diverse set of presumed indicators of repressed memories of abuse (e.g., depressed mood, tension in the presence of a male relative, sudden images of a penis). None had any explicit, autobiographical memories of trauma. Finally, we compared the directed forgetting performance of the repressed and recovered memory groups with that of a nonabused control group. In this experiment, we did not do psychiatric diagnostic interviews to assess for PTSD, although psychometric assessments on recovered and especially repressed memory subjects in our research program indicate elevated levels of PTSD, depressive, and dissociative symptoms (McNally, Clancy, Schacter, & Pitman, 2000; for a review of this research program on the cognitive psychology of recovered memories, see McNally, 2001, 2003b).

Using the same methods as in our previous study, we tested whether superior forgetting of trauma words would occur in the recovered and (especially) repressed memory groups. If anyone should exhibit superior forgetting of trauma words, it should be subjects who had repressed and recovered memories of abuse. However, we found entirely "normal" memory functioning in these groups: They recalled trauma, positive, and neutral words they were told to remember more often than the trauma, positive, and neutral words they had been told to forget. They did not show impaired or enhanced memory for trauma-related words.

These two experiments indicate that none of the groups exhibited the predicted superior ability to forget material related to abuse. Survivors with PTSD remembered trauma words all too well, whereas those reporting repressed or recovered memories of sexual abuse exhibited neither enhanced nor impaired ability to forget these words. To be sure, the directed forgetting paradigm concerns mere words, not the autobiographical memories of abuse. Nevertheless, if trauma survivors were capable of forgetting memories of abuse, they should have been capable of forgetting mere words related to their trauma—pale proxies of the real thing.

Other researchers have used directed forgetting methods with other diagnostic groups who often report histories of early physical and sexual abuse. In fact, Cloitre and her colleagues were the first clinical research team to apply directed forgetting methods in trauma survivors (Cloitre, Cancienne, Brodsky, Dulit, & Perry, 1996). They found that women with borderline personality disorder who had been physically or sexually abused during childhood exhibited better recall for R words than did women with borderline personality disorder who had not been abused during childhood. However, Cloitre et al. did not include abuse-related words in this study, nor did they assess for PTSD.

Korfine and Hooley (2000), however, did use disorder-relevant material in an item-cuing directed forgetting experiment in which they tested women with borderline personality disorder. Relative to psychiatrically healthy control subjects, borderline personality subjects exhibited no deficits for negative (e.g., suicidal, abandon, enraged, reject), positive (e.g., celebrate, charming, sincere, creative), or uncategorized neutral (e.g., listen, collect, actually, consider) words they had been instructed to remember. Indeed, they exhibited heightened recall for negative F words relative to other words and relative to control subjects.

Some psychopathologists believe that severe physical and sexual abuse during childhood is an important cause of dissociative identity disorder (formerly multiple personality disorder) in adulthood (Putnam, Guroff, Silberman, Barban, & Post, 1986)—a view trenchantly criticized by others (Lilienfeld et al., 1999). In any event, clinical lore holds that these patients are capable of blocking out years of horrific abuse, only to recall it later during therapy (Young, Sachs, Braun, & Watkins, 1991). Elzinga and her colleagues tested these patients in a directed forgetting experiment (Elzinga, de Beurs, Sergeant, van Dyck, & Phaf, 2000). Dissociative identity disorder patients exhibited an inability to forget words they had been instructed to forget, especially sexual words. Once again, individuals who might have been expected to forget emotionally charged material had difficulty doing so.

Moulds and Bryant (2002) have published the only study suggesting that trauma survivors might be good at forgetting disturbing material. They tested patients who had recently been exposed to either a motor vehicle accident or a nonsexual assault. Patients with acute stress disorder recalled significantly fewer trauma F words relative to trauma-exposed people without the disorder and relative to non-trauma-exposed control subjects. However, the groups did not differ in their recall of trauma R words. It is unclear why a recently traumatized person would exhibit superior forgetting for trauma words, whereas those with chronic PTSD seem to exhibit dysfunction in the ability to expel disturbing material from awareness. It is possible that people still numb from the recent traumatic event may possess an edge in forgetting this material—an edge that vanishes once chronic PTSD develops.

Panic Disorder

People with anxiety disorders often exhibit an attentional bias for threatening words, without exhibiting a corresponding memory bias for these words (Williams et al., 1997). This effect has been most apparent for patients with generalized anxiety disorder (GAD). Threatening words capture attention in GAD (e.g., MacLeod, Mathews, & Tata, 1986), but seldom do GAD patients preferentially recall threat words relative to nonthreat words (Mogg, Mathews, & Weinman, 1987). Mogg et al. suggested that a two-stage process might be operative: rapid, attentional capture by threat cues followed by active expulsion of threatening material from awareness. An ability to disengage attention from threat cues, following early attentional capture, might explain why GAD patients do not exhibit an explicit memory bias for threat despite exhibiting an early attentional bias for threat.

Mogg et al.'s (1987) hypothesis about cognitive avoidance was a reasonable inference from the data. To test whether anxiety patients are, indeed, characterized by heightened ability to disengage attention from threat cues, cease encoding them, and therefore forget them, we used an item-cuing directed forgetting procedure (McNally, Otto, Yap, Pollack, & Hornig, 1999). We asked our panic disorder patients and psychiatrically healthy control subjects to view a series of words on a computer screen. Each word appeared for two seconds and was replaced by a string of letters instructing the subject either to remember the word (RRRR) or to forget it (FFFF). The words were drawn from three categories: threat (e.g., suffocate, insane, collapse, coronary), positive (e.g., confident, healthy, cheerful, relaxed), and neutral (e.g., household words: stairs, curtain, table, cabinet). Immediately after this encoding phase, subjects were asked to write down as many words as they could remember, irrespective of original encoding instructions (remember versus forget).

The results revealed a robust directed forgetting effect: R words were recalled much more often than were F words. Contrary to the cognitive avoidance hypothesis, panic patients did not exhibit superior forgetting of threat words relative to other words or relative to control subjects. However, Mogg et al. (1987) proposed their cognitive avoidance hypothesis in reference to GAD patients who exhibit an attentional bias for threat but no memory bias. We tested panic disorder patients who often exhibit attentional (e.g., McNally, Riemann, & Kim, 1990) and (sometimes) memory biases for threat (McNally, Foa, & Donnell, 1989). Our data do not refute Mogg et al.'s hypothesis about cognitive avoidance in GAD, but they do question its applicability to panic disorder.

Obsessive–Compulsive Disorder

Patients with OCD experience intrusive, distressing, unwanted thoughts, images, and impulses (obsessions). Accordingly, it is possible that patients with this disorder may experience a breakdown in the ability to expel and forget disturbing material from awareness. We tested this hypothesis by using methods similar to those of our panic disorder study, except that the threat category was OCD-relevant (e.g., infected, shit, filthy, accident; Wilhelm, McNally, Baer, & Florin, 1996). In contrast to control subjects, OCD patients exhibited difficulty forgetting negative F words relative to either positive or neutral F words. Not only did OCD patients exhibit heightened recall of negative F words, but this pattern was preserved on a recognition test, thereby implying that patients had difficulty ceasing to encode negative F words—a finding consistent with the phenomenology of OCD. Emotionality ratings of the words indicated that OCD patients rated F words they recalled as having greater personal, negative emotional significance than those F words they managed to forget.

Extending this work further, Tolin et al. (2002) tested OCD patients, patients with generalized social phobia, and healthy control subjects. Using an idiographic stimulus selection method, they had OCD patients select both negative and positive words relevant to their obsessions from a long list of possible words. For example, a patient with contamination obsessions and washing compulsions might select filthy and clean as personally relevant stimuli. Patients were also free to generate their own items if those on the list were not relevant. A recognition (but not recall) test revealed that OCD patients, relative to the other two groups, exhibited difficulty forgetting OCD-relevant words, irrespective of valence. Positive words relevant to their obsessions were just as difficult to forget as were negative ones.

DIRECTED FORGETTING EXPERIMENTS: THE LIST METHOD

Researchers studying how people forget emotional material have seldom used the list method. As Golding (see chap. 11, this volume) points out, the list method is apt for testing hypotheses about retrieval inhibition rather than differential encoding.

Using the list method, Myers, Brewin, and Power (1998) compared the ability of repressors and nonrepressors to inhibit negative emotional words (e.g., grieving, selfish, worried) versus positive emotional words (e.g., ecstatic, sociable, relaxed). Repressors are individuals who score low on self-report measures of anxiety, but high on self-report measures of social desirability. The subjects were female college students. In two experiments, repressors forgot more negative F words than did nonrepressors. Myers et al. concluded that people characterized by a repressive style of coping are especially talented at inhibiting disturbing information from entering awareness.

Power, Dalgleish, Claudio, Tata, and Kentish (2000) used similar methods in a study comparing patients with major depressive disorder, anxiety disorder (mainly panic disorder), and healthy control subjects. Similar to previous research on panic disorder (McNally et al., 1999), the anxiety disorder group did not exhibit either enhanced or impaired forgetting of negative adjectives (e.g., guilty, ugly). Strikingly, the depressed patients exhibited enhanced recall of negative F words. Attempts to forget these negative words actually enhanced their subsequent memorability.

My research group is currently applying the list method to test whether people reporting repressed or recovered memories of childhood sexual abuse can inhibit trauma-related words better than other words, relative to people who have always remembered their abuse or who have never been abused.

CONCLUSIONS

With the exception of a single study documenting heightened forgetting of threat cues in acute stress disorder (Moulds & Bryant, 2002), research has revealed breakdowns in the ability to forget disturbing material in PTSD (McNally et al., 1998), OCD (Tolin et al., 2002; Wilhelm et al., 1996), dissociative identity disorder (Elzinga et al., 2000), and borderline personality disorder (Korfine & Hooley, 2000). Individuals with panic disorder (McNally et al., 1999) or individuals reporting either repressed or recovered memories of childhood sexual abuse (McNally et al., 2001) exhibit neither impaired nor heightened ability to expel disturbing material from awareness. The content of the disturbing material has, of course, varied across studies because the clinical groups have varied. But otherwise the methods have varied little; researchers have almost always used the item method. Therefore, variations in the ability to forget are most likely attributable to variations in disorder.

There are several directions for future research on people with clinical disorders. First, Mogg et al.'s (1987) original hypothesis regarding cognitive avoidance in GAD has yet to be tested with directed forgetting methods. Second, directed forgetting methods might usefully be applied to study differences among people with mood disorders. For example, individuals with melancholic major depression are supposedly more plagued by rumination than are those with nonmelancholic major depression. If so, then the former group ought to exhibit great difficulty disengaging attention from negative self-referent words in a directed forgetting task. Third, researchers have seldom used the list method to study retrieval inhibition for encoded material that varies in emotional valence. If people with dissociative identity disorder, for example, are especially good at keeping encoded material out of awareness, as clinical lore has it, then they should exhibit heightened ability to forget trauma-related words in the list paradigm.

Experimental psychopathologists attempt to isolate cognitive mechanisms in the laboratory that presumably generate the signs and symptoms of emotional disorder in everyday life. To accomplish this aim, they must standardize materials and take other steps to ensure the internal validity of the study. But there is a risk to this approach: The results may not apply to the real world. In fact, some therapists question the relevance of these kinds of experiments for understanding repression, dissociation, and other putative mechanisms for banishing disturbing personal memories from awareness

(Brown, Scheflin, & Hammond, 1998, p. 98). The word *incest*, for example, cannot fully capture the sensory and narrative complexity of autobiographical memories of molestation. Yet experimentalists assume that the ability to remember or forget the word *incest* engages the same mechanisms involved in remembering or forgetting actual abuse episodes denoted by this word. Is this assumption justified? On the one hand, the differences between remembering the word *incest* and remembering an abuse episode seem to outweigh any similarities between them. On the other hand, using mere words as proxies for autobiographical memories may underestimate how the mechanisms play out in the real world. For example, if someone cannot expel the word *incest* from awareness, how can we expect them to expel autobiographical memories of trauma from consciousness?

For more than 30 years, experimental cognitive psychologists have studied the mechanisms of directed forgetting. Surprisingly, experimental psychopathologists, most of whom are clinicians, have only recently begun to apply these methods to investigate the ability (or inability) of clinical populations to expel unwanted material from mind. Unburdened by the baggage of repression and related psychoanalytic concepts, we can now investigate forgetting of emotional information with the rigor it deserves.

REFERENCES

Breuer, J., & Freud, S. (1955). Studies on hysteria. In J. Strachey (Ed. & Trans.), *The standard edition of the complete psychological works of Sigmund Freud* (Vol. 2, pp. 21–319). London: Hogarth Press. (Original work published 1895)

Brown, D., Scheflin, A. W., & Hammond, D. C. (1998). *Memory, trauma treatment, and the law*. New York: Norton.

Chaplin, J. P. (1968). *Dictionary of psychology*. New York: Dell.

Cloitre, M., Cancienne, J., Brodsky, B., Dulit, R., & Perry, S. W. (1996). Memory performance among women with parental abuse histories: Enhanced directed forgetting or directed remembering? *Journal of Abnormal Psychology, 105*, 204–211.

Constantine, R., McNally, R. J., & Hornig, C. D. (2001). Snake fear and the pictorial emotional Stroop paradigm. *Cognitive Therapy and Research, 25*, 757–764.

Elzinga, B. M., de Beurs, E., Sergeant, J. A., van Dyck, R., & Phaf, R. H. (2000). Dissociative style and directed forgetting. *Cognitive Therapy and Research, 24*, 279–295.

Erdelyi, M. H. (1990). Repression, reconstruction, and defense: History and integration of the psychoanalytic and experimental frameworks. In J. L. Singer (Ed.), *Repression and dissociation: Implications for personality theory, psychopathology, and health* (pp. 1–31). Chicago: University of Chicago Press.

Eysenck, M. W. (1992). *Anxiety: The cognitive perspective*. Hillsdale, NJ: Erlbaum.

Francis, W. N., & Kučera, H. (1982). *Frequency analysis of English usage*. Boston: Houghton Mifflin.

Freud, S. (1957). On narcissism: An introduction. In J. Strachey (Ed. & Trans.), *The standard edition of the complete psychological works of Sigmund Freud* (Vol. 14, pp. 73–102). London: Hogarth Press. (Original work published 1914)

Freud, S. (1962). Repression. In J. Strachey (Ed. & Trans.), *The standard edition of the complete psychological works of Sigmund Freud* (Vol. 14, pp. 146–158). London: Hogarth Press. (Original work published 1915)

Herman, J. L., & Schatzow, E. (1987). Recovery and verification of memories of childhood sexual trauma. *Psychoanalytic Psychology, 4*, 1–14.

Hope, D. A., Rapee, R. M., Heimberg, R. G., & Dombeck, M. J. (1990). Representations of the self in social phobia: Vulnerability to social threat. *Cognitive Therapy and Research, 14*, 177–189.

Kaspi, S. P., McNally, R. J., & Amir, N. (1995). Cognitive processing of emotional information in posttraumatic stress disorder. *Cognitive Therapy and Research, 19*, 433–444.

Korfine, L., & Hooley, J. M. (2000). Directed forgetting of emotional stimuli in borderline personality disorder. *Journal of Abnormal Psychology, 109*, 214–221.

Lilienfeld, S. O., Lynn, S. J., Kirsch, I., Chaves, J. F., Sarbin, T. R., Ganaway, G. K., & Powell, R. A. (1999). Dissociative identity disorder and the sociocognitive model: Recalling the lessons of the past. *Psychological Bulletin, 125*, 507–523.

MacLeod, C., Mathews, A., & Tata, P. (1986). Attentional bias in emotional disorders. *Journal of Abnormal Psychology, 95*, 15–20.

McNally, R. J. (1994). *Panic disorder: A critical analysis*. New York: Guilford Press.

McNally, R. J. (1996). Cognitive bias in the anxiety disorders. *Nebraska Symposium on Motivation, 43*, 211–250.

McNally, R. J. (2001). The cognitive psychology of repressed and recovered memories of childhood sexual abuse: Clinical implications. *Psychiatric Annals, 31*, 509–514.

McNally, R. J. (2003a). Progress and controversy in the study of posttraumatic stress disorder. *Annual Review of Psychology, 54*, 229–252.

McNally, R. J. (2003b). Recovering memories of trauma: A view from the laboratory. *Current Directions in Psychological Science, 12*, 32–35.

McNally, R. J. (2003c). *Remembering trauma*. Cambridge, MA: Belknap Press/Harvard University Press.

McNally, R. J., Clancy, S. A., & Schacter, D. L. (2001). Directed forgetting of trauma cues in adults reporting repressed or recovered memories of childhood sexual abuse. *Journal of Abnormal Psychology, 110*, 151–156.

McNally, R. J., Clancy, S. A., Schacter, D. L., & Pitman, R. K. (2000). Personality profiles, dissociation, and absorption in women reporting repressed, recovered, or continuous memories of childhood sexual abuse. *Journal of Consulting and Clinical Psychology, 68*, 1033–1037.

McNally, R. J., Foa, E. B., & Donnell, C. D. (1989). Memory bias for anxiety information in patients with panic disorder. *Cognition & Emotion, 3*, 27–44.

McNally, R. J., Hornig, C. D., Hoffman, E. C., & Han, E. M. (1999). Anxiety sensitivity and cognitive biases for threat. *Behavior Therapy, 30*, 51–61.

McNally, R. J., Kaspi, S. P., Riemann, B. C., & Zeitlin, S. B. (1990). Selective processing of threat cues in posttraumatic stress disorder. *Journal of Abnormal Psychology, 99*, 398–402.

McNally, R. J., Luedke, D. L., Besyner, J. K., Peterson, R. A., Bohm, K., & Lips, O. J. (1987). Sensitivity to stress-relevant stimuli in posttraumatic stress disorder. *Journal of Anxiety Disorders, 1*, 105–116.

McNally, R. J., Metzger, L. J., Lasko, N. B., Clancy, S. A., & Pitman, R. K. (1998). Directed forgetting of trauma cues in adult survivors of childhood sexual abuse with and without posttraumatic stress disorder. *Journal of Abnormal Psychology, 107*, 596–601.

McNally, R. J., Otto, M. W., Yap, L., Pollack, M. W., & Hornig, C. D. (1999). Is panic disorder linked to cognitive avoidance of threatening information? *Journal of Anxiety Disorders, 13*, 335–348.

McNally, R. J., & Ricciardi, J. N. (1996). Suppression of negative and neutral thoughts. *Behavioural and Cognitive Psychotherapy, 24*, 17–25.

McNally, R. J., Riemann, B. C., & Kim, E. (1990). Selective processing of threat cues in panic disorder. *Behaviour Research and Therapy, 28*, 407–412.

Mogg, K., Mathews, A., & Weinman, J. (1987). Memory bias in clinical anxiety. *Journal of Abnormal Psychology, 96*, 94–98.

Moulds, M. L., & Bryant, R. A. (2002). Directed forgetting in acute stress disorder. *Journal of Abnormal Psychology, 111*, 175–179.

Myers, L. B., Brewin, C. R., & Power, M. J. (1998). Repressive coping and the directed forgetting of emotional material. *Journal of Abnormal Psychology, 107*, 141–148.

Power, M. J., Dalgleish, T., Claudio, V., Tata, P., & Kentish, J. (2000). The directed forgetting task: Application to emotionally valent material. *Journal of Affective Disorders, 57*, 147–157.

Putnam, F. W., Guroff, J. J., Silberman, E. K., Barban, L., & Post, R. M. (1986). The clinical phenomenology of multiple personality disorder: Review of 100 recent cases. *Journal of Clinical Psychiatry, 47*, 285–293.

Reiss, S., Peterson, R. A., Gursky, D. M., & McNally, R. J. (1986). Anxiety sensitivity, anxiety frequency and the prediction of fearfulness. *Behaviour Research and Therapy, 14*, 1–8.

Riemann, B. C., & McNally, R. J. (1995). Cognitive processing of personally relevant information. *Cognition & Emotion, 9*, 325–340.

Shipherd, J. C., & Beck, J. G. (1999). The effects of suppressing trauma-related thoughts on women with rape-related posttraumatic stress disorder. *Behaviour Research and Therapy, 37*, 99–112.

Terr, L. C. (1991). Childhood traumas: An outline and overview. *American Journal of Psychiatry, 148*, 10–20.

Tolin, D. F., Hamlin, C., & Foa, E. B. (2002). Directed forgetting in obsessive-compulsive disorder: Replication and extension. *Behaviour Research and Therapy*, *40*, 793–803.

Wegner, D. M. (1994). Ironic processes of mental control. *Psychological Review*, *101*, 34–52.

Wenzlaff, R. M., & Wegner, D. M. (2000). Thought suppression. *Annual Review of Psychology*, *51*, 59–91.

Westen, D. (1998). The scientific legacy of Sigmund Freud: Toward a psychodynamically informed psychological science. *Psychological Bulletin*, *124*, 333–371.

Wilhelm, S., McNally, R. J., Baer, L., & Florin, I. (1996). Directed forgetting in obsessive-compulsive disorder. *Behaviour Research and Therapy*, *34*, 633–641.

Williams, J. M. G., Watts, F. N., MacLeod, C., & Mathews, A. (1997). *Cognitive psychology and the emotional disorders* (2nd ed.). Chichester, England: Wiley.

Young, W. C., Sachs, R. G., Braun, B. G., & Watkins, R. T. (1991). Patients reporting ritual abuse in childhood: A clinical syndrome. Report of 37 cases. *Child Abuse and Neglect*, *15*, 181–189.

V

AUTOBIOGRAPHICAL
MEMORY TASKS

13

AUTOBIOGRAPHICAL MEMORY TASKS: SIX COMMON METHODS

DAVID C. RUBIN AND AMY WENZEL

Of all the areas of cognition described in this book, the methods used to study autobiographical memory are those based least on traditional laboratory research. Historically, they owe their roots more to Galton, a founder of individual differences research, than to Ebbinghaus, a founder of the dominant laboratory memory tradition (Robinson, 1986). Recent developments have been influenced nearly as much by concepts and methods from life span developmental psychology as by cognitive psychology. In autobiographical memory, the information to be recalled is about events that occurred outside the laboratory and long before the test session. Moreover, there is usually no correct answer, or a least none known to the experimenter. Nonetheless, there are many similarities with the other methods considered in this volume.

In chapters 14 and 15, we review six ways autobiographical memory has been studied, as summarized in Table 13.1. The most common method in both experimental and clinical research, and the one to which we devote the most attention, is the word-cue method from experimental work (and its parallel Autobiographical Memory Test in clinical work). In this procedure, participants are presented with a cue, usually a single word, and instructed to

TABLE 13.1
Summary of Autobiographical Memory Methods

Method	Conditions of Retrieval	Stimulus	Clinical Application
Word-Cue	Free association	Words or pictures	Analysis of memory specificity, retrieval latency, and affective tone and its relation to pathology
Life Narrative	Free association	"Tell me your story"	Analysis of coherence of trauma narratives and their relation to pathology
Involuntary Memory Diary	Free association	Daily circumstances	Correlation between self-reported ratings of intrusive memories and pathology
Autobiographical Memory Interview	Structured interview	Questions probing successive life stages	Examination of semantic and autobiographical memory in pathology groups
Diary Recall	Probes from diary	Diary entries	None at present
Questionnaire	On-line judgments about memories	Structured questions	Examination of properties of traumatic memories

recall the first autobiographical memory that comes to mind. We also discuss two diary methods that, though they are less used in the experimental literature and are used hardly at all in clinical research, are appropriate for addressing fundamental questions of interest to clinical research, particularly the way memory content changes over time and the nature of the involuntary memories. Moreover, we examine a structured interview for assessing different types of autobiographical memories (e.g., episodic and semantic), a life narrative method, and questionnaire items designed to assess properties of autobiographical memories, such as the accompanying sensory experience.

Because of the richness and variety of methods used to study autobiographical memory, which method to use and how to adapt it to the questions at hand are not easy decisions. It is important for researchers to carefully consider the questions they wish to answer and the relevant theory before selecting and adapting a method. Although we describe established autobiographical memory protocols that exist in the literature to date, these methods are flexible and can be modified to examine new research questions. The information listed in the table under clinical application summarizes the manner in which the methods have been used with clinical populations to date. As work continues to progress in these areas, we expect to see these methodologies adapted and used with additional populations.

Autobiographical memory research reflects a unique balance of rigorous methodological implementation in contexts closer to real-world tasks. On the one hand, stimuli included in tasks must be carefully normed, and coding schemes to assess aspects of participants' must demonstrate acceptable reliability. On the other hand, in autobiographical memory research, participants' recollections potentially can lead to the uncovering of important variables relevant to the etiology and maintenance of psychopathology in a more open-ended and direct fashion than can more controlled modes of investigation. We invite researchers to apply existing methods with clinical populations as well as to modify these methods for their own purposes to add to this rich source of data.

REFERENCE

Robinson, J. A. (1986). Autobiographical memory: A historical prologue. In D. C. Rubin (Ed.), *Autobiographical memory* (pp. 19–24). Cambridge, England: Cambridge University Press.

14

AUTOBIOGRAPHICAL MEMORY TASKS IN COGNITIVE RESEARCH

DAVID C. RUBIN

In contrast to the topics considered in some of the other chapters in this volume, autobiographical memory is not defined by a single prototypical method or task, as is the Stroop task, nor is it a well-defined concept in a global theory as implicit memory can be. Exactly what is and is not an auto-biographical memory depends on the definitions and goals of the particular researchers. For everyone it is memory about the self (Conway & Pleydell-Pearce, 2000); some add no further constraints (e.g., Butters & Cermak, 1986). The most common two additional restrictions are of theoretical importance. The first is that the memory is of a specific event (Crovitz & Schiffman, 1974); that is, the memory is an episodic memory rather than semantic knowl-edge about oneself (Tulving, 1972, 1983). The second is that the memory comes with a sense of recollection or reliving of the original event (Baddeley, 1992; Brewer, 1996; Greenberg & Rubin, 2003; Wheeler, Stuss, & Tulving, 1997). These two restrictions are what separate autobiographical memory from other forms of memory in most theories. The methods described in this

---

I thank Dorthe Berntsen for comments on this chapter and support from National Institute on Aging Grant R01 AG 16340, National Institute of Mental Health Grant R01 MH 066079.

chapter, however, vary regarding the extent to which these added restrictions are used: Most methods require a specific event whereas none require a sense of recollection. But even if the definition of autobiographical memory is restricted to be a store of specific recollected events, autobiographical memory cannot simply be viewed as a particular kind of abstract memory system. As will follow from some of the methods reviewed in this chapter and the experimental and clinical literature, having an autobiographical memory involves integration among at least emotion, narrative, language, and imagery in several sensory modalities (Rubin, 1998; Rubin, Schrauf, & Greenberg, 2003). Thus, the study of autobiographical memory involves much of cognition and its relation to emotion.

Six methods have been commonly used to study autobiographical memory. The first method is the *word-cue method,* in which participants are asked to think of autobiographical memories cued by words or other stimuli. The second method is the *life-narrative method,* in which participants are simply asked to tell the experimenter about their lives. The third is the *involuntary-memory-diary method,* in which the request for willful retrieval found in the first two methods is replaced by the request for participants to record involuntary, or unbidden, autobiographical memories as they occur; participants may return to them later if needed to provide additional information. These first three methods are intended to be as open-ended as possible and to provide as unconstrained a view of memory as possible, both of which qualities are at the same time their main strengths and weaknesses. All fit naturally into clinical studies.

The fourth method is the *Autobiographical Memory Interview,* which was devised for the study of neuropsychological patients, but is applicable in other situations. It is the only method that is capitalized because, unlike the others, it is a formal copyrighted test. In contrast to the others, it asks for specific kinds of memories from specific time periods that are determined by the experimenter and not the participant. The fifth method is the *diary recall method,* in which participants record events for themselves or others and are later tested on their memory of the events. The events are recorded either at the end of each day or when the participant is signaled by a beeper. In contrast to the first four methods, this method allows the comparison of the original record and later retrieved versions of the same episode and thus can provide some measure of the accuracy of the memories and of which aspects of the memories are forgotten under a variety of cuing conditions. Finally, the sixth method is the *questionnaire method,* in which participants are asked to report on a series of properties of autobiographical memories. We discuss it last because it usually is used in combination with the other methods reviewed. In this method, the definition of autobiographical memory can be kept open, and participants can report whether their autobiographical memories were of a single episode or a combination of them and whether they had a sense of recollection. How these aspects of autobiographical memory affect other properties or vary across participant population can then be viewed as empirical findings that test theoretical distinctions.

The six methods discussed do not allow for the direct investigation of the clinically relevant substantive issues of accuracy versus suggestibility of memory, memory under hypnosis, eyewitness testimony, and the ease of recalling of once-forgotten memories (except as measured in diary studies). These are questions of memory in general, as opposed to autobiographical memory in particular, and have tended to develop their own literatures. I have also excluded studies of the dating of autobiographical memories (for reviews, see Friedman, 1993; Thompson, Skowronski, Larsen, & Betz, 1996), an active area of research, because it seems less relevant to studies of psychopathology. The following sources offer a more general review of the literature: Schacter (1996) places autobiographical memory in the context of memory in general, Conway's (1990) text reviews the experimental work on autobiographical memory, and several edited books provide tutorial chapters (Conway, Rubin, Spinnler, & Wagenaar, 1992; Rubin, 1986, 1996; Thompson et al., 1998). An excellent summary of much of the data and theoretical arguments can be found in Brewer (1996). The role of narrative in autobiographical memory is reviewed from several different perspectives in Neisser and Fivush (1994) and Rubin and Greenberg (2003). Flashbulb memories are reviewed in Conway (1995) and Winograd and Neisser (1992).

THE WORD-CUE METHOD

The word-cue method (also known as the Crovitz method, the Galton method, and the Galton–Crovitz method) was invented by Galton (1879) and revived in modern times by Crovitz and Schiffman (1974) and Robinson (1976). It can be seen as a precursor to Freud's free association method (Robinson, 1986). It is probably the most widely used method in experimental and clinical work and so receives the most attention here. The technique is simple and intended to give a sample of autobiographical memories that come to mind most easily. Participants are presented with stimuli, usually common words, and then asked to produce an autobiographical memory for each. Unless detailed descriptions of the memories are collected for later analysis, in the interests of time and confidentiality participants are informed that their descriptions should be brief and need be intelligible to only themselves, and that descriptions of any potentially illegal or embarrassing events should be coded so only they will understand them. After all memories are obtained, participants are asked to return to each memory description and date it. The dating is usually done last because dating a memory often requires accessing more memories related to it. Dating thereby would change the search for later memories and could lead participants to dwell on one time period. However, when many questions are asked about each memory, as in the questionnaire method, the date of the memory is obtained after each memory. In these cases, the distribution of memories is not usually of major theoretical interest and the other questions direct participants' attention in a number of directions.

The technique is flexible and has been used in varied ways. As few as one (Rubin, 1982) and as many as 900 (Rubin & Schulkind, 1997a) memories per person have been analyzed, the number depending on the goals of the experimenter and the time available. When a large number of memories are collected, it is typically to obtain a distribution of memories over the life span or to obtain enough memories from each participant to do within-individual analyses. Typical instructions have been as follows: "This is a study of autobiographical memory, that is, memory for events in your life that you can specify as occurring at one particular place and time. Shortly I will ask you to inspect each of the words on the following pages, one at a time, until a specific memory associated with that word comes to mind. As soon as you think of such a memory you should write it down in the space provided. One or two words should be sufficient, so you can later refer back to what you wrote" (Rubin, 1982, p. 24).

The three typical schemes for dating memories have been to ask the participant to record (a) their age at the time of the event (Berntsen & Rubin, 2002), (b) the exact date on which the event occurred (Rubin & Schulkind, 1997a, 1997b), and (c) how long ago the event occurred, using the standard time markers of English (e.g., 5 minutes ago, 2 months ago, 10 years ago; Crovitz & Schiffman, 1974; Rubin, 1982). Asking for the age of the participant at the event is simple and quick, but as about half of word-cued memories come from the most recent year, it is not precise for recent memories. When cuing is expected to produce fewer memories in the past year, it is an excellent technique. Asking for the exact date takes time and requires participants to estimate, which is difficult for some people, but for college students who are willing to spend the time, it is an excellent technique if the temporal distribution of memories is important. Asking how long ago events occurred is a good compromise, but produces a large number of memories at round numbers because the participants wish to communicate a lack of precision in their estimates. Thus, many more memories will be reported at 10 years ago than at 9 or 11 years ago.

The dates from all three methods can be used directly in most analyses, though it is often useful to convert the responses from the first two methods into time ago (i.e., time before the experimental session) to measure the retention interval. The procedure for plotting a distribution of memories over time is a bit more complex. For the first measure of asking the age of the participant at the time of the event, all that need be done is plot the number of memories at each age or, if a retention function is desired, the number of memories that occurred 0, 1, 2, 3, . . . years ago. As the average participant is six months from a birthday, the number of memories reported at the participant's current age is an underestimate and as an approximation could be doubled. For the second method of asking for exact dates, the dates are rank-ordered, and bins of an odd number of reported memories are formed. The range time of each bin is used to determine the density of memories and the median date of each bin to determine the times ago. For example, once the memories are rank-ordered, if there are 11 memories in a bin and the last memory occurs 5 days later than the first, there would be $5/11$ memories per day and that would be plotted at the time ago of the sixth memory in the bin (for details see Rubin, 1982). Finally, for the third method of asking how long ago the event occurred, Crovitz and Schiffman (1974) assumed that when a respondent reported that a memory occurred n time-units ago, the implied precision meant that the memory could be distributed evenly over $\pm \frac{1}{2}$ of the time-unit. Thus, a memory that was reported as occurring 24 hours ago was assigned to a bin ranging from 23.5 to 24.5 hours ago, whereas a memory reported as occurring one day ago was assigned to a bin ranging from 12 to 36 hours ago. Crovitz and Schiffman plotted these densities at each time marker of English from 1 hour to 17 years ago using the time-units of hours, days, weeks, months, and years. Often the distributions as a whole are fit to a theoretical curve (Rubin, 1982, 1986) though occasionally those of individual participants are fit (Rubin, 1982). Statistical tests are usually done with analysis of variance comparing theoretically interesting differences in specific periods of life or comparing the mean age of the memories across conditions. In the latter comparison, a logarithmic transformation is often used because of the highly skewed nature of the distribution, but this transformation seems to make little practical difference.

The words used as cues have varied. The properties of cue words have been studied, and words with high imagery value produce fewer missing memories and faster reaction times (Rubin, 1980; Rubin & Schulkind, 1997c). In college students, but not in older adults, words higher in imagery and meaningfulness produce memories from earlier in life (Rubin & Schulkind, 1997c). Rubin and his colleagues have used 125 words or subsets of them. The words, which are rated on 51 properties (Rubin, 1980), are listed here rank ordered by the number of valid responses they produced in an autobiographical memory cue word tasks. When fewer than 125 words are needed, those that produced the greatest number of memories are a reasonable sample though some words may not be appropriate for all populations. The 125 words are fire, wine, death, hospital, kiss, mountain, ocean, sickness, candy, city, doctor, dress, horse, lake, love, mother, party, plant, poetry, ambulance, church, dirt, friend, health, money, river, tobacco, window, anger, anxiety, book, flower, paper, pencil, salad, warmth, water, baby, bird, history, home, orchestra, ship, tree, vision, agility, corpse, cottage, engine, errand, green, ink, star, violation, clothing, dream, hammer, hide, street, thief, trouble, trumpet, vehicle, boy, breast, door, excuse, frog, fur, salute, vanity, blossom, butter, comedy, girl, kindness, bowl, grief, humor, joy, time, village, chair, child, memory, table, truth, army, opinion, pride, seat, hatred, jelly, month, priest, square, beggar, earth, theory, butterfly, comparison, justice, custom, hostage, industry, revolt, woman, person, shadow, kerosene, world, king, power, menace, rattle, patent, capacity, moment, contents, prairie, nectar, virtue, glacier, malice, and context.

In addition to words in one language, researchers have provided the words in two languages in order to examine the role of cuing in one language or another, testing in each language on different days (Schrauf & Rubin, 1998, 2000; see Schrauf, 2000, for clinical implications of retrieval in different languages). Odors and pictures (Chu & Downes, 2000; Herz & Cupchik, 1992; Rubin, Groth, & Goldsmith, 1984) and even no stimuli with a request for "50 events from your life . . . just let your mind wander until you happen on them" have also been used (Rubin, 1982, p. 27). To examine particular kinds of memories, instead of using word cues, researchers have asked participants for their most vivid (Fitzgerald, 1988), most important memories (Rubin & Schulkind, 1997c); memories to go into the book of their life (Fitzgerald, 1996); and their most happy, sad, or traumatic autobiographical memory (Berntsen & Rubin, 2002). Such cues are not intended to sample autobiographical memory in as neutral a way as are random words, pictures, or odors, but to sample cultural norms or the narrative structure of memory and emotion. The distribution of such memories over the life span has been the common question in these studies, with additional questions intended to address other issues. Variations such as these, but selected to probe a particular psychopathology, such as a specific phobia or clinical issue, would be easy extensions.

Here and in most autobiographical memory research outside the flash-bulb memory and eyewitness literatures, the accuracy of the memory and even the existence of the event remembered are not verified. The dating of the memories in college students, however, has been checked and appears quite good. Rubin (1982) reported on nine undergraduates who were keeping and had kept diaries for an average of six years and who could find more than a quarter of their word-cued memories in their diaries. The median error was 0 days, indicating that the errors were not biased. The median of the absolute error was three days, with 74% of the dates within one month of the date found in the diary, which indicates that the errors were in general small.

In terms of the distribution of memories over the life span, the word-cue method, though it lacks much in the way of experimental control, has provided extremely regular results. There is a childhood amnesia component for the early years of life, a retention component for the most recent two decades, and, for participants over 40, a reminiscence bump in the form of an increase in memories from adolescence and early adulthood. The first two components are extremely regular. Results from different studies with the word-cued and other methods provide remarkably similar plots for childhood amnesia, in which there are few memories from the first years of life

(Rubin, 2000). The retention component is fit by a power function with r^2 values above .95 (Crovitz & Schiffman, 1974; Rubin, 1982). The bump varies in form a bit more, but appears in many methods (Rubin, 2002; Rubin, Rahhal, & Poon, 1998; Rubin & Schulkind, 1997a, 1997b), though it does not occur when participants are asked to produce their saddest or most traumatic memory (Berntsen & Rubin, 2002).

Reaction times have often been measured, but there are no clear effects as a function of the age of the memories, though as with other cognitive tasks older adults are slower (Rubin & Schulkind, 1997a). Other properties also do not vary with the age of the memory including vividness, pleasantness, emotionality significance, novelty of the event, and frequency of rehearsal (Conway & Haque, 1999; Jansari & Parkin, 1996; Rubin & Schulkind, 1997a). Whether participants have a recollective experience as opposed to just knowing about the event without any sense of reliving it also does not vary with the age of the memory in older adults (Rybash & Monaghan, 1999). Although decay in many properties would be expected, it seems that asking for any memory that pops into mind works against this. Memories that are easy to recall are rated equally on many properties regardless of their age. Thus, one advantage of the word-cued memories is that variability in such measures is not typically confounded with the age of the memory. In addition, there have been no reports of gender differences in the distribution of memories or in ratings, and explicit attempts to find them have failed (Rubin, Schulkind, & Rahhal, 1999).

THE LIFE-NARRATIVE METHOD

Instead of being cued with words or other stimuli to provide autobiographical memories, people can simply be asked to relate their life in narrative form. This method has the advantage of using a natural request; people are often asked for a version of their life story, either directly or implicitly in a social situation (Linde, 1993). Moreover, being able to do this task is an important developmental landmark (Habermas & Bluck, 2000). The request for a life narrative is less likely to sample a wide range of memories because there is an implied request for important life events that form a coherent story and that tell the interviewer about important traits of the participant that are inherent parts of a narrative (Rubin & Greenberg, 2003). This difference is either an advantage or disadvantage depending on the goals of the study. Narratives that are generated by a structured interview, that are for time periods shorter than a lifetime, or that involve groups (e.g., Bruner & Feldman, 1996; Hirst & Manier, 1996) are less common than the open-ended method reviewed here. A variety of related methods exist in the literature on life review and reminiscence, which unfortunately is a separate literature with few cross citations to the cognitive literature (for a review and discussion of this separation see Fitzgerald, 1996).

Fromholt and Larsen and their colleagues have used the life narrative method in autobiographical memory research with older participants (Fromholt & Larsen, 1991, 1992; Fromholt, Larsen, & Larsen, 1995; Fromholt et al., 2003). Participants in these studies are asked to "Tell about the events that have been important in your life." The participants are told about the 15-minute time limit in the instructions so that they can plan the length of their life stories. Narratives end naturally or when the allotted time is used. In contrast, Schrauf and Rubin (2001) provided less guidance with respect to time, letting social expectations provide them with 30- to 45-minute narratives. Interviews are tape-recorded and later transcribed for analyses. Questions (such as the dating of events and those discussed later in the questionnaire method) can be asked after the life narrative is obtained in the same session if the interviewer, or interviewers, make notes in order to isolate and provide a brief description of each event in the narrative. Researchers must take care not to influence the participants during the interview by showing special interest in certain issues or life periods, although interest and social encouragement are provided.

In the cue-word technique, the response to each cue is considered to be a memory. The life-narrative method produces a continuous stream of memories, and so the first step in analyzing the data is to divide the life narrative into distinct events. In practice, this can be accomplished fairly easily. Each memory is defined as "a thematically delimited set of information that referred to a past event, the content of which separated it from prior and succeeding information" (Fromholt & Larsen, 1991, p. 88). Thus, in this method a brief event, an extended episode such as a vacation, and a repisodic memory (Neisser, 1981) such as going fishing repeatedly over the course of several years are all considered as autobiographical memories, with dating of the longer periods at their midpoint. The following dependent variables have been considered once the life narrative was divided into events or memories, with many variables showing differences among groups (e.g., Fromholt et al., 2003): (a) the number of memories in the life narrative; (b) the amount of detail in each memory scored with a three-point scale, in which events expressed in a single sentence receive one point, events with up to three additional pieces of information receive two, and events with more elaborated contents receive three; (c) repetitions of memories, though this variable is considered mainly in demented patients (Fromholt & Larsen, 1991); (d) the number of transitional events, that is, events that signify a major change in life (e.g., starting school, getting married, or being widowed); (e) emotional valence scored on a three-point scale of positive, neutral, and negative (For such judgments, Fromholt, Larsen, and colleagues adopted a strict criterion to avoid false attributions of emotionality. All memories in which the participant did not specifically express emotional quality were scored as neutral.); (f) the memories are dated, and either the age of the respondent during the reported event or how long ago the reported event occurred is analyzed, both to examine the distribution of memories over the life span and to note changes in the other measures over the life span; and finally (g) backward searches are a violation of a strict temporal order and thus can be seen as one measure of disorder in the telling of the life narrative. Once the memories are dated, those that do not fall in strict temporal order can be easily noted. A normalized measure can be obtained by dividing the number of memories occurring earlier in real time than the one that was before it in the narrative by the number of memories occurring later in real time than the one that occurred before it in the narrative (Schrauf & Rubin, 2001).

Another form of life narrative analysis is the *sequence and templates in narrative* method developed and standardized by Luborsky and colleagues (Luborsky, 1987, 1990, 1993, 1998). The first of two questions is "I'd like to know more about you and your life. Would you describe your life for me, whatever comes to mind about it? Start where you like; take as much time as you need." No framework is imposed by the interviewer. No suggestion is made that a chronological approach be taken. Phrases such as "important events of your life" are not used to avoid generating an account indexed to social norms. The interviewer listens without interruption until the person has finished. Luborsky's experience is that once they have begun, people will talk uninterruptedly for 20 to 30 minutes about their own lives. The first step in his analysis, as with the one developed by Fromholt and Larsen, is to divide the continuous narrative into individual events or memories.

In the second section of the interview, the researcher asks that the participant depict his or her whole life with a pair of contrasting images or structures: a sequence of book chapters and a mural with many scenes and themes. These frames are purposely provided in order to "probe a person's affinity for a particular image. The chapters provide a linear chronology of socially normative and bounded categories. The mural image provides for the simultaneous presentation of diverse experiences and events without attention to sequence, boundaries, and coherence" (Luborsky, 1998, pp. 321–322). Luborsky has found that how individuals impose narrative coherence on their life-stories sorts into general types. Some individuals organize their life-stories according to the dominant *cultural life-course* reflected in their ethnic socialization. The cultural life-course (Fry, 1990) includes expected transitions (e.g., graduate college at 23, marriage in the late 20s, children in the 30s, retirement at age 65). Other individuals, whose lives challenge the cultural patterns, adopt *personal themes* in organizing their narratives and use other metaphors for shaping their narratives (e.g., "life is sweet," "the bitter life," "the devoted, silent life," "life as a hurdle race"; Ruth & Oberg, 1996). Still others employ a *recursive* strategy and tell their stories by domain, beginning at some appropriate point and following the thread to the stop-point (or present moment) of that domain: life at home, life at school, work history, marriage and family (Luborsky, 1990, 1998). This choice of narrative framework on the part of the individual can change over time, of course, and may be indicative in any given moment of the individual's sense of adjustment to life's challenges.

THE INVOLUNTARY MEMORY DIARY METHOD

Although Ebbinghaus considered them as one of the three main types of memory, modern cognitive psychologists have generally not studied involuntary memories. Nonetheless, involuntary memories are observed in clinical settings and are symptoms in a range of disturbances—especially posttraumatic stress disorder. Moreover, studies have indicated that most undergraduates have involuntary memories at least several times a week (Berntsen, 1996; Brewin, Christoulides, & Hutchinson, 1996). A survey study of a representative sample of the Danish population showed that most people knew about involuntary memories and rated them as being common (Berntsen & Rubin, 2002). Because many involuntary memories vanish quickly, recording them as they occur as opposed to retrospectively provides a description less biased toward those involuntary memories that are themselves especially memorable.

A diary method has recently been used to study such memories at the time that they occur (Berntsen, 1996, 1998, 2001). Two demands are in conflict in this method. The first is to make the recording of involuntary memories as quick and easy as possible so that the act of recording them as they occur will not put too much of a burden on participants. The second is to record as much information as possible about each memory. The compromise is to record at the time of the involuntary memory the information that is most important to the study and that is most likely to change or be forgotten with the passage of a few hours and to provide other information later that day. To accomplish this, the participant carries a small notebook with some questions. In Berntsen's studies, participants are able to provide a brief description of each involuntary memory and complete 10 rating-scale questions without difficulty. An additional set of questions is filled out at the participants' convenience later during the same day. In some studies a comparison word-cued memory task is added, in which the experimenter provides a cue word and the same set of questions answered about the involuntary memory.

At the start of the task, participants in Berntsen's studies were given individual detailed instructions. An involuntary memory was defined as a memory about a past event that is brought to consciousness with no preceding attempts at retrieving the memory. The participants were informed that an involuntary memory could be cued by their surroundings or aspects of current thought, but if an autobiographical memory were cued by current thoughts, it was to be considered involuntary only if the cuing of the memory had occurred without voluntary attempts. It was stressed that involuntary memories could deal with all kinds of personal experiences, pleasant as well as unpleasant, recent as well as remote. Emotionally neutral examples were used as illustrations during the instruction. Participants were informed that it was legitimate to skip a record if it appeared too intimate and embarrassing. As there was no possible way of preventing the participant from excluding records, making such exclusions a possible part of the procedure allowed the experimenter to ask, subsequent to recording, whether or not the participant had censored responses. In Berntsen's (1996) study, only a few reported that they had skipped one or two records, because the record was too intimate or too difficult to describe in words. In Berntsen's studies, participants are limited to the first two involuntary memories that occur each day. Although the particular questions changed for each study, questions answered immediately have included the following rating scales: vividness of the memory, impact on mood, physical reactions, emotional valence, and relation to a previous trauma.

In most cases, the involuntary memories are found to have recognizable environmental cues. Recent and distinctive events are found to dominate, and the majority of the memories are rated emotionally positive or neutral. Nonetheless, undergraduates' most traumatic memories occur more frequently among involuntary memories than do memories of their most positive events. Compared with voluntary word-cued memories, involuntary memories refer more frequently to specific episodes and are less rehearsed (Berntsen, 1998). Although this method is new and has been used by only a few laboratories, it is included here because of its potential to examine how active concerns, as well as environmental stimuli, cue memories without conscious effort. Such a technique is especially relevant for clinical research in which involuntary memories (as either intrusive memories or rumination) can be an important symptom and can provide a window on ongoing thought processes that occasionally break into and interrupt conscious thought.

THE AUTOBIOGRAPHICAL MEMORY INTERVIEW

In the word-cue, life-narrative, involuntary-memory-diary, and diary recall methods the participant generates the events. Participant generation is ideal if the researcher wants to know what memories come to mind under various situations or what events tend to occur or be distinct enough to be noted. However, it is often useful to document what people can remember rather than what they (consciously or unconsciously) select to remember, and it is often desirable to distinguish semantic memory from episodic memory. For this reason Kopelman, Wilson, and Baddeley (1989, 1990) developed the Autobiographical Memory Interview. It divides life into three periods—

childhood, early adult life, and recent events—and asks for three autobiographical memories for specific incidents from each period and three personal semantic memories from each period as well as for semantic background information. Thus, for early adulthood, participants would be asked for a memory of a specific incident concerning (a) their first job or their time at college, (b) their or someone else's wedding during their 20s, and (c) meeting someone during their 20s. For the same period they would be asked for personal semantic questions with similar cues. For example, for their first job, participants would be asked for the name of the firm, their colleagues, their supervisor, and so forth. Set prompts are used if participants fail to produce a memory. For instance, failure to remember an event from a first job would evoke questions about the first day on the job or an event with a friend.

Because the questions for autobiographical and semantic memory are similar, comparisons of loss in these kinds of memories can be more direct. Because specific time periods are queried, the failure to be able to recall from one time period cannot be attributed to a bias to avoid that time period. These advantages come at the expense of the more open-ended probing of autobiographical memory of the first three methods.

THE DIARY RECALL METHOD

In all of the methods discussed so far, no attempt is made to examine how the contents of a memory change over time; little experimental research has been done on which aspect of the memory provides good cues to the memory as a whole. However, by asking people to record events in a diary each day and not to examine them again until testing, researchers can note changes in the contents of memory over time. To the extent to which a record from the time of an event can be considered accurate, the diary method offers an approximation to a measure of accuracy. Similarly, through selection of particular aspects from the initial recording of a memory as cues for the later recall, the value of these aspects as memory cues can be measured and used to infer how memory is organized. Many diary recall studies, and all of the early ones, developed to study autobiographical memory were done on a single participant, the author of the study (Linton, 1975, 1982, 1986; Wagenaar, 1986; White, 1982). Later studies used undergraduates as diary keepers (see Thompson et al., 1996, for a review).

Linton called her heroic effort "the take-two-items-a-day-for-five-years study" (1975, p. 87). It focused more on dating accuracy than did later studies, but set the main parameters of the method. The basic procedure is to make diary entries each day and then later select randomly from among these entries either to query the participant about some recorded properties of an event given other recorded properties or to provide ratings of a memory of the event given its description. For instance, Wagenaar (1986) might cue himself with who was present at an event and then see if he could remember all the other aspects of the memory; if this failed he could add another cue such as when the event occurred. For long-term studies such as Linton's or Wagenaar's the only person the experimenter could rely on to do the recording regularly and be available years later for testing was the experimenter. Thus, the study is very labor intensive, but this time is often well spent. The single-experimenter-as-participant approach has provided the experimenter with a rich sense of how memory works that is obtained from considering all the issues of how to record events and the intensive testing and data analysis that follow. The combination of first person, participant, knowledge of the processes involved in memory search and retrieval; and third person, experimenter, knowledge of the results has led to especially rich discussions of how memory functions (see especially Linton, 1982, 1986; Wagenaar, 1986). For instance, a major problem that Linton uncovered for herself was that in real life, events cannot be fully appreciated until well after they occur, so testing the accuracy or the meaning of an event recorded in a diary can be problematic (Robinson, 1996). Descriptions including "for the first time" are good ways to uniquely identify an event for later testing, but descriptions such as "I Xeroxed the final draft of the statistics book and mailed it" (Linton, 1982, p. 82) turned out to be a problem when Linton later mailed her third "final draft." Similarly, meeting a shy scholar is an event whose meaning and importance is changed significantly when they decide to marry (1986).

Wagenaar (1986), in his six-year study, recorded who, what, where, when, and a critical detail for each diary entry, which allowed him to cue himself first with one of the wh- questions first and then add a second, third, and fourth wh- question to measure their effectiveness as cues alone and in combination. Although it was expected that dates would be a good cue in a database as there was usually only one and at most two entries per day, dates were of little use to Wagenaar as cues (see Brewer, 1996, and Thompson et al., 1996, for an argument on why dates are not integral aspects of autobiographical memories). He also recorded salience, emotional involvement, and pleasantness, finding like Linton that pleasant events were better retained. Like all other diary studies, he found forgetting to be much slower than would be expected from laboratory work and to have a much more linear curve. He also noted that he had no evidence that any memory he recorded was ever completely forgotten. He found 10 memories that he failed to recall when he examined all the cues but that were likely to be recalled by the person recorded in the *who* slot. He then took each of those diary entries to that person and asked him or her to provide more details of the event. In all 10 cases, he reported that he eventually was able to recall the event.

An especially clever modification was introduced by Thompson (1982). In addition to recording events from their lives for a 14-week semester, undergraduates recorded events from their roommates' lives. At the end of the recording period, the roommates were asked whether the experimenters could look at the recordings of their lives and prepare questions for them to answer.

In this way, the objection that the diary keepers spent unusual effort trying to recall their lives or that the act of recording memories distorted normal processing could be overcome. Thompson found no difference between the diary keepers' and the roommates' memory performance even though the roommates were unaware that they would be tested until a week before the test.

The studies reviewed so far have one major limitation. The events participants enter in a diary are intended to be unique. Linton noted that a stranger examining her diary entries would not be aware of the repetitive events, such as lecturing, that made up much of her life. Thus, the autobiographical memories queried in the diary method are a small biased subset of all autobiographical memories, often just the most interesting or troublesome. If routine events are of interest or are the crux of a clinical problem, they will be greatly underrepresented or omitted completely. If one really wants to sample autobiographical memory, then one has to sample the events to be remembered. To do this, Brewer (1988) had undergraduates carry a beeper that went off at random intervals during their waking hours. When the beeper signaled, the participant recorded information about ongoing activity or thoughts including when, where, and what in the form of a summary sentence about thoughts and actions, and a host of ratings about the event. Thoughts as well as actions were specifically requested because, as a pilot subject, Brewer found that in many cases the event that was occurring at the time the beeper sounded was primarily a thought that was unrelated to his ongoing actions. Participants were asked to record enough information to distinguish the event from similar events that might occur that week, including the weather, what they were wearing, and other details.

One type of diary study is underrepresented in the cognitive literature. Many people keep diaries, especially in adolescence (Burt, 1994; Rubin, 1982; Thompson, 1982). These could be available for research. Rubin (1982) had undergraduate diary keepers check the dates of their memory descriptions in their own diaries. In this way, he never needed access to the diaries. Thompson reported that 12% of keepers of journals not required for a course "were interested in having their memory tested using their journal" (1982, p. 11). Thus, a rich source of material for testing may be existing diaries or diaries kept as part of therapy (Burt, 1994). Such diaries would not contain descriptions neatly formatted with specific information and in some cases may have been read at intervals after they were initially recorded, but they would not require the extra effort needed in the more controlled experimental diary studies and would focus on issues of importance to participants.

THE QUESTIONNAIRE METHOD

In all of the previous methods, except the Autobiographical Memory Interview, questions are often asked about aspects of the memories in addition to when they occurred. Usually, only a few questions that are central to the research project are used, but for some studies, responses to a fixed set of questions are the main data of the study. The questions most often used have been fairly stable from the earliest studies of autobiographical and flashbulb memories because they probe theoretical issues that have endured. Sample collections of such questions can be found in Brewer (1988); Johnson, Foley, Suengas, and Raye (1988); Sheen, Kemp, and Rubin (2001); Rubin, Schrauf, and Greenberg (2003); and Talarico and Rubin (2003).

Often questions about only one memory of a given type can be asked of each person, such as "What was your most traumatic memory?" However, when multiple memories are obtained, such as to cue words or requests for 10 happy memories, the responses to questions can be averaged. If each memory is considered as a separate item on a test, reliability can be calculated and in general is high, with Cronbach's alphas of about .9 with 20 memories. Also, when answers to questions on many memories are obtained from each participant, it is possible to examine the relation among the responses to the question within individuals and summarize those relations (e.g., Rubin et al., 2003) In this way, the relations of variables can be investigated within individuals.

The exact wording of the questions has been fluid, and there has been little systematic work to ensure that the questions really measure the concept they ask about in the manner done in the development of a standardized clinical test. Questions are sometimes asked both for the present time and the times when the event reported in the memory occurred. When *now* and *then* questions both are asked, the two responses usually are highly correlated (e.g., Rubin et al., 1984). It is reasonable to assume that part of the correlation can be attributed to stability over time and another part to current attitudes affecting reports of past attitudes. Thus, any differences in *now* and *then* measures can be seen as an indication both of actual change and of how the participant now views that change.

Questions About the Memories Themselves

The most commonly asked question is how old the memory is, a question discussed in detail earlier. In addition to this question's importance in assessing the distribution of memories over the life span, measuring the age of the memory ensures that differences in other measures are not due to differences in the retention interval. Another common question has been how often a memory has been thought or talked about in the past. For cognitive psychologists this is a measure of rehearsal, but it may also reflect the importance of the memory to the individual. The response is assumed to be monotonically related to the actual number of rehearsals. A measure that is often correlated with rehearsal is the importance of the event reported in the memory to the individual, or the significance to his or her life.

Perhaps the most important question for clinical research is whether the memory is of a specific event or is the merging of several memories that are from an extended time period or are merged because they are similar in content (Williams, 1996). Most of the discussion of this question is deferred until the next chapter. However, in terms of cognitive psychology, the question has important theoretical consequences for how one views autobiographical memory. Tulving's (1972) widely accepted distinction divides memory into semantic and episodic components. Semantic memory stores items such as language rules, word definitions, and general facts. Episodic memory contains the store of "personally experienced unique episodes" that are "distinctive and separate although part of a larger series"; they are "always stored in terms of its autobiographical reference to . . . already existing" memories (Tulving, 1972, pp. 385, 387). Thus, according to Tulving's definition, an autobiographical memory should be identified as a single, isolated event, not as a concatenation of several prior experiences, and so merged or extended memories are excluded from autobiographical memory. This more atomistic verbal-learning approach can be contrasted with schema-based approaches. Although Brewer (1986, 1996) preserves a once-versus-many-times distinction, he holds that both single and repeated events that form a schema can lead to a recollective memory. Similarly, Neisser (1981) coined the term *repisodic memory* for the merging of memories of events into one representative event and argued that people may confuse such repisodic memories with those caused by memories for single occurrences. Both kinds of memories can be observed, but merged memories, which are especially important in the study of depression and posttraumatic stress disorder, are considered outside the realm of autobiographical memory for some theoretical approaches.

Questions About the Phenomenological Properties of the Memories

There are two main issues: reliving or recollection of the memory and belief in the accuracy of the memory. A key distinction introduced in the beginning of the chapter and one used to define autobiographical memory for many philosophers is that of recollection, the idea that in a sense, a person relives the memory. An extreme version of reliving is the clinical phenomenon of flashbacks. Typical questions have asked for ratings of the extent that the event is being relived and, on the basis of Wheeler et al. (1997), asking whether the participant travels back in time to the event and feels as a participant rather than as an observer (see Sheen et al., 2001, and Talarico & Rubin, 2003, for examples). Belief in the accuracy of memories has been central to many debates and has been examined in the reality monitoring research of Johnson and colleagues (Johnson et al., 1988; Johnson, Hashtroudi, & Lindsay, 1993; Johnson & Raye, 1981) and in direct questions (Rubin et al., 2003; Sheen et al., 2001; Talarico & Rubin, 2003). In laboratory research, a *remember* versus *know* choice is often used to study recollection, but in autobiographical memory studies this distinction seems more closely related to belief in the accuracy of the memory (Rubin et al., 2003).

Questions About Components of the Memories

Autobiographical memory involves at least emotion, narrative, language, and imagery in several sensory modalities and questions have been asked about all of these components. As visual imagery is a central feature of autobiographical memory, many questions have centered on it. In addition to asking how vivid the visual image of the memory is, researchers have asked about the spatial layout and setting. In Brown and Kulik's (1977) paper introducing the term *flashbulb memory*, knowledge of the setting was stressed and so questions about it entered early into consideration of autobiographical memory. Although setting can be considered visual and correlates with questions about vividness of the image, the setting is also part of a multimodal spatial property of the memory. The separation of visual and spatial can be made on the basis of both behavioral and neuropsychological data for autobiographical memory (Greenberg & Rubin, 2003; Rubin et al., 2003) and is most clearly distinguished in autobiographical memory studies of the blind (Ogden & Barker, 2001).

One of the most interesting visual questions is whether the memory is seen from a field (i.e., out of one's own eyes) or an observer perspective (i.e., as an outsider would). This dimension, which was used by Freud (1899/1950) to argue for the constructive nature of autobiographical memory, has been studied by cognitive psychologists (Nigro & Neisser, 1983; Robinson & Swanson, 1993) and is important in clinical studies, as it may be a way of distancing oneself from the event and, in the extreme, be part of an out-of-body experience. In my own experience, a two-point dichotomous question is much less useful than a more continuous five-point scale (e.g., Berntsen, Willert, & Rubin, 2003; Talarico & Rubin, 2003).

In addition to visual imagery, questions have been asked about other modalities. The vividness of auditory images is usually lower than for visual images and those of smell and taste are often near the floor, except for some memories noted in the trauma literature. Questions on emotion have included three aspects: (a) the extent to which the original emotion is felt now, (b) emotional intensity, and (c) valence. Language, especially narrative, plays an important role in autobiographical memory. Questions about language have included the extent to which the memory comes in words and whether there is talking in the memory. Narrative can be considered separate from language in general on both behavioral and neural grounds (Rubin & Greenberg, 2003). Narrative questions have centered on whether the memory is coherent, but to determine clinical relevance one can also ask whether the memory is central to the life story (Berntsen et al., 2003). One way to gain a better understanding of the role of language and narrative in autobiographical memory is to test participants who are bilingual and bicultural. Just as dreams can come to people in one language or another, so can autobiographical memories. Both the language being used in the testing session and the language in which the memory is felt to come can be examined (Schrauf & Rubin, 1998, 2000). The language used to relate the memory can be of importance in distancing oneself from the event recalled in experimental and clinical settings (Schrauf, 2000).

A FINAL NOTE

The methods used in the experimental literature to study autobiographical memory place relatively few constraints on the responses participants can make and thus may be especially suitable for uncovering changes in memory processes that occur in clinical populations. They are flexible in that few fixed parameters or stimuli are set. The results obtained are robust, in spite of this lack of experimental control. These virtues, however, require the experimenter to be especially thoughtful in choosing a method and in analyzing the data obtained. Few procedures exist that are applicable without modification in the way that the administration of a standardized test is; decisions must be made that will have effects on the success of the research. In writing this chapter, I kept wanting to be able to say "here are the stimuli to use" or "25 trials are ideal" but could not; the details depend on the goals of the research. It is a challenging and exciting time to be investigating autobiographical memory. Guidelines are not strict, and there is much to discover.

REFERENCES

Baddeley, A. D. (1992). What is autobiographical memory? In M. A. Conway, D. C. Rubin, H. Spinnler, & W. A. Wagenaar (Eds.), *Theoretical perspectives on autobiographical memory* (pp. 13–29). Dordrecht, The Netherlands: Kluwer Academic.

Berntsen, D. (1996). Involuntary autobiographical memory. *Applied Cognitive Psychology, 10,* 435–454.

Berntsen, D. (1998). Voluntary and involuntary access to autobiographical memory. *Memory, 6,* 113–141.

Berntsen, D. (2001). Involuntary memories of emotional events. Do memories of traumas and extremely happy events differ? *Applied Cognitive Psychology, 15,* 135–158.

Berntsen, D., & Rubin, D. C. (2002). Emotionally charged memories across the life span: The recall of happy, sad, traumatic, and involuntary memories. *Psychology of Aging, 17,* 636–652.

Berntsen, D., Willert, M., & Rubin, D. C. (2003). Splintered memories or vivid landmarks? Qualities and organization of traumatic memories with and without PTSD. *Applied Cognitive Psychology, 17,* 675–693.

Brewer, W. F. (1986). What is autobiographical memory? In D. C. Rubin (Ed.), *Autobiographical memory* (pp. 25–49). Cambridge, England: Cambridge University Press.

Brewer, W. F. (1988). Memory for randomly sampled autobiographical events. In U. Neisser & E. Winograd (Eds.), *Remembering reconsidered: Ecological and traditional approaches to the study of memory* (pp. 21–90). Cambridge, England: Cambridge University Press.

Brewer, W. F. (1996). What is recollective memory? In D. C. Rubin (Ed.), *Remembering our past: Studies in autobiographical memory* (pp. 19–66). Cambridge, England: Cambridge University Press.

Brewin, C. R., Christoulides, J., & Hutchinson, G. (1996). Intrusive thoughts and intrusive memories in a nonclinical sample. *Cognition & Emotion, 10,* 107–112.

Brown, R., & Kulik, J. (1977). Flashbulb memories. *Cognition, 5,* 73–99.

Bruner, J., & Feldman, C. F. (1996). Group narratives as a cultural context of autobiography. In D. C. Rubin (Ed.), *Remembering our past: Studies in autobiographical memory* (pp. 291–317). Cambridge, England: Cambridge University Press.

Burt, C. D. B. (1994). An analysis of self-initiated coping behavior: Diary keeping. *Child Study Journal, 24,* 171–189.

Butters, N., & Cermak, L. S. (1986). A case study of forgetting of autobiographical knowledge: Implications for the study of retrograde amnesia. In D. C. Rubin (Ed.), *Autobiographical memory* (pp. 253–272). New York. Cambridge University Press.

Chu, S., & Downes, J. J. (2000). Long live Proust: The odour-cued autobiographical memory bump. *Cognition, 75,* B41–B50.

Conway, M. A. (1990). *Autobiographical memory: An introduction.* Milton Keynes, UK: Open University Press.

Conway, M. A. (1995). *Flashbulb memories.* Hove, England: Erlbaum.

Conway, M. A., & Haque, S. (1999). Overshadowing the reminiscence bump: Memories of a struggle for independence. *Journal of Adult Development, 6,* 35–44.

Conway, M. A., & Pleydell-Pearce, C. W. (2000). The construction of autobiographical memories in the self-memory system. *Psychological Review, 107,* 261–268.

Conway, M. A., Rubin, D. C., Spinnler, H., & Wagenaar, W. A. (Eds.). (1992). *Theoretical perspectives on autobiographical memory.* Dordrecht, The Netherlands: Kluwer Academic.

Crovitz, H. F., & Schiffman, H. (1974). Frequency of episodic memories as a function of their age. *Bulletin of the Psychonomic Society, 4,* 517–518.

Fitzgerald, J. M. (1988). Vivid memories and the reminiscence phenomenon: The role of a self narrative. *Human Development, 31,* 261–273.

Fitzgerald, J. M. (1996). Intersecting meanings of reminiscence in adult development and aging. In D. C. Rubin (Ed.), *Remembering our past: Studies in autobiographical memory* (pp. 360–383). Cambridge, England: Cambridge University Press.

Freud, S. (1950). Screen memories. In J. Strachey (Ed. & Trans.), *Collected papers: Vol. 5., Miscellaneous Papers 1888–1938* (pp. 47–69). London: Hogarth Press. (Original work published 1899)

Friedman, W. J. (1993). Memory for the time of past events. *Psychological Bulletin, 113,* 44–66.

Fromholt, P., & Larsen, S. F. (1991). Autobiographical memory in normal aging and primary degenerative dementia (dementia of the Alzheimer type). *Journal of Gerontology: Psychological Sciences, 46,* 85–91.

Fromholt, P., & Larsen, S. F. (1992). Autobiographical memory and life-history narratives in aging and dementia (Alzheimer type). In M. A. Conway, D. C. Rubin, H. Spinnler, & W. Wagenaar (Eds.), *Theoretical perspectives on autobiographical memory* (pp. 413–426). Utrecht, The Netherlands: Kluwer Academic.

Fromholt, P., Larsen, P., & Larsen, S. F. (1995). Effects of late-onset depression and recovery on autobiographical memory. *Journal of Gerontology: Psychological Sciences, 50,* 74–81.

Fromholt, P., Mortensen, D., Torpdahl, P., Bender, L., Larsen, P., & Rubin, D. C. (2003). Life-narrative and word-cued autobiographical memories in centenarians: Comparisons with 80-year old control, depressed, and dementia groups. *Memory, 11,* 81–88.

Fry, C. L. (1990). The life course in context: Implications of comparative research. In R. Rubinstein (Ed.), *Anthropology and aging* (pp. 129–149). Dordrecht, The Netherlands: Kluwer Academic.

Galton, F. (1879). Psychometric experiments. *Brain, 2,* 149–162.

Greenberg, D. L., & Rubin, D. C. (2003). The neuropsychology of autobiographical memory. *Cortex, 39,* 687–728.

Habermas, T., & Bluck, S. (2000). Getting a life: The emergence of the life story in adolescence. *Psychological Bulletin, 126,* 748–769.

Herz, R. S., & Cupchik, G. C. (1992). An experimental characterization of odor-evoked memories in humans. *Chemical Senses, 17,* 519–528.

Hirst, W., & Manier, D. (1996). Remembering as communication: A family recounts its past. In D. C. Rubin (Ed.), *Remembering our past: Studies in autobiographical memory* (pp. 271–290). Cambridge, England: Cambridge University Press.

Jansari, A., & Parkin, A. J. (1996). Things that go bump in your life: Explaining the reminiscence bump in autobiographical memory. *Psychology and Aging, 11,* 85–91.

Johnson, M. K., Foley, M. A., Suengas, A. G., & Raye, C. L. (1988). Phenomenal characteristics of memories for perceived and imagined autobiographical events. *Journal of Experimental Psychology: General, 117,* 371–376.

Johnson, M. K., Hashtroudi, S., & Lindsay, D. S. (1993). Source monitoring. *Psychological Bulletin, 114,* 3–28.

Johnson, M. K., & Raye, C. L. (1981). Reality monitoring. *Psychological Review*, 88, 67–85.

Kopelman, M. D., Wilson, B. A., & Baddeley, A. D. (1989). The autobiographical memory interview: A new assessment of autobiographical and personal semantic memory in amnesic patients. *Journal of Clinical and Experimental Neuropsychology*, 11, 724–744.

Kopelman, M. D., Wilson, B. A., & Baddeley, A. D. (1990). *The autobiographical memory interview*. Bury St. Edmund, Suffolk, England: Thames Valley Test Company.

Linde, C. (1993). *Life stories: The creation of coherence*. New York: Oxford University Press.

Linton, M. (1975). Memory for real-world events. In D. A. Norman & D. E. Rumelhart (Eds.), *Explorations in cognition* (pp. 376–404). San Francisco: W. H. Freeman.

Linton, M. (1982). Transformations of memory in everyday life. In U. Neisser (Ed.), *Memory observed: Remembering in natural contexts* (pp. 77–91). San Francisco: W. H. Freeman.

Linton, M. (1986). Ways of searching and the contents of autobiographical memory. In D. C. Rubin (Ed.), *Autobiographical memory* (pp. 202–221). Cambridge, England: Cambridge University Press.

Luborsky, M. (1987). Analysis of multiple life history narratives. *Ethos*, 15, 366–381.

Luborsky, M. (1990). Alchemists' visions, conceptual templates, and narrative sequences in life histories. *Journal of Aging Studies*, 4, 17–29.

Luborsky, M. (1993). The romance with personal meaning in gerontology, cultural aspects of life themes. *The Gerontologist*, 33, 445–452.

Luborsky, M. (1998). Creative challenges and the construction of meaningful life narratives. In C. Adams-Price (Ed.), *Creativity and successful aging: Theoretical and empirical approaches* (pp. 311–337). New York: Springer.

Neisser, U. (1981). John Dean's memory: A case study. *Cognition*, 9, 1–22.

Neisser, U., & Fivush, R. (1994). *The remembering self: Construction and accuracy of life narrative*. Cambridge, England: Cambridge University Press.

Nigro, G., & Neisser, U. (1983). Point of view in personal memories. *Cognitive Psychology*, 15, 467–482.

Ogden, J. A., & Barker, K. (2001). Imagery used in autobiographical recall in early and late blind adults. *Journal of Mental Imagery*, 25, 153–176.

Robinson, J. A. (1976). Sampling autobiographical memory. *Cognitive Psychology*, 8, 578–595.

Robinson, J. (1986). Autobiographical memory: A historical prologue. In D. C. Rubin (Ed.), *Autobiographical memory* (pp. 19–24). Cambridge, England: Cambridge University Press.

Robinson, J. A. (1996). Perspective, meaning, and remembering. In D. C. Rubin (Ed.), *Remembering our past: Studies in autobiographical memory* (pp. 199–217). Cambridge, England: Cambridge University Press.

Robinson, J. A., & Swanson, K. L. (1993). Field and observer modes of remembering. *Memory, 1*, 169–184.

Rubin, D. C. (1980). 51 properties of 125 words: A unit analysis of verbal behavior. *Journal of Verbal Learning and Verbal Behavior, 19*, 736–755.

Rubin, D. C. (1982). On the retention function for autobiographical memory. *Journal of Verbal Learning and Verbal Behavior, 21*, 21–38.

Rubin, D. C. (Ed.). (1986). *Autobiographical memory.* Cambridge, England: Cambridge University Press.

Rubin, D. C. (Ed.). (1996). *Remembering our past: Studies in autobiographical memory.* Cambridge, England: Cambridge University Press.

Rubin, D. C. (1998). Beginnings of a theory of autobiographical remembering. In C. P. Thompson, D. J. Herrmann, D. Bruce, J. D. Reed, D. G. Payne, & M. P. Toglia (Eds.), *Autobiographical memory: Theoretical and applied perspectives* (pp. 47–67). Mahwah, NJ: Erlbaum.

Rubin, D. C. (2000). The distribution of early childhood memories. *Memory, 8*, 265–269.

Rubin, D. C. (2002). Autobiographical memory across the lifespan. In P. Graf & N. Ohta (Eds.), *Lifespan development of human memory* (pp. 159–184). Cambridge, MA: MIT Press.

Rubin, D. C., & Greenberg, D. L. (2003). The role of narrative in recollection: A view from cognitive and neuropsychology. In G. Fireman, T. McVay, & O. Flanagan (Eds.), *Narrative and consciousness: Literature, psychology, and the brain* (pp. 53–85). New York: Oxford University Press.

Rubin, D. C., Groth, L., & Goldsmith, D. (1984). Olfactory cuing of autobiographical memory. *American Journal of Psychology, 97*, 493–507.

Rubin, D. C., Rahhal, T. A., & Poon, L. W. (1998). Things learned in early adulthood are remembered best. *Memory & Cognition, 26*, 3–19.

Rubin, D. C., Schrauf, R. W., & Greenberg, D. L. (2003). Belief and recollection of autobiographical memories. *Memory & Cognition, 31*, 887–901.

Rubin, D. C., & Schulkind, M. D. (1997a). The distribution of autobiographical memories across the lifespan. *Memory & Cognition, 25*, 859–866.

Rubin, D. C., & Schulkind, M. D. (1997b). The distribution of important and word-cued autobiographical memories in 20-, 35-, and 70-year-old adults. *Psychology and Aging, 12*, 524–535.

Rubin, D. C., & Schulkind, M. D. (1997c). Properties of word cues for autobiographical memory. *Psychological Reports, 81*, 47–50.

Rubin, D. C., Schulkind, M. D., & Rahhal, T. A. (1999). A study of gender differences in autobiographical memory: Broken down by age and sex. *Journal of Adult Development, 6*, 61–72.

Ruth, J.-E., & Oberg, P. (1996). Ways of life: Old age in a life history perspective. In J. F. Birren, G. M. Kenyon, J.-E. Ruth, J. J. F. Schroots, & T. Svensson (Eds.), *Aging and biography: Explorations in adult development* (pp. 167–186). New York: Springer.

Rybash, J. M., & Monaghan, B. E. (1999). Episodic and semantic contributions to older adults' autobiographical recall. *Journal of General Psychology, 126*, 85–96.

Schacter, D. L. (1996). *Searching for memory: The brain, the mind, and the past.* New York: Basic Books.

Schrauf, R. W. (2000). Bilingual autobiographical memory: Experimental studies and clinical cases. *Culture & Psychology, 6*, 387–417.

Schrauf, R. W., & Rubin, D. C. (1998). Bilingual autobiographical memory in older adult immigrants: A test of cognitive explanations of the reminiscence bump and the linguistic encoding of memories. *Journal of Memory and Language, 39*, 437–457.

Schrauf, R. W., & Rubin, D. C. (2000). Identification of internal languages of retrieval: The bilingual encoding of memories for the personal past. *Memory & Cognition, 28*, 616–623.

Schrauf, R. W., & Rubin, D. C. (2001). Effects of voluntary immigration on the distribution of autobiographical memory over the lifespan. *Applied Cognitive Psychology, 15*, S75–S88.

Sheen, M., Kemp, S., & Rubin, D. C. (2001). Twins dispute memory ownership: A new false memory phenomenon. *Memory & Cognition, 29*, 779–788.

Talarico, J. M., & Rubin, D. C. (2003). Confidence, not consistency, characterizes flashbulb memories. *Psychological Science, 14*, 455–461.

Thompson, C. P. (1982). Diary-keeping as a sex-role behavior. *Bulletin of the Psychonomic Society, 20*, 11–13.

Thompson, C. P., Herrmann, D. J., Bruce, D., Reed, J. D., Payne, D. G., & Toglia, M. P. (Eds.). (1998). *Autobiographical memory: Theoretical and applied perspectives.* Mahwah, NJ: Erlbaum.

Thompson, C. P., Skowronski, J. S., Larsen, S. F., & Betz, A. L. (1996). *Autobiographical memory: Remembering what and remembering when.* Hillsdale, NJ: Erlbaum.

Tulving, E. (1972). Episodic and semantic memory. In E. Tulving & W. Donaldson (Eds.), *Organization of memory.* New York: Academic Press.

Tulving, E. (1983). *Elements of episodic memory.* Oxford, England: Oxford University Press.

Wagenaar, W. A. (1986). My memory: A study of autobiographical memory over six years. *Cognitive Psychology, 18*, 225–252.

Wheeler, M. A., Stuss, D. T., & Tulving, E. (1997). Toward a theory of episodic memory: The frontal lobes and autonoetic consciousness. *Psychological Bulletin, 121*, 331–354.

White, R. T. (1982). Memory for personal events. *Human Learning, 1*, 171–183.

Williams, J. M. G. (1996). Depression and the specificity of autobiographical memory. In D. C. Rubin (Ed.), *Remembering our past: Studies in autobiographical memory* (pp. 244–267). Cambridge, England: Cambridge University Press.

Winograd, E., & Neisser, U. (Eds.) (1992). *Affect and accuracy in recall: Studies of "flashbulb" memories.* New York: Cambridge University Press.

15

AUTOBIOGRAPHICAL MEMORY TASKS IN CLINICAL RESEARCH

AMY WENZEL

Autobiographical memory is of central importance in the field of clinical psychology. Clients rely on their autobiographical memories to communicate information about their lives to therapists as well as to place their current difficulties into a historical context. Part of the diagnostic criteria for one specific type of psychopathology, posttraumatic stress disorder (PTSD), requires that individuals experience intrusive memories of traumatic events. Theoretical work has shown that the failure to retrieve specific positive memories worsens the course of depression (cf. Williams, 1996) and is related to deficits in social problem solving (e.g., Goddard, Dritschel, & Burton, 1996). Unlike cognitive psychologists, clinical psychology researchers are less concerned with the definition of autobiographical memory than the manner in which the phenomenological experience of personal memories influences affective and cognitive expressions of psychopathology.

To date, much of the clinically relevant autobiographical memory research has been conducted with a specific adaptation of the word-cue method (Williams & Broadbent, 1986), although small lines of research have been developed to assess autobiographical memory in clinical populations with some of the other methods outlined by Rubin (see chap. 14, this volume).

For example, a variation of the life narrative method has been used to examine aspects of trauma narratives and the manner in which aspects of these trauma narratives predict PTSD symptomatology posttreatment (Foa, Molnar, & Cashman, 1995). Although no clinical researchers have adopted Berntsen's (1996, 1998, 2001) involuntary memory diary method, Brewin and his colleagues have assessed the impact of intrusive memories using a self-report inventory to predict subsequent symptoms of depression (e.g., Brewin, Reynolds, & Tata, 1999). At least one study (Meesters, Merckelbach, Muris, & Wessel, 2000) has investigated semantic autobiographical memory in a manner similar to that of Kopelman, Wilson, and Baddeley's (1989) Autobiographical Memory Inventory. Moreover, recent work has adopted the questionnaire method to compare the structure of autobiographical memory in individuals with symptoms of psychopathology and healthy individuals (e.g., Berntsen, Willert, & Rubin, 2003). The purpose of this chapter is to describe these methods in detail, evaluate particular methodological choices, and make recommendations for future researchers who wish to consider autobiographical memory in pathology groups.

THE WORD-CUE METHOD

The most common way the word-cue procedure has been applied to clinical autobiographical memory research is through the Autobiographical Memory Test (AMT), first described by Williams and Broadbent (1986). The AMT is a procedure in which participants are presented with an alternating order of positive and negative single cue words on index cards and instructed to indicate the first specific personal memory that comes to mind. In many studies, participants are presented with five positive and five negative cue words (e.g., Williams & Broadbent, 1986). The five most commonly used positive words are happy, safe, interested, successful, and surprised, and the five most commonly used negative words are sorry, angry, clumsy, hurt, and lonely (e.g., Kuyken & Brewin, 1995; Kuyken & Dalgleish, 1995; Phillips & Williams, 1997; Sidley, Calam, Wells, Hughes, & Whitaker, 1999; Sidley, Whitaker, Calam, & Wells, 1997; Swales, Williams, & Wood, 2001; Wessel, Meeren, Peeters, Arntz, & Merckelbach, 2001; Williams & Broadbent, 1986). Some researchers have included 6 (e.g., Brittlebank, Scott, Williams, & Ferrier, 1993) or 10 (Williams & Dritschel, 1988) stimuli for each type of cue valence, and others have included a set of neutral stimuli (e.g., Croll & Bryant, 2000). Additional examples of positive, neutral, and negative stimuli can be found in Brittlebank et al. (1993); Croll and Bryant (2000); Harvey, Bryant, and Dang (1998); Jones et al. (1999); Kaney, Bowen-Jones, and Bentall (1999); Mackinger, Loschin, and Leibestseder (2000); Mackinger, Pachinger, Leibestseder, and Fartacek (2000); McNally, Lasko, Macklin, and Pitman (1995); McNally, Litz, Prassas, Shin, and Weathers (1994); Williams and

Dritschel (1988); and Williams, Williams, and Ghadiali (1998). Other positive and negative words—such as energetic, healthy, fit, ill, and fatigued—have been identified for studies examining depression and autobiographical memory in medically ill samples (Leung & Bryant, 2000).

As can be observed from the examples above, in most autobiographical memory studies, the positive and negative stimuli consist of words that are quite abstract. In contrast, the neutral words tend to be much more concrete. It is questionable as to whether the neutral words are appropriate comparison stimuli, as often they do not have the same properties as the valenced stimuli. Specifically, Rubin and Schulkind (1997) found that concrete words elicit faster reaction times and result in fewer instances of missing data than do abstract words. In addition, several autobiographical memory researchers match different types of stimuli for their frequency in the English language and the degree of emotional tone (e.g., Brittlebank et al., 1993; Wenzel, Jackson, & Holt, 2002).

Participants generally are allowed a predefined time frame to respond to each cue word, and if they are unable to identify a *specific* memory within that time frame, then their response is regarded as an omission. Williams and Scott (1988) considered a memory as being specific if a participant is able to "give a date, day of the week, or time of day when the episode occurred" (p. 691). The importance of prompting a specific memory cannot be understated, as theories linking autobiographical memory with psychopathology suggest that the degree to which individuals with psychopathology can retrieve specific memories is uniquely predictive of future symptomatology (Williams, 1996). If a participant is unable to comply with instructions and instead retrieves a *general* memory, then the experimenter responds with a sentence such as "Can you think of a specific time—one particular event?" to prompt a specific occurrence (Williams & Broadbent, 1986).

In most instances, recall of autobiographical memories is done in a verbal format with the experimenter in the room. This procedure is necessary if participants are to be prompted to retrieve specific memories on trials in which their first response is a general memory. However, other researchers have implemented different protocols. For example, Wessel et al. (2001) used Williams and Broadbent's (1986) version of the AMT, but they asked participants to provide a written rather than a verbal response. Although participants in this study were trained to produce specific memories in one to two practice trials, they were not prompted to retrieve specific memories once the experimental trials had commenced. Similar to other studies, these researchers found that individuals diagnosed with major depressive disorder failed to retrieve specific memories in response to positive cues; this finding provided at least preliminary evidence that the written autobiographical memory procedure produces effects that are similar to those observed with the oral method. In Wenzel's (2000) study of autobiographical memory in individuals with panic disorder and individuals with social phobia, an experimenter trained participants to retrieve specific memories in five practice trials, after which time participants were left alone in the room to complete the AMT. Stimuli were presented by a voice on a computer, and participants verbalized their memories out loud so that they could be audio-recorded. This elaborate procedure was adopted so that social phobic participants would not inhibit the expression of certain memories because of the presence of the experimenter. In general, it is recommended that the standard protocol for the AMT be used when possible, as it has the greatest amount of research evidence supporting its efficacy. However, if a researcher is concerned about the sensitive nature of personal memories that might be retrieved, then there is precedence for the use of written or computer-administered protocols.

One variable that differs from study to study is the time frame that participants are given in which to retrieve memories. Most commonly, participants are allowed 60 seconds (e.g., Goddard et al., 1996; Kuyken & Brewin, 1995; Leung & Bryant, 2000; Phillips & Williams, 1997; Williams & Broadbent, 1986; Williams et al., 1998) to retrieve a specific personal memory. If participants are unable to retrieve a specific autobiographical memory in this time, then the experimenter moves on to the next trial. However, some researchers have allowed only 30 seconds to retrieve a specific personal memory (e.g., Jones et al., 1999; Startup et al., 2001; Swales et al., 2001; Watkins & Teasdale, 2001; Williams & Dritschel, 1988), and participants in one study were allowed just 15 seconds (Burke & Mathews, 1992). In general, older clinical autobiographical memory studies adopt a 60-second time frame, and newer clinical autobiographical memory studies adopt a 30-second time frame. Thus, there is justification for either choice. However, from my experience, participants tend to become frustrated when they have to struggle for an entire minute to retrieve a specific personal memory.

In most autobiographical memory studies, participants simply are told to retrieve the first specific memory that comes to mind, which implies that they can indicate a memory from any period of their lives. Bryant and his colleagues, on the other hand, have adopted a different strategy; they instruct participants to retrieve memories in both *unconstrained* (i.e., from any time in one's life) and *constrained* (i.e., from a specified time period) conditions. The nature of the constrained time period depends on the particular clinical population being studied. This variable (i.e., unconstrained vs. constrained) has the potential to be an important manipulation that can enable differentiation of specific pathology-related autobiographical memory distortions from general autobiographical memory distortions. For example, in his case report of an individual with dissociative identity disorder (DID), Bryant (1995) included this manipulation in order to assess the manner in which DID symptoms influenced the retrieval of traumatic childhood memories of abuse. Moreover, in their investigation of autobiographical memory in motor vehicle accident survivors with and without acute stress disorder (ASD), Harvey et al.'s (1998) constrained time period pertained to the period of the trauma. Although participants with ASD retrieved fewer specific positive memories in both constrained and unconstrained conditions, they were slower than non-ASD participants to retrieve specific positive memories in the constrained condition only. Thus, results suggested that individuals with ASD are characterized by "both a general and a trauma-related deficit in the retrieval of specific memories" (Harvey et al., 1998, p. 504).

Variables of Interest

Overgenerality (Versus Specificity)

The most commonly studied variable in clinical investigations that use the AMT is the extent to which participants' first responses are specific versus general in nature (cf. Healy & Williams, 1999, and Williams, 1996, for comprehensive discussions). A *specific* memory is defined as a particular recollection that takes place during a period of no longer than one day. In contrast, there are two basic types of *general* memories that a participant might retrieve. A *categoric* memory is defined as a recollection of a summary of a recurring event, such as "visits to my parent's house" or "playing racquetball games." In contrast, an *extended* memory refers to an event that takes place over a period of more than one day, such as "my vacation to France." Research shows that categoric memories, as opposed to extended memories, are important in differentiating depressed from nondepressed individuals (Williams & Dritschel, 1992) and delusional from nondelusional participants (Kaney et al., 1999). However, no known research has assessed the extent to which individuals with other pathologies who are free of depression retrieve memories that are categoric versus extended in nature.

Despite the fact that relatively uniform schemes have been adopted to code for the general versus specific nature of memories, the actual dependent variable of interest varies from study to study. Most commonly, studies consider the number of specific memories (Croll & Bryant, 2000; Goddard et al., 1996; Goddard, Dritschel, & Burton, 1997; McNally et al., 1995) or the number of general memories (Brittlebank et al., 1993; Dalgleish, Spinks, Yiend, & Kuyken, 2001; McNally et al., 1994). Williams and Dritschel (1988) suggested that researchers should consider the ratio of specific positive memories retrieved to specific negative memories retrieved. They examined autobiographical memory in patients who had recently attempted suicide by overdosing, ex-patients, and controls. Overdose patients' memories were more overgeneral than those of controls, and they exhibited the normal tendency to retrieve more specific positive memories than specific negative memories. In contrast, ex-patients' memories also were more overgeneral than those of controls, but they retrieved fewer specific positive memories than specific negative memories. Thus, the ratio of specific positive memories to specific negative memories was crucial in distinguishing overdose patients from ex-patients.

Overgenerality (versus specificity) usually is rated in a categorical fashion. That is, coders categorize memories as either specific or general, and in studies examining differences between categoric and extended memories, those categories are included in the coding scheme. Dependent variables of interest are either the number or percentage of memories included in these categories. Nearly all researchers adopting this approach to coding obtain some sort of reliability coefficient to ensure that their classifications are accurate. Statisticians often recommend kappa coefficients for this purpose, as they ensure that coders are classifying participants' responses to a degree that is well above chance level (Cohen, 1960). In contrast, Phillips and Williams (1997) used a 0–3 scale to classify overgenerality (0 = omission; 1 = categoric response; 2 = extended response; 3 = specific response), in which codes were treated in an ordinal fashion rather than in a categorical fashion. The scores represented increasing degrees of specificity. For one of their analyses, they calculated *specificity rating scores* for positive and negative stimuli by computing a sum of responses in those categories.

Latency to Retrieve a Specific Memory

Another variable often considered is the latency to retrieve autobiographical memories. It is important to note that many clinical autobiographical memory researchers measure the latency to retrieve the first specific memory rather than simply the latency to retrieve the first memory. Thus, in many studies, participants might verbalize a memory rather quickly in these procedures, but they will continue to be timed if their response is not judged by the experimenter to be a specific memory.

A second issue which researchers must decide a priori is the manner in which they will treat omissions, or instances in which a participant does *not* retrieve a memory within a specified time period. The manner in which omissions are dealt with in latency data is not specified in many articles. Several researchers indicate that if participants do not retrieve a specific memory within a particular time frame, such as 60 seconds, then that maximum time period is recorded for that trial (e.g., Goddard et al., 1996). Other researchers simply omit the trial from their analysis of latency data (e.g., Leung & Bryant, 2000). This arbitrary choice can have a significant impact on obtained results. For example, Burke and Mathews (1992) failed to find differences in the latency to retrieve *anxious* and *nonanxious* memories in their generally anxious and nonanxious participants. However, when null responses were set to 15 seconds (the maximum time period allowed in their study), then they found that generally anxious individuals retrieved anxious memories faster than did nonanxious individuals. On the other hand, Kuyken and Brewin (1995) also analyzed their latency data both ways, and they failed to find a significant effect with either approach. If one assumes that participants would find memories for omissions if they were given enough time, then using the maximum amount of time makes sense. If one assumes that participants would never find memories, then missing values are appropriate. As we are not sure of the proportion of times each assumption holds, it makes sense to report results from both methods of calculating latency.

A final methodological note concerns the manner in which latencies are timed. In some studies, the experimenter times the latency to participants' first specific response, presumably using a handheld stopwatch (e.g., Kuyken & Brewin, 1995). It is argued here that such a procedure might result in substantial error, as experimenters must direct resources to conducting the experimental session as well as to timing participants' responses. In addition, experimenters need to hear enough of the memory in order to classify its overgeneral versus specific nature, which will determine whether they will continue timing. In contrast, other researchers determine the latency to retrieve specific memories by listening to an audio tape (e.g., McNally et al., 1994). In Wenzel's autobiographical memory studies (2000; Wenzel et al., 2002; Wenzel, Jackson, Brendle, & Pinna, 2003), two separate coders make two passes through the audiotaped data in order to obtain an average latency to first specific response. Coders are instructed to listen to audio tapes in a quiet room free from distraction. They first must listen to the tape to determine at which point in the trial participants verbalize specific memories. Next, they make their two passes through the data to obtain the precise latency to retrieve a specific memory, taking care not to be diverted by paraverbal expressions (e.g., um, uh) and phrases indicating that participants are processing a memory (e.g., "This is a hard one," "I'm trying to think of a time. . . ." Correlations between coders for this method range from .64 to 1.0 (mean ≈ .90), which suggests that timing is generally accurate (but far from perfect), even in this setting.

Number of Omissions

Although participants rarely are able to identify a specific personal memory for all stimuli that are presented, few researchers specify the number of omissions made by participants or the manner in which omissions are handled in the calculation of the main dependent variables. However, it is argued that the number of omissions has the potential to be an important dependent variable in its own right. For example, one of the main findings in a report by Jones et al. (1999) was that individuals diagnosed with borderline personality disorder made more omissions than did nonpsychiatric control individuals. Omissions might be particularly important to consider in individuals with certain types of psychopathology characterized by avoidance behaviors, such as social phobia or agoraphobia.

Memory Age

Few autobiographical memory researchers have considered the age of memories retrieved by participants despite this age being a variable of major interest to cognitive psychology researchers. Results from existing studies lend mixed evidence to the utility of dating memories with clinical populations. For example, in their study with patients who had overdosed, ex-patients, and controls, Williams and Broadbent (1986) instructed participants to date their autobiographical memories as accurately as possible. There were no differences between groups as to the periods of their lives from which they retrieved memories. On the other hand, a different pattern of results was reported by McNally et al. (1995) in their study of Vietnam veterans with and without PTSD. These researchers instructed participants to indicate whether their memory had occurred in the past month, past year, past 5 years, past 10 years, or over 10 years ago. They discovered that Vietnam veterans with PTSD who wore regalia were more likely to recall memories from over 10 years ago than did veterans who did not wear regalia, which occurred largely because they recalled personal memories from the Vietnam War. Although it is difficult to make recommendations on the basis of the results of only two studies, it is suggested tentatively that memory age would be important to consider when theoretically appropriate. Moreover, as Rubin (see chap. 14, this volume) described, memory age has an effect on the properties of autobiographical memories retrieved in some instances.

Content-Related Variables

To date, much more emphasis has been placed on the structure of retrieved memories in clinical participants, especially the extent to which memories are overgeneral versus specific, than on the actual contents of memories. It is argued here that the contents of memories are just as important to examine in clinical populations, as it is well established that individuals with psychopathology often exhibit cognitive distortions that do not adequately characterize the reality of their experience (e.g., Beck & Emery, 1985; Beck, Rush, Shaw, & Emery, 1979). The few studies that have examined aspects of memory content have uncovered interesting aspects of cognitive processes in particular types of pathology (e.g., Burke & Mathews, 1992; Croll & Bryant, 2000).

Affective Tone

Participants in most clinical autobiographical memory studies are cued with generally positive and generally negative single words. Although the assumption might be that this procedure would prompt participants to retrieve either positive or negative memories, this assumption is an empirical question that generally has not been scrutinized to date. Moreover, if participants indeed retrieve affectively toned memories that are relevant to the valence of the cue word, it is of interest to assess the degree to which the affect reflected in the memory is exaggerated or blunted as compared with control participants without pathology.

Research considering the affective tone of memories retrieved by anxious and nonanxious individuals has yielded fruitful results. In their examination of autobiographical memory in individuals diagnosed with generalized anxiety disorder (GAD), Burke and Mathews (1992) presented 24 neutral single word cues to participants and asked them to retrieve the first personal memory that came to mind. Participants then supplied an adjective that best described the emotion associated with that memory. Results indicated that participants with GAD were more likely to use descriptors consistent with being nervous and less likely to use descriptors consistent with being pleased than were nonanxious control participants. Interestingly, when neutral raters classified participants' memories according to their affective tone, there was no difference in the emotional tone associated with memories retrieved by the two groups. This finding suggests that perhaps anxious individuals are not characterized by distorted memory per se but that, instead, they interpret memories in a more negative and less positive light than do nonanxious individuals. Wenzel and her colleagues (Wenzel, 2000; Wenzel et al., 2002; Wenzel et al., 2003) found that negative affective tone, as coded by raters naive to diagnostic status of participants, was the only variable to reliably differentiate the autobiographical memories of anxious and nonanxious individuals. However, more research in this area needs to be conducted; Wenzel did not gather participants' ratings of the affective tone associated with their memories, so any discrepancies could not be noted.

Thus, results from these studies suggest that affective tone is a variable that potentially differentiates autobiographical memories retrieved by individuals with psychopathology from those retrieved by individuals without psychopathology. Two reasons why affective tone might not be considered as much as it should be is because (a) it is more labor intensive than coding the specific versus overgeneral nature of memories and (b) there is not a well-defined coding scheme in the literature. Wenzel et al. (2003) categorized the autobiographical memories of individuals with social phobia and nonanxious individuals into five groups. Memories coded under *positive affect* and *negative affect* contained specific references to emotions represented on the Positive Affect and Negative Affect Schedule (PANAS; Watson, Clark, & Tellegen, 1988). Memories describing clearly positive or negative experiences with no overt references to emotion were categorized as *positive tone* and *negative tone*. Memories that reflected no affective tone or valence were categorized as *neutral*. This coding scheme is relatively easy to implement and requires coders to attend approximately six hours of meetings to attain an acceptable level of interrater reliability (kappa = .70 or greater). Thus, Wenzel and her colleagues (2002) added two categories—*positive tone* and *negative tone*— to the more conservative three-category method used by Fromholt et al. (2003) in their research reviewed in Rubin (see chap. 14, this volume), and this may be one method by which autobiographical memory researchers can consider the affective tone of memories retrieved by their participants.

Other Memory Contents

Croll and Bryant (2000) measured the latency to retrieve parent-related memories in new mothers with and without postpartum depression and coded the extent to which participants retrieved specific memories related to parenting. Participants were cued with six positive, six neutral, and six negative cue words. When the researchers considered the full range of autobiographical memories retrieved, they found no group by valence interaction for the latency to retrieve specific memories or the number of specific memories retrieved. However, when they limited their analyses only to memories that had a parent-related theme, they found that mothers with postpartum depression retrieved more negative memories and fewer positive memories than did mothers without postpartum depression. Because parenting concerns are frequent in mothers with postpartum depression, it made intuitive sense that the authors would focus on this domain of recollection. However, if they had ignored the contents of the memories that participants in their sample retrieved, then they would have failed to uncover an important dimension in the cognitive processes associated with postpartum depression. Thus, results from this study raise the possibility that memories reflecting content related to a particular pathology group are especially important to consider.

THE LIFE-NARRATIVE METHOD

Clinical psychology researchers have used the life narrative method to examine participants' memories of pathology-relevant experiences, particularly those related to trauma. The major difference between the experimental and clinical approaches is that in experimental research, one's entire life story is requested, whereas in clinical research, usually only the clinically relevant areas are examined. Foa and Riggs (1993) speculated that individuals with PTSD have disorganized, fragmented narratives of their traumatic experience and that successful treatment should facilitate the integration of these narratives, which should in turn improve symptoms. To investigate this issue, Foa et al. (1995) developed a coding scheme to measure the coherence of participants' descriptions of the trauma during exposure therapy. Therapy sessions were audiotaped, and portions of the therapy sessions that were of interest to the investigators were transcribed so that participants' references to threatening parts of the trauma could be coded. Thus, unlike methods from the cognitive psychology literature in which participants are specifically instructed to provide a narrative about their lives, participants in clinical psychology studies provide narratives in the context of their treatment. Transcripts are broken down into a series of utterances, or units, and each unit is assigned one of the categories below.

Units are characterized as *repetition* when an utterance is repeated within five lines. Three types of thoughts are coded: (a) *desperate thoughts*, or indications that nothing can be done; (b) *disorganized thoughts*, or indications of confusing or disjointed thinking; and (c) *organized thoughts*, or indications of realization, decision making, or planning. A unit is categorized as a *negative feeling* when it makes reference to unpleasant emotions, including dissociation, and as a *sensation* when it makes reference to an experience of one of the five senses, including a taste, smell, vision, sound, or touch. Additional categories include references to *actions* of the victim or the perpetrator, *dialogues*, *speech fillers* such as "um," and *details*. Subsequently, data are reduced into five groups: (a) *fragmentation* (unfinished thoughts, speech fillers), (b) *organization* (organized and disorganized thoughts analyzed separately), (c) *internal events* (all categories of thoughts, negative feelings, sensations), (d) *external events* (actions), and (e) *dialogues and details*. Interrater reliability should be obtained both for the categorization of these variables and for the manner in which coders divide the transcripts into units.

This coding scheme has been used in only a handful of studies; however, results to date suggest that it is useful in assessing change in trauma narratives pre- and posttherapy. For example, although there was not a significant reduction in fragmentation of trauma narratives after treatment as was expected, Foa et al. (1995) reported that patients exhibited more organized thoughts posttherapy than they did pretherapy, which was related to a reduction in depression. In an attempt to replicate Foa's work, van Minnen, Wessel, Dijkstra, and Roelofs (2002) reported that improved patients demonstrated fewer disorganized thoughts at the posttherapy assessment than did nonimproved patients. However, van Minnen et al. (2002) cautioned that the coherence of memory could have improved simply through the practice of discussing traumatic events in treatment, rather than through improvement in the organization of memory itself. It is important for future research to examine this possibility, either by the comparison of narrative organization in individuals assigned to treatment and that of individuals assigned to a no-treatment condition, or by the examination of narrative organization in individuals who have endured multiple traumas but who focus on only one in the course of treatment.

Recently, other schemes to quantify data obtained from the life narrative methodology have been tested (Amir, Stafford, Freshman, & Foa, 1998; Gray & Lombardo, 2001; Zoellner, Alvarez-Conrad, & Foa, 2002). These studies calculated reading level and reading ease to approximate level of articulation, with the assumption that higher levels of articulation reflect better organization of trauma narratives. Results of studies that used these approaches to analyze the structure of trauma narratives have been mixed. Although Amir et al. (1998) reported that the reading level that characterized narratives obtained two weeks posttrauma predicted PTSD symptoms 10 weeks later, Gray and Lombardo (2001) were unable to replicate this association, which they attributed to the fact that they controlled for writing skill and cognitive ability. These researchers suggested that the results obtained by Amir et al. (1998) simply reflected differences in cognitive ability often observed in comparisons of pathology and healthy samples. However, there were several subtle differences in the design of these two studies, most notably the fact that Amir et al. (1998) transcribed oral narrative accounts, whereas Gray and Lombardo (2001) instructed their participants to write out their narratives. Gray and Lombardo (2001) speculated that their written procedure might have reduced the variability often seen in oral communication, which is characterized by frequent sentence fragments and disorganization. Zoellner et al. (2002) used a procedure similar to that of Amir et al. (1998) and found that the narratives of individuals characterized by peritraumatic dissociation reflected a higher grade level but lower reading ease than did the narratives of individuals not characterized by peritraumatic dissociation regardless of whether or not they were speaking specifically of the traumatic incident. Clearly, this line of research requires additional study, and Gray and Lombardo's (2001) work underscores the importance of controlling for variables that might affect cognitive performance (e.g., cognitive ability) when pathology and healthy groups are compared.

The methodologies described above focused on the *structure* of trauma narratives; however, the *contents* of trauma narratives might provide important information about the severity of psychopathology. Recently, Alvarez-Conrad, Zoellner, and Foa (2001) analyzed the linguistic content of trauma narratives using the Linguistic Inquiry and Word Count computer program described by Pennebaker and Francis (1999). With this software, transcripts of female assault victims being treated for PTSD were scanned for the following variables: (a) indications of cognitive processes, defined as "words suggestive of causal and insightful thinking" (p. S163); (b) negative emotions; (c) positive emotions; (d) words about death and dying; (e) total word count; (f) ratio of number of different words to total number of words; and (g) speech fillers. Each of these variables was calculated for (a) prethreat material, or material indicated before the "first expressed realization of danger"; threat material; and (b) postthreat material, or material indicated "after the first expressed realization that the threat had terminated" (Alvarez-Conrad et al., 2001, p. S163). A number of variables were associated with symptoms of psychopathology and functioning posttreatment, but the most striking finding was that references to death during threat narratives were correlated positively with PTSD and depressive symptoms. Zoellner et al. (2002) examined references to negative emotions, sensations, and dissociative experiences and found that the latter variable (dissociative experiences) distinguished between individuals high and low in peritraumatic dissociation. In sum, variables measuring coherence reading level as well as contents of narratives have been useful in relating life narratives to symptoms of psychopathology, at least in individuals who have endured some sort of trauma. This method shows great promise in characterizing pathology groups, predicting success in treatment, and assessing gains made in treatment.

THE INVOLUNTARY MEMORY DIARY METHOD

The involuntary memory diary method has not yet been adopted by clinical psychology researchers to assess the frequency and effects of intrusive memories in the daily lives of individuals with psychopathology, but its clinical implications are obvious. In contrast, many clinical studies have used retrospective reports of intrusive memories. Recently, Brewin and his colleagues (see Brewin, 1998, for a comprehensive discussion) have examined the nature of intrusive memories of traumatic events in depressed individuals, similar to memories often reported by individuals with PTSD, and have related these memories to the course of depressive episodes. They have created a life events and memories interview that elicits information such as deaths of loved ones, major life events linked with the onset of depression, and aversive childhood experiences, including harsh discipline (see Brewin et al., 1999; Brewin, Watson, McCarthy, Hyman, & Dayton, 1998). Participants indicate whether they view memories elicited from this interview as intrusive (i.e., "consisting of a visual image of a specific scene that has actually taken place" [Brewin et al., 1999, p. 513]), rate the extent to which these memories are distressing (0 = not distressing at all; 10 = extremely distressing), and complete the Impact of Events Scale (IES; Horowitz, Wilner, & Alvarez, 1979) with regard to each memory. The IES, which is a common self-report inventory that assesses symptoms of traumatic stress, consists of two subscales: intrusion and avoidance of thoughts pertaining to the traumatic event.

Brewin and his colleagues analyze their data for two main purposes: (a) to examine the manner in which intrusive memories relate to symptoms of psychopathology and (b) to examine the manner in which intrusive memories relate to the retrieval of overgeneral memories in the AMT. For example, Brewin et al. (1998) reported that avoidance of intrusive memories, as assessed by the IES-Avoidance scale, predicted anxiety symptoms in depressed cancer patients six months later even after they controlled for baseline anxiety and stage of illness. In a subsequent study, Brewin et al. (1999) found that baseline IES-Total scores predicted depression above and beyond baseline depression scores. With regard to AMT performance, Kuyken and Brewin (1995) and Wessel et al. (2002) found that IES-Avoidance scores were associated with the retrieval of overgeneral positive memories, although Brewin et al. (1999) reported that IES-Intrusion was related to the retrieval of both positive and negative overgeneral memories.

This line of research clearly has demonstrated that intrusive memories and the retrieval of overgeneral autobiographical memories correlate and that both are characteristic of depressed individuals. Although Brewin et al. (1999) proposed two competing explanations to account for the relation between these variables, much work needs to be done to determine the mechanism through which disruptions of autobiographical memory cause symptoms of psychopathology. One way to draw a firmer conclusion about the nature of intrusive memories in psychopathology is to move beyond the intentional retrieval of these memories in the laboratory, which may or may not be similar to the phenomenological experience of these memories when they occur in one's daily life. The involuntary memory diary method is one well-defined methodology that could be used for this purpose.

THE AUTOBIOGRAPHICAL MEMORY INTERVIEW

To date, the Autobiographical Memory Interview (AMI; Kopelman et al., 1989) has been used primarily with patients exhibiting some organic brain damage, such as Alzheimer's disease, and has not been adopted to examine autobiographical memory in individuals with psychopathology. For this reason, applications of the AMI will not be considered further in this chapter. Nevertheless, it is important for clinical researchers to be aware that this methodology exists as an alternative to Williams and Broadbent's (1986) AMT. If there are theoretical reasons to suspect that episodic and/or semantic memory from different periods of a person's life might vary as a function of psychopathology, then this might be an useful tool to adapt to the population in question.

Although the AMT itself has not been used to examine autobiographical memory in pathology groups, it has influenced the manner in which autobiographical memory was studied in at least one case. Meesters et al. (2000) constructed a test of autobiographical semantic facts, influenced by the AMT, to administer to adolescent psychiatric patients with and without a history of trauma. They chose to assess semantic autobiographical memory to provide empirical evidence to support or refute clinical lore suggesting that individuals who have experienced trauma in childhood have a poor memory for childhood information. The authors included their Semantic Autobiographical Memory Test in an appendix; it contained 22 items including, "Do you remember the name of your elementary school? If so, what was its name?" Each item is scored a 1 or a 0 depending on whether the participant is able to provide the particular detail in question. A total score is calculated by summing the number of responses in which a participant provides a correct detail and dividing this sum by the total number of relevant items. Results indicated that adolescents with a history of trauma recalled fewer autobiographical facts than did adolescents who were hospitalized for psychiatric symptoms but had not experienced trauma, which suggests this method is useful in distinguishing traumatized from nontraumatized individuals.

THE DIARY RECALL METHOD

There are no known studies that have adopted the diary recall method for use with clinical populations. Implementation of this method would be difficult, as the likelihood that one could identify a sample of individuals with a particular psychiatric diagnosis who *also* faithfully maintain a diary is quite small. On the other hand, this method could be implemented with patients once they enter therapy. It is not uncommon for therapists to instruct their patients to keep journals to record problematic incidents and associated thoughts, feelings, and behaviors (Stone, 1998). A clinical psychology researcher might make use of this journal in order to compare patients' memory for particular events when they are experiencing psychopathology with their memory for those same events after they have recovered from their episode. Similar to diary studies described in the cognitive psychology literature, variables of interest might be accuracy of memory and the influence of certain types of cues (e.g., emotions, thoughts) upon the retrieval of memories. It would be of interest to clinical psychologists to determine which cues elicit negative or traumatic memories that exacerbate the course of psychopathology as well as cues that are likely to elicit memories leading to relapse.

THE QUESTIONNAIRE METHOD

The questionnaire method is useful in assessing qualities of autobiographical memories that are difficult for objective raters to code, such as the clarity of the recollection and the extent to which individuals recall associated sensory experiences. Although the reliance on participants' self-report might appear to be a limitation of this method, it provides information about individuals' phenomenological experience of the recollection. It is this aspect of autobiographical memory that has the potential to be most important to clinicians, as one's subjective experience with the recollection of difficult life events is likely to be highly associated with subsequent symptoms of psychopathology.

The questionnaire method is a flexible one in which researchers either borrow questions used in other studies or develop their own to investigate particular questions of interest. For example, Byrne, Hyman, and Scott (2001) and Koss, Figueredo, Bell, Tharan, and Tromp (1996) instructed female participants to identify their most traumatic experience and to rate them using a modified version of the Memory Characteristics Questionnaire (Johnson,

Foley, Suengas, & Raye, 1988). Koss et al. (1996) selected items that distinguish real from imagined experiences, such as clarity and vividness. Byrne et al. (2001) used a broader range of questions, including those that pertained to the sensory characteristics of the memory (e.g., smell), emotions related to the event, importance of the event, and confidence in the accuracy of the memory. In both studies, all questions were rated on a seven-point scale. Some of the results from both studies suggested that trauma-related memories were less clear and coherent than other memories, which confirmed the research conducted by Foa and her colleagues (e.g., Foa et al., 1995).

The questionnaire method has the potential to answer important theoretical questions about the manner in which negative or traumatic memories affect psychopathology, as evidenced by a recently completed study. Berntsen et al. (2003) constructed questions to differentiate between two competing theories of traumatic memories—that traumatic memories are fragmented and poorly integrated into one's identity, and that traumatic memories serve as a reference point to process less distinctive events. They constructed questions that corresponded with their questions of interest, such as "I feel that the traumatic event has become part of my identity," which participants rated on a 1–5 scale (1 = totally disagree, 5 = totally agree). Consistent with the latter theory, participants rated traumatic memories as being vivid recollections that organized subsequent experiences and became a part of their identities. Thus, this method has the potential to shed light on theories of psychopathology, and it is flexible in that researchers can instruct participants to retrieve memories associated with specific pathologies and can develop their own theoretically motivated questions.

METHODOLOGICAL NOTE: PARTICIPANT SELECTION

As in all studies with clinical samples, participant selection is a crucial issue to which researchers must attend, and the nature of the sample often affects the pattern of results that a researcher obtains. Carefully defining characteristics of one's sample is especially important in conducting autobiographical memory research. For example, there is much evidence that depressed individuals show deficits in retrieving specific positive autobiographical memories (e.g., Healy & Williams, 1999). In contrast, individuals with other types of psychopathology, including generalized anxiety disorder (Burke & Mathews, 1992), social phobia (Wenzel et al., 2002), and obsessive–compulsive disorder (Wilhelm, McNally, Baer, & Florin, 1997), do not demonstrate such a deficit *unless* participants report elevated levels of depressive symptoms (cf. Wilhelm et al., 1997). Thus, if a research study is examining the extent to which a particular clinical condition is characterized by deficits in autobiographical memory, it is critically important to measure and subsequently control for the level of depressive symptoms in the sample.

Results from other studies suggest that the nature of an individual's parasuicidal behavior affects the type of autobiographical memory distortions that are found. Startup et al. (2001) administered the AMT to 23 individuals with borderline personality disorder and 23 control individuals. In contrast with results from other studies suggesting that overgenerality is positively correlated with parasuicidal behavior (e.g., Williams & Broadbent, 1986; Williams & Dritschel, 1988), these authors reported that overgenerality was inversely related to parasuicidal behavior. Startup et al. made an important distinction between the participants in their sample and participants in these other samples. Participants in other studies were recruited from hospitals after they had made serious suicide attempts, whereas the borderline participants in Startup et al.'s study engaged in self-harm behavior that would not necessarily be regarded as suicidal, or with the intent to die. Thus, overgeneral memory may have served a protective function in Startup et al.'s sample, which suggests that the symptom expression and their underlying motivational features are important factors to consider in interpreting results from autobiographical memory studies.

Another important issue that cuts across many dimensions of cognition and psychopathology research involves the decision to use participants with clinical diagnoses as opposed to participants screened to be high and low on a particular trait associated with psychopathology. Research that uses the latter type of participants generally suggests that it is more difficult to find a significant effect than when clinical samples are used (Logan & Goetsch, 1993). The state of nonclinical participants in the autobiographical memory literature is no different. Several autobiographical memory studies that use undergraduate participants screened to be high and low on a particular analogue to psychopathology found either no differences between groups (Levy & Mineka, 1998) or only partially confirmed hypotheses (Goddard et al., 1997; Richards & Whittaker, 1990). If a researcher is interested in generalizing results to psychopathology but does not have access to a clinical sample (and therefore must use an analogue sample), it is important to select participants to be as stable on the analogue construct as possible. One way of doing this, for example, is to screen analogue participants with at least two well-validated measures of a particular construct, and require them to score at least one standard deviation above the mean on both inventories and to continue to score in that range at the time of the experimental session (e.g., Wenzel et al., 2003).

CONCLUSION

Autobiographical memories provide rich accounts into the nature and possible etiology of psychopathology. Not only are differences between the autobiographical memories of individuals with some types of psychopathology, such as depression, and those of healthy individuals robust and striking, but there is evidence that deficits in some aspects of autobiographical memory retrieval predict the course of a disorder. Although the existing methodologies generally used to study autobiographical memory in clinical populations are well validated, there clearly are other established methods from the cognitive psychology literature (see chap. 14, this volume) that potentially have just as much clinical relevance. It is incumbent upon clinical researchers to be familiar with models of autobiographical memory from the cognitive psychology literature and demonstrate the precise manner in which their pathology samples deviate. I hope that this chapter, in combination with Rubin's (see chap. 14, this volume), will serve as the basis for future autobiographical memory researchers to do so.

REFERENCES

Alvarez-Conrad, J., Zoellner, L. A., & Foa, E. B. (2001). Linguistic predictors of trauma pathology and physical health. *Applied Cognitive Psychology, 15*, S159–S170.

Amir, N., Stafford, J., Freshman, M. S., & Foa, E. B. (1998). Relationship between trauma narratives and trauma pathology. *Journal of Traumatic Stress, 11*, 385–392.

Beck, A. T., & Emery, G. (1985). *Anxiety disorders and phobias: A cognitive perspective*. New York: Basic Books.

Beck, A. T., Rush, A. J., Shaw, P. M., & Emery, G. (1979). *Cognitive therapy of depression*. New York: Guilford.

Berntsen, D. (1996). Involuntary autobiographical memory. *Applied Cognitive Psychology, 10*, 435–454.

Berntsen, D. (1998). Voluntary and involuntary access to autobiographical memory. *Memory, 6*, 113–141.

Berntsen, D. (2001). Involuntary memories of emotional events: Do memories of traumas and extremely happy memories differ? *Applied Cognitive Psychology, 15*, S135–S158.

Berntsen, D., Willert, M., & Rubin, D. C. (2003). Splintered memories or vivid landmarks? Reliving and coherence of traumatic memories in PTSD. *Applied Cognitive Psychology, 17*, 675–693.

Brewin, C. R. (1998). Intrusive autobiographical memories in depression and posttraumatic stress disorder. *Applied Cognitive Psychology, 12*, 359–370.

Brewin, C. R., Reynolds, M., & Tata, P. (1999). Autobiographical memory processes in the course of depression. *Journal of Abnormal Psychology, 108*, 511–517.

Brewin, C. R., Watson, M., McCarthy, S., Hyman, P., & Dayson, D. (1998). Memory processes and the course of anxiety and depression in cancer patients. *Psychological Medicine, 28*, 219–224.

Brittlebank, A. D., Scott, J., Williams, J. M. G., & Ferrier, I. N. (1993). Autobiographical memory in depression: State or trait marker? *British Journal of Psychiatry, 162*, 118–121.

Bryant, R. A. (1995). Autobiographical memory across personalities in dissociative identity disorder: A case report. *Journal of Abnormal Psychology, 104*, 625–631.

Burke, M., & Mathews, A. (1992). Autobiographical memory and clinical anxiety. *Cognition & Emotion, 6*, 23–35.

Byrne, C. A., Hyman, I. E., & Scott, K. L. (2001). Comparisons of memories for traumatic events and other experiences. *Applied Cognitive Psychology, 15*, S119–S133.

Cohen, J. (1960). A coefficient of agreement for nominal scales. *Educational and Psychological Measurement, 20*, 37–46.

Croll, S., & Bryant, R. A. (2000). Autobiographical memory in postnatal depression. *Cognitive Therapy and Research, 24*, 419–426.

Dalgleish, T., Spinks, H., Yiend, J., & Kuyken, W. (2001). Autobiographical memory style in seasonal affective disorder and its relationship to future symptom remission. *Journal of Abnormal Psychology, 110*, 335–340.

Foa, E. B., Molnar, C., & Cashman, L. (1995). Change in rape narratives during exposure therapy for posttraumatic stress disorder. *Journal of Traumatic Stress, 8*, 675–690.

Foa, E. B., & Riggs, D. S. (1993). Posttraumatic stress disorder and rape. In J. M. Oldham, R. B. Riba, & A. Tasman (Eds.), *Review of psychiatry* (p. 12). Washington, DC: American Psychiatric Press.

Fromholt, P., Mortensen, D., Torpdahl, P., Bender, L., Larsen, P., & Rubin, D. C. (2003). Life-narrative and word-cued autobiographical memories in centenarians: Comparisons with 80-year-old control, depressed, and dementia groups. *Memory, 11*, 81–88.

Goddard, L., Dritschel, B., & Burton, A. (1996). Role of autobiographical memory in social problem solving and depression. *Journal of Abnormal Psychology, 105*, 609–616.

Goddard, L., Dritschel, B., & Burton, A. (1997). Social problem solving and autobiographical memory in non-clinical depression. *British Journal of Clinical Psychology, 36*, 449–451.

Gray, M. J., & Lombardo, T. W. (2001). Complexity of trauma narratives as an index of fragmented memory in PTSD: A critical analysis. *Applied Cognitive Psychology, 15*, S171–S186.

Harvey, A. G., Bryant, R. A., & Dang, S. T. (1998). Autobiographical memory in acute stress disorder. *Journal of Consulting and Clinical Psychology, 66*, 500–506.

Healy, H., & Williams, J. M. G. (1999). Autobiographical memory. In T. Dalgleish & M. Powers (Eds.), *Handbook of cognition and emotion* (pp. 229–242). New York: Wiley.

Horowitz, M. J., Wilner, N., & Alvarez, W. (1979). Impact of Event Scale: A measure of subjective stress. *Psychosomatic Medicine, 41*, 209–218.

Johnson, M. K., Foley, M. A., Suengas, A. G., & Raye, C. L. (1988). Phenomenal characteristics of memories for perceived and imagined autobiographical events. *Journal of Experimental Psychology: General, 117*, 371–376.

Jones, B., Heard, H., Startup, M., Swales, M., Williams, J. M. G., & Jones, R. S. P. (1999). Autobiographical memory and dissociation in borderline personality disorder. *Psychological Medicine, 29*, 1397–1404.

Kaney, S., Bowen-Jones, K., & Bentall, R. P. (1999). Persecutory delusions and autobiographical memory. *British Journal of Clinical Psychology, 38*, 97–102.

Kopelman, M. D., Wilson, B. A., & Baddeley, A. D. (1989). The Autobiographical Memory Interview: New assessment of autobiographical and personal semantic information in amnesic patients. *Journal of Clinical and Experimental Neuropsychology, 11*, 724–744.

Koss, M. P., Figueredo, A. J., Bell, I., Tharan, M., & Tromp, S. (1996). Traumatic memory characteristics: A cross-validated mediational model of response to rape among employed women. *Journal of Abnormal Psychology, 105*, 421–432.

Kuyken, W., & Brewin, C. R. (1995). Autobiographical memory functioning in depression and reports of early abuse. *Journal of Abnormal Psychology, 104*, 585–591.

Kuyken, W., & Dalgleish, T. (1995). Autobiographical memory and depression. *British Journal of Clinical Psychology, 34*, 89–92.

Leung, P., & Bryant, R. A. (2000). Autobiographical memory in diabetes mellitus patients. *Journal of Psychosomatic Research, 49*, 435–438.

Levy, E. A., & Mineka, S. (1998). Anxiety and mood-congruent autobiographical memory: A conceptual failure to replicate. *Cognition & Emotion, 12*, 625–634.

Logan, A. C., & Goetsch, V. L. (1993). Attention to external threat cues in anxiety states. *Clinical Psychology Review, 13*, 541–559.

Mackinger, H. F., Loschin, G. G., & Leibestseder, M. M. (2000). Prediction of postnatal affective changes by autobiographical memories. *European Psychologist, 5*, 52–61.

Mackinger, H. F., Pachinger, M. M., Leibestseder, M. M., & Fartacek, R. R. (2000). Autobiographical memories in women remitted from major depression. *Journal of Abnormal Psychology, 109*, 331–334.

McNally, R. J., Lasko, N. B., Macklin, M. L., & Pitman, R. K. (1995). Autobiographical memory disturbance in combat-related posttraumatic stress disorder. *Behaviour Research and Therapy, 33*, 619–630.

McNally, R. J., Litz, B. T., Prassas, A., Shin, L. M., & Weathers, F. W. (1994). Emotional priming of autobiographical memory in post-traumatic stress disorder. *Cognition & Emotion, 8*, 351–367.

Meesters, C., Merckelbach, H., Muris, P., & Wessel, I. (2000). Autobiographical memory and trauma in adolescents. *Journal of Behavior Therapy and Experimental Psychiatry, 31*, 29–39.

Pennebaker, J. W., & Francis, M. E. (1999). *Linguistic inquiry and word count*. Mahwah, NJ: Erlbaum.

Phillips, S., & Williams, J. M. G. (1997). Cognitive impairment, depression, and the specificity of autobiographical memory in the elderly. *British Journal of Clinical Psychology, 36*, 341–347.

Richards, A., & Whittaker, T. M. (1990). Effects of anxiety and mood manipulation in autobiographical memory. *British Journal of Clinical Psychology, 29*, 145–153.

Rubin, D. C., & Schulkind, M. D. (1997). Properties of word cues for autobiographical memory. *Psychological Reports, 81*, 47–50.

Sidley, G. L., Calam, R., Wells, A., Hughes, T., & Whitaker, K. (1999). The prediction of parasuicide repetition in a high-risk group. *British Journal of Clinical Psychology, 38*, 375–386.

Sidley, G. L., Whitaker, K., Calam, R. M., & Wells, A. (1997). The relationship between problem-solving and autobiographical memory in parasuicide patients. *Behavioural and Cognitive Psychotherapy, 25*, 195–202.

Startup, M., Heard, H., Swales, M., Jones, B., Williams, J. M. G., & Jones, R. S. P. (2001). Autobiographical memory and parasuicide in borderline personality disorder. *British Journal of Clinical Psychology, 40*, 113–120.

Stone, M. (1998). Journaling with clients. *Journal of Individual Psychology, 54*, 535–545.

Swales, M. A., Williams, J. M. G., & Wood, P. (2001). Specificity of autobiographical memory and mood disturbance in adolescents. *Cognition & Emotion, 15*, 321–331.

van Minnen, A., Wessel, I., Dijkstra, T., & Roelofs, K. (2002). Changes in PTSD patients' narratives during prolonged exposure therapy: A replication and extension. *Journal of Traumatic Stress, 15*, 255–258.

Watkins, E., & Teasdale, J. D. (2001). Rumination and overgeneral memory in depression: Effects of self-focus and analytic thinking. *Journal of Abnormal Psychology, 110*, 353–357.

Watson, D., Clark, L. A., & Tellegen, A. (1988). Development and validation of a brief measure of positive and negative affect: The PANAS scales. *Journal of Personality and Social Psychology, 54*, 1063–1070.

Wenzel, A. (2000). *An evaluation of schema-based models of information processing in anxiety disorders*. Unpublished doctoral dissertation, University of Iowa, Iowa City.

Wenzel, A., Jackson, L. C., Brendle, J. R., & Pinna, K. (2003). Autobiographical memories associated with feared stimuli in fearful and nonfearful individuals. *Anxiety, Stress, and Coping: An International Journal, 16*, 1–15.

Wenzel, A., Jackson, L. C., & Holt, C. S. (2002). Social phobia and the recall of autobiographical memories. *Depression and Anxiety, 15*, 186–189.

Wessel, I., Meeren, M., Peeters, F., Arntz, A., & Merckelbach, H. (2001). Correlates of autobiographical memory specificity: The role of depression, anxiety, and childhood trauma. *Behaviour Research and Therapy, 39*, 409–421.

Wessel, I., Merckelbach, H., & Dekkers, T. (2002). Autobiographical memory specificity, intrusive memory, and general memory skills in Dutch-Indonesian survivors of the World War II era. *Journal of Traumatic Stress, 15*, 227–234.

Wilhelm, S., McNally, R. J., Baer, L., & Florin, I. (1997). Autobiographical memory in obsessive-compulsive disorder. *British Journal of Clinical Psychology, 36,* 21–31.

Williams, J. M. G. (1996). Autobiographical memory in depression. In D. Rubin (Ed.), *Remembering our past: Studies in autobiographical memory* (pp. 244–267). Cambridge, England: Cambridge University Press.

Williams, J. M. G., & Broadbent, K. (1986). Autobiographical memory in suicide attempters. *Journal of Abnormal Psychology, 93,* 144–149.

Williams, J. M. G., & Dritschel, B. H. (1988). Emotional disturbance and the specificity of autobiographical memory. *Cognition & Emotion, 2,* 221–234.

Williams, J. M. G., & Dritschel, B. H. (1992). Categoric and extended autobiographical memories. In M. A. Conway, D. C. Rubin, H. Spinnler, & W. A. Wagenaar (Eds.), *Theoretical perspectives on autobiographical memory* (pp. 391–412). London: Kluwer Academic.

Williams, J. M. G., & Scott, J. (1988). Autobiographical memory in depression. *Psychological Medicine, 18,* 689–695.

Williams, W. H., Williams, J. M. G., & Ghadiali, E. J. (1998). Autobiographical memory in traumatic brain injury: Neuropsychological and mood predictors of recall. *Neuropsychological Rehabilitation, 8,* 43–60.

Zoellner, L. A., Alvarez-Conrad, J., & Foa, E. B. (2002). Peritraumatic dissociative experiences, trauma narratives, and trauma pathology. *Journal of Traumatic Stress, 15,* 49–57.

AUTHOR INDEX

Numbers in italics refer to entries in the reference sections.

Murdock, T. B., 44, 56
Muris, P., 48, 60, 244, 262
Murphy, F. C., 42, 45, 60
Murphy, K., 26, 38
Myers, L. B., 207, 211

Näätänen, R., 76, 95
Naparstek, J., 44, 61
Navon, D., 24, 38
Neely, J. H., 44, 57, 132, 147
Neisser, U., 85, 95, 221, 226, 234, 235, 239, 241
Nelson, D. L., 132, 149
Neri, M., 153, 167
Nigro, G., 235, 239
Nordgren, J. C., 44, 59
Nulty, D. D., 45, 59, 62

Ober, B. A., 157, 169, 170
Oberg, P., 227, 240
O'Brien, C. P., 42, 56
Ogden, J. A., 235, 239
Öhman, A., 105, 106, 115, 116
Ohta, K., 43, 61
Ohta, N., 146, 148, 150
Okada, R., 181, 192
Öst, L., 46, 47, 58,160, 161, 169
Otto, M. W., 52, 59, 206, 211

Pachella, R. G., 23, 38
Pachinger, M. M., 244, 262
Paivio, A., 29, 38
Paller, K. A., 180, 181, 188, 194
Parasuraman, R., 76, 94, 95
Park, S. M., 157, 170
Parkin, A. J., 225, 238
Parzer, P., 42, 55
Pascual, J., 160, 167
Pashler, H., 75, 76, 95
Pashler, H. E., 75, 82, 95
Paul, E., 164, 168
Pauli, P., 42, 60
Paykel, E. S., 60
Payne, D. G., 241
Peeters, F., 244, 263
Pennebaker, J. W., 254, 262
Perpina, C., 46, 60
Perruchet, P., 158, 167
Perry, S. W., 204, 209
Peterson, J., 18, 38
Peterson, R. A., 199, 211
Petruk, R., 181, 193

Petty, R. E., 184, 189, 192, 194, 195
Phaf, R. H., 33, 38, 205, 209
Phillips, M. L., 52, 56
Phillips, S., 244, 246, 248, 263
Pihl, R. O., 44, 61
Pilotti, M., 132, 149
Pinna, K., 249, 263
Pitman, R. K., 201, 204, 210, 211, 244, 262
Pleydell-Pearce, C. W., 219
Poirier, M. F., 169
Poirier, M.-F., 127
Pollack, M. H., 52, 59
Pollack, M. W., 206, 211
Pollatsek, A., 99, 116
Poon, L. W., 225, 240
Pope, R. S., 187, 188, 193
Portin, R., 157, 169
Posner, M. I., 17, 38, 49, 60, 70, 77, 85, 86, 95, 98, 103, 116
Post, R. M., 205, 211
Powell, R. A., 210
Power, M., 9
Power, M. J., 207, 211
Prassas, A., 244, 262
Preston, M. S., 43, 60
Proctor, R. W., 102, 109, 115, 116
Purcell, D. G., 106, 116
Pury, C. L. S., 108, 116
Putnam, F. W., 205, 211
Pylyshyn, Z. W., 70, 84, 86, 95

Quero, S., 43, 60

Race, J. H., 45, 56
Radach, R., 99, 115
Radvansky, G., 188, 196
Rahhal, T. A., 225, 240
Rajaram, S., 132–134, 142, 147, 149
Ramponi, C., 103
Rapee, R. M., 43, 50, 57, 160, 170, 200, 210
Rappold, V. A., 131, 147
Ratcliff, R., 23, 38
Rau, H., 42, 60
Rauch, S. L., 35
Ravenscroft, H., 160, 170
Ray, C., 28, 38
Raye, C. L., 233, 234, 238, 239, 258, 262
Raymond, J. E., 71, 82, 95
Rayner, K., 71, 99, 116
Redding, G. M., 22, 38
Reed, H., 187, 194, 195
Reed, J. D., 241

SUBJECT INDEX

ABOUT THE EDITORS

Amy Wenzel, PhD, is on the faculty in the Department of Psychiatry at the University of Pennsylvania. She received her AB with honors in psychology and religion from Duke University, and her MA and PhD in psychology from the University of Iowa. Dr. Wenzel has held positions as an assistant professor at the University of North Dakota and visiting professor at the American College of Norway. With John Harvey, she has coedited *Close Relationships: Maintenance and Enhancement, A Clinician's Guide to Maintaining and Enhancing Close Relationships*, and *The Handbook of Sexuality in Close Relationships* (also with Susan Sprecher). She has coauthored more than 40 articles and chapters on cognitive biases in anxiety disorders, postpartum anxiety disorders, and the impact of anxiety on close relationships.

David C. Rubin, PhD, is Professor of Psychological and Brain Sciences and Senior Fellow in the Center for the Study of Aging and Human Development at Duke University. He received his BS in physics and psychology from Carnegie Mellon University, and his MA and PhD in psychology from Harvard University. Professor Rubin has held positions as an aerospace engineer for the National Aeronautics and Space Association (NASA); assistant professor at Lawrence University; visiting professor at the University of Aarhus, Denmark; visiting scientist at the Medical Research Council Applied Psychology Unit and at the Max Planck Institute for Human Development, Berlin; a Fellow-in-Residence at the Netherlands Institute for Advanced Study in the Humanities and Social Sciences; and an Erskine Fellow at the University of Canterbury. His 1995 book, *Memory in Oral Traditions: The Cognitive Psychology of Epic, Ballads, and Counting-Out Rhymes* was awarded the American Association of Publishers' Best New Professional/Scholarly Book in Psychology for 1995 and the William James Award from the American Psychological Association. His research interests are in the neural, behavioral, and cultural basis of memory for complex material and events, especially autobiographical memory.